Self and Wisdom in Arts-Based Contemplative Inquiry in Education

By foregrounding a first-person perspective, this text enacts and explores self-reflection as a mode of inquiry in educational research and highlights the centrality of the individual researcher in the construction of knowledge.

Engaging in particular with the work of Thomas Merton through a dialogical approach to his writings, *Self and Wisdom in Arts-Based Contemplative Inquiry in Education* offers rich examples of personal engagement with text and art to illustrate the pervasive influence of the personal in reflective, narrative and aesthetic forms of inquiry. Chapters consider methodological and philosophical implications of self-study and contemplative research in educational contexts and show how dialogic approaches can enrich empirical forms of inquiry and inform pedagogical practice. In its embrace of a contemplative voice within an academic treatise, the text offers a rich example of arts-based contemplative inquiry.

This unique text will be of interest to postgraduate scholars, researchers and academics working in the fields of educational philosophy, arts-based and qualitative research methodologies and Merton studies.

Giovanni Rossini, PhD (University of Toronto/OISE) is a philosopher and independent scholar whose research interests span the fields of holistic and contemplative studies in education and, in particular, the terrain of arts-based contemplative inquiry. Core to his research is the intersection of narrative study and the imaginal and how it is foundational to the constructing of self and the ethos of knowledge as wisdom.

Routledge International Studies in the Philosophy of Education

A Democratic Theory of Educational Accountability
From Test-Based Assessment to Interpersonal Responsibility
Derek Gottlieb

Confucian Philosophy for Contemporary Education
Charlene Tan

Virtues as Integral to Science Education
Understanding the Intellectual, Moral, and Civic Value of Science and Scientific Inquiry
Edited by Wayne Melville and Donald Kerr

A Platonic Theory of Moral Education
Cultivating Virtue in Contemporary Democratic Classrooms
Mark E. Jonas & Yoshiaki Nakazawa

Exploring Materiality in Childhood
Body, Relations and Space
Edited by Maarit Alasuutari, Marleena Mustola and Niina Rutanen

Self and Wisdom in Arts-Based Contemplative Inquiry in Education
Narrative, Aesthetic and the Dialogical Presence of Thomas Merton
Giovanni Rossini

Reading Plato's Dialogues to Enhance Learning and Inquiry
Exploring Socrates' Use of Protreptic for Student Engagement
Mason Marshall

For more information about this series, please visit: www.routledge.com/Routledge-International-Studies-in-the-Philosophy-of-Education/book-series/SE0237

Self and Wisdom in Arts-Based Contemplative Inquiry in Education

Narrative, Aesthetic and the Dialogical Presence of Thomas Merton

Giovanni Rossini

Routledge
Taylor & Francis Group
NEW YORK AND LONDON

First published 2021
by Routledge
52 Vanderbilt Avenue, New York, NY 10017

and by Routledge
2 Park Square, Milton Park, Abingdon, Oxon, OX14 4RN

Routledge is an imprint of the Taylor & Francis Group, an informa business

© 2021 Taylor & Francis

The right of Giovanni Rossini to be identified as author of this work has been asserted by him in accordance with sections 77 and 78 of the Copyright, Designs and Patents Act 1988.

All rights reserved. No part of this book may be reprinted or reproduced or utilised in any form or by any electronic, mechanical, or other means, now known or hereafter invented, including photocopying and recording, or in any information storage or retrieval system, without permission in writing from the publishers.

Trademark notice: Product or corporate names may be trademarks or registered trademarks, and are used only for identification and explanation without intent to infringe.

Library of Congress Cataloging-in-Publication Data
A catalog record for this book has been requested

ISBN: 978-0-367-41974-5 (hbk)
ISBN: 978-0-367-81705-3 (ebk)

Typeset in Times New Roman
by Apex CoVantage, LLC

**For
Gianna & Oriana**

Contents

List of Images		viii
Foreward by John P. Miller		x
Acknowledgements		xii
	A Necessary Letter to the Reader: On the Ethos of Arts-Based Contemplative Inquiry	1
1	Narrative Beginnings: The Seeds of Inquiry and the Imperative of Story	12
2	Meditations on Merton's Paradox: Narrative, Aesthetics and the Emergence of the Wisdom Image	34
3	The Journey of the *"Perpetual Seeker"*: Of Emerging Questions on the Dialogical Ethos of Wisdom and Art	81
4	The Friendship of Texts: Beyond a Referential Relation With Texts Onto the Dialogical in Inquiry	96
5	Towards a Methodology of One: The Personal Versus the Socio-Empirical in Inquiry	118
6	The Imaginal as a Pathway Onto Wisdom: A Prolegomenon for a Classroom Practice	157
7	The Journey of *Gionitus* and *"Newton's Child"*: Concluding Reflections on the Imperative of the Personal and Aesthetical in Arts-Based Contemplative Inquiry	169
Bibliography		177
Index		187

Images

The artwork included in the book consists of original images created by the author and images by Gianna Di Rezze and photographer Edward Burtynsky.

1.1	Unknown. (c. 1962). *John's Journey*. [Digitally Recaptured & Edited Photograph]. Ontario, Canada	12
1.2	Rossini, G. (c. 1966). *Beginning Inquiry, My Grade 3 Workbook*. [Photograph of Page From G. Rossini's Grade 3 Workbook]. Ontario, Canada	17
1.3	Rossini, G. (2017). *Clock Mechanism*. [Photographic Detail]. Museo Galileo. Florence, Italy	23
1.4	Rossini, G. (2017). *The Fluidity of Inquiry. A Narrow Street in Venice Known as a Calle*. [Digital Photograph]. Venice, Italy	27
1.5	Rossini, G. (2017). *The "Centred Self"*. Image of Fra Angelico (1440). *Mocking of Christ*. [Digital Photograph]. Convent of San Marco. Florence, Italy	31
2.1	Rossini, G. (2017). *I Turn Inwards in Order to Look out Onto the World*. [Digital Photograph]. Monk's Cell, Convent of San Marco. Florence, Italy	34
2.2	Rossini, G. (2018). *Looking Onto Others to See Myself. Reflection Upon Robert Smithson's Mirage No. 1*. [Digitally edited photograph]. Museum of Contemporary Art, Los Angeles, California	40
2.3	Burtynsky, Edward. (2012). *Pivot Irrigation No. 39* [Chromogenic print]	67
2.4	Burtynsky, Edward. (2012). *Borromini No. 21, 1999* [Chromogenic print]	67
2.5	Rossini, G. (2017). *Electrostatic Machine*. Anonymous. (c. 1890). *Modified Carré Electrical Machine*. [Photographic Detail]. Museo Galileo. Florence, Italy	72
2.6	Rossini, G. (2017). Ghirlandaio, Domenico. (1487). *Adoration of the Magi*. [Digital Photograph]. Uffizi Gallery. Florence Italy	72

2.7	Burtynsky, Edward. (2013). *Navajo Reservation/Suburb: Phoenix, Arizona, USA, 2011* [Chromogenic Print]	75
3.1	Rossini, G. (2017). *Gionitus, The Beginning of Astronomy*. Relief by Pisano, Andrea & Assistant. (1341–1348). [Digital Photograph]. Opera del Duomo Museum. Florence, Italy	81
3.2	Rossini, G. (2017). *A Voice of Contemplative Solitude. A Courtyard in the Convent of San Marco*. [Digital Photograph]. Convent of San Marco. Florence, Italy	91
4.1	Rossini, G. (c. 1966). *Merton's "Vague Fragments," Building the Big Picture*. [Photograph of Page From G. Rossini's Grade 4 Workbook]. Ontario, Canada	96
4.2	Rossini, G. (2017). *The Journey*. Detail of Fresco by di Bonaiuto, Andrea. (1365–1367). *The Triumph of Christian Doctrine*. [Digital Photograph]. Spanish Chapel. Florence, Italy	100
4.3	Rossini, G. (2017). *Transformation*. Sculpture by di Lodovico Buonarroti, Michelangelo. (1512–1530). *Atlas Slave*. [Digital Photograph]. Galleria dell'Accademia, Florence, Italy	114
5.1	Di Rezze, G. (2017). *Pentimento*. Image Based on Damien Hirst's *Treasures From the Wreck of the Unbelievable*. [Digitally Edited Photograph by G. Rossini]. Palazzo Grassi. Venice, Italy	118
5.2	Rossini, G. (2018). *A Formation of My Being-in-the-Moment*. Image Based on Frank Gehry's *Walt Disney Concert Hall*. [Digital Photograph Superimposed With Text]. Los Angeles, California	154
6.1	Burtynsky, Edward. (2000). *Manufacturing No. 18. Cankun Factory, Zhangzhou Fujian Province, 2005*. [Chromogenic Print]	157
6.2	Unknown. (2011). *Student Group Reflections on Paper of a Burtynsky Photograph*. [Digital photograph by G. Rossini]	167

Foreward

In the second chapter of this book, Giovanni (John) Rossini refers to an exercise that I use in my class, The Holistic Curriculum, where I ask students to read and discuss six different definitions of holistic education. One of these is by Thomas Merton:

> The purpose of education is to show a person how to define himself authentically and spontaneously in relation to his world-not to impose a prefabricated definition of the world, still less an arbitrary definition of the individual. . . . Thus, the fruit of education,. . . was the activation of that inmost center, that *scintilla anima*, that "apex" or "spark" which is a freedom beyond freedom, an identity beyond essence, a self beyond all ego, a being beyond the created realm, and a consciousness that transcends all division, all separation.

Very few students choose this definition but this brief encounter with Merton was a spark that led to John's doctoral thesis and this book. Merton was one of the greatest contemplatives of the 20th century, and John engages Merton to assist in his exploration of the relationship between art and wisdom. Contemplation is essential to the development of wisdom which cannot be developed by logic. Merton's "center" or "spark" is a source of wisdom and can be nurtured through contemplative practices such as meditation, yoga and tai chi. It can also be nourished through art. However, the relationship between art and wisdom has not often been explored, particularly in philosophy. John writes about arts-based inquiry as a form of contemplative practice and shows how this kind of inquiry can lead to wisdom.

John brings together a diverse literature from holistic education, contemplative education, philosophy, ethics and narrative inquiry. He also includes visual art that has touched him in different ways ranging from religious art from the middle ages to the contemporary art of Edward Burtynsky. John writes in the last chapter

> Art awakens us, and within such moments when we reflect upon our being in the world, is seeded its transformative promise. For Merton,

such promise resides in the artist within us (Merton, 1972) and one whose transformative potential, as the indigenous educator Gregory Cajete observes, lives in all of us (Cajete, 2019). For Cajete the divine which resides within is made manifest through the encounter with art, in kindred manner with Merton who speaks of the inner artist (Merton, 1972). Or, in Burtynsky's depictions of landscapes which he describes as a seeking of the divine; but also ones where we, as witnesses, begin to reflect upon our being in the world.

There is so much in this book to explore and contemplate. The writing itself has a contemplative quality and can bring the reader to a more contemplative space. So I invite you to explore this text and contemplate all that is presented here.

John (Jack) P. Miller, author of
The Holistic Curriculum

Acknowledgements

While transformation is marked by shifts of consciousness, another marker of such movement is the presence of those in our lives who have accompanied such shifts and illuminated its journey. In my journey there are many to whom I am grateful for their support.

Amongst them is the Holistic Educators Group, affiliated with the Department of Curriculum, Teaching and Learning in the Ontario Institute for Studies in Education, whose members both welcomed and encouraged my project. I thank them for their friendship and support of my project.

I am also grateful for the constellation of teachers who sparked my academic transit. Amongst them my first teacher at OISE, Kari Dehli, who welcomed my return to graduate school with warmth and kindness and Roger Simon with whom I pondered the power of images and whose touch continues to be present in my work.

My book emerges from my doctoral dissertation, amongst the scintillae its constellation enriched by my committee members. Michel Ferrari guided me onto the arc of wisdom studies while Grace Feuerverger supported the spark of narrative. Susan Schiller nurtured the intersection of my writing with spirituality while David Booth provided generative insights into the visual composition of my project. I am grateful for their support.

At the core of the constellation is my supervisor John P. Miller, whose presence guided me as I contemplated Merton's scintilla on the purpose of education. Jack's presence became central to the transformative spirit of my own educational journey. I thank him for his support and guidance.

I am indebted to Dr. Avram Sussman for nurturing both my mind and soul as I journeyed through inquiry. Thank you also to Eri Oshima for fostering my creativity while supporting my wellness. My project is also indebted to my friends and colleagues Jude Ulysse and Ricky Varghese; their journeys onto the terrain of inquiry in the University of Toronto illuminated my own.

I am also grateful for the many artists and curators who supported my project. Amongst them is Greg Manuel, with whom I started a conversation on Edward Burtynsky's work which remains ongoing. A talk by Edward Burtynsky in conversation with William Ewing on the publication of *Essential Elements* in October 2016 was a seminal moment in that conversation. An excerpt from it is included in the book courtesy of the Nicholas Metivier Gallery. My thanks to Caroline Pearson of the gallery for assistance with transcription of the talk. I am also indebted to Marcus Schubert and Alanna Joanne of the Edward Burtynsky studio for their support of my project and permissions to use selected images from Burtynsky's photographic work.

My book would not have emerged were it not for the support of my editors at Routledge. I am grateful to Elsbeth Wright for her encouraging critiques of my writing and, with her editorial assistants Rebecca Collazo, AnnaMary Goodall and copy editor Stacy Lavin, for guiding me through the publication journey.

The journey began with my parents, Antonio and Agata, who encouraged my sister Lucia and me to love learning. I thank them for this gift.

As I travelled the arc of inquiry, I was accompanied by my wife Gianna; her presence was the original scintilla which nurtured the transformative journey.

A Necessary Letter to the Reader
On the Ethos of Arts-Based Contemplative Inquiry

Following Merton's "Summonses to Awareness"

> *To speak of the summonses describes a powerful request when one is called upon; a calling marked by the imperative of the demand. In my summonses such imperative is configured within the domain of narrative; one in which the presence of story is foundational to both epistemological discourse and the promise of learning and transformation.*
>
> *Narrative seeds the summonses with a necessary presence which I must face. My summonses cannot be without my narrative; and from the demand of narrative emerges my summonses onto inquiry.*
>
> *Being and narrative entwined wherein my being in the world is a being in narrative.*

In *Raids on the Unspeakable* (1966) Thomas Merton offers us his Zen-like sketches and speaks of their aesthetical presence as "summonses to awareness" (Merton, 1966, p. 182). Within an aesthetical encounter, Merton seeks to traverse into a place of awareness. His retelling of his own aesthetical journey in turn became a starting point for my own reflections upon the character of inquiry. Following Merton I ponder: *what summons me to awareness in this inquiry?* What conveys me to the question of the relation of wisdom and art?

Understandings of wisdom are diverse and straddle millennia and cultures; an observation which has led some commentators to observe that wisdom defies a singular understanding (Curnow, 2015, 2008; Walsh, 2015, 2011). *How does one begin inquiry when its key word defies a consensus on its definition?*

Seeking to emerge from such a conundrum follows Curnow's suggestion that, in lieu of a universal definition, we select one from the many, though our selection may depart from other understandings of wisdom (Curnow, 2015). In this study, a working definition is broadly informed by Hadot's historical exploration of wisdom as both "a discourse and a way of life" (Hadot, 2002, p. 4). Wisdom is not knowledge of the world; instead it is "a mode of being" (Hadot, 2002, p. 220). Of wisdom as a way of being in the world, Hadot observes

> If philosophy is that activity by means of which philosophers train themselves for wisdom, such an exercise must necessarily consist not

merely in speaking and discoursing in a certain way, but also in being, acting, and seeing the world in a specific way. If, then, philosophy is not merely discourse but a choice of life, an existential option, and a lived exercise, this is because it is the desire for wisdom.

(Hadot, 2002, p. 220)

While such an understanding of wisdom is rooted in Hadot's study of ancient philosophy, a second aspect of its working definition is informed by recent work in the spirituality research paradigm (Lin, Oxford, & Culham, 2016), one which ponders wisdom through such notions as Oxford's thesis of "deep education and mysticism" (Oxford, 2016, p. 207), or Miller's reflections upon wisdom as embodied (Miller, 2016). While these notions configure understandings of wisdom, they also enrich the question of the relation of wisdom and the aesthetical.

With my working understanding of wisdom as a starting point, my study begins its reflections upon this question. However, while an inquiry into the exploring of the relation of art and wisdom may follow the path of historical chronicle or philosophical investigation, my study seeks to traverse a different terrain. Departing from the inquirer-subject dualism which marks the methodological canon of such research my study seeks to meditate upon the relation of wisdom and art within a different territory, one which departs from the methodological binary and is instead nested within a contemplative ethos informed by the presence of narrative and the aesthetical.

The "contemplative turn" (Ergas, 2016, p. 2) is one onto the self: a turn which stands apart from the binary by its will to map its own path onto inquiry. In this study, such seeking witnessed by acts of writing within encounters with texts and experiences with art that collectively seeded a terrain from which my map began to emerge. Its contours formed a dialogical landscape wherein my passage onto inquiry emerged from within discourses with *myself* and Thomas Merton.

My method was born within such a landscape. Its inward turn, while dialogical in spirit, was also paradoxical yet necessary, as I needed to turn inwards onto my narrative in order to turn outwards onto the understanding I sought of the world beyond. And within such territory of turns and paradoxes formed of dialogical reflections, narrative presences and aesthetical encounters my method emerged. Its core formed of the intimacy of aesthetics with ethics, a view which I extend from Heesoon Bai (1997), onto the question of how the understanding of wisdom, as ethical knowledge, is enriched by the presence of the artful. It is an inward turn sculpting a way of contemplative inquiry whose witness is a map formed of the interweaving of the aesthetical with narrative and the dialogical— and whose tools for inquiry emerge organically from within them.

My Being in Narrative

I introduce my *necessary letter* with a reflection upon the imperative of narrative in my study. The thesis of the necessity by which inquiry is informed by narrative builds upon Mary Beattie's observation, following Bruner, about how "narrative is at the heart of our meaning-making structures, and that we understand the events of our lives in the context of stories that have beginnings, middles, and ends (Bruner)" (Beattie, 2019, p. 252). By engaging with narrative through such strategies as storytelling, conversation and arts-based practices Beattie observes how it nurtures reflection upon our lives and seeds transformation and wholeness.

Narrative forges our reality (Bruner, 1991); and if stories are central to our being in the world, then our stories are also the seedbed of wisdom. In this I cycle back to Hadot and reflect upon how he entwines the idea of wisdom, not with discourse, but with life as a "lived exercise" (Hadot, 2002, p. 220). To Hadot's idea I add the necessary presence of narrative, in the construct of reality which Beattie and Bruner speak of, and am guided towards the view of how the promise of wisdom emerges from the interweaving of our being in the world with our stories.

Though the study of wisdom is not central to Bruner's research, the essence of such interweaving is elegantly captured in his observation that a "life as led is inseparable from a life as told" (Bruner, 2004, p. 708). To engage with story is to engage with what Bruner describes as "life making" (Bruner, 2004, p. 692). But, as Bruner also observes, the reflective nature of narrative is complicated as the storyteller is also the story's character (Bruner, 2004). Narrative poses a methodological conundrum in narrative research; and as the psychologist Donald Polkinghorne (2007) observes cycles about the not insurmountable problem of validity in such research.

Bruner's dilemma underscores a conundrum which is central to my study. My summonses onto inquiry emerges from the demand of my narrative yet such demand is not exempt from its paradox. I look out onto the world by a reflexive turn onto my self; a turn formed of my stories and within kindred moments of dialogical engagement with Merton's writings and works of art that I feel towards. The narrative turn becoming the construct of my being in the world; yet, one which is also paradoxical as the inward turn is also outward in ethos. I heed the summonses of narrative by turning onto the imperative of my story. The construct of my world which stands beyond is predicated upon my stories which emerge from within.

My *being in narrative in the world* is constructed within such conundrum. And while the crossing onto such terrain is paradoxical, such transit is not a desolate one. I am present within my narrative universe as are others within theirs as I engage them in the classroom or pass them on the street or wait patiently within a queue. We are configured by the imperative of our own stories and taken together inviting conjecture that the domain of *beings in the world* is nested within a mysterious amalgam of such stories.

To dwell upon such conjecture, while interesting in its implication for a sociological interpretation of narrative, extends beyond the scope of the present inquiry into wisdom's relation to art. Instead my study has a more modest methodological goal and is guided by the thesis that while narrative is imperative to the construct of reality, contemplative inquiry is a vehicle whereby we may begin to interpret such edifice.

4 A Necessary Letter to the Reader

Although this thesis touches upon methodological themes which are explored in Chapter 5 of this study, it is introduced here to observe that while wisdom research, grounded in historical chronicle, empirical psychological investigation or philosophical study, can inform the question of wisdom's relation to art, my study is not guided by the methods of these research disciplines. Instead, my exploration endeavours to follow in the spirit of Tobin Hart's proposal, within the field of transformative learning in education, of "a third way of knowing" (Hart, 2004, p. 29), that is, of contemplative knowing—one which departs from the rationalist and empirical paradigms and that, as Hart observes, dominates the understanding of what counts as legitimate knowing today.

Instead of eroding the phenomenon in order to understand it, contemplative knowing embraces the fullness of its complexity within a strategy which is inclusive, about connection and non-dualistic. Instead of the binary of inquirer and subject which marks empirical methodology, contemplative knowing seeks another path: one which is reflected in Merton's critique of Cartesian thinking in *New Seeds of Contemplation* (Merton, 1972), Walsh's and Bai's meditative engaging with writing through "writing witness consciousness" (Walsh & Bai, 2015, p. 25) or Parker Palmer's observation that we embrace the "voice of the subject" (Palmer, 1993, p. 98) within a spirit of connection. Within such an embrace, binaries dissolve and inquiry, within a contemplative strategy, is in turn nurtured, as Hart observes, "through a wide range of approaches—from pondering to poetry to meditation" (Hart, 2004, p. 29) which extend beyond the narrower lens of empirical investigation.

Whereas such research strategies defy accommodation with analytical methodologies they are suited to explore the complexity of narrative and how, following Beattie and Bruner, it is core to the construction of meaning (Beattie, 2019). Entangled within its paradoxical domain, where it is configured about an inward presence which also looks outwards, narrative summons us with its imperative demand—one which is interpreted in this study, following Hart, through a contemplative methodology configured about aesthetical encounters and dialogical engagements with texts.

At its core, narrative study "*re*-searches lived experience" (Bai, Elza, Kovacs, & Romanycia, 2010. p. 351) and is intimate with the spirit of contemplative inquiry. Our stories sculpt our way of being in the world with their imperative presence; to engage them touches the core life questions or "ultimate concerns" which philosophers Peter London (London, 2004, p. 5) and Paul Tillich (Hart, 2004, p. 37) observe respectively. To be with them within such moments when we reflect upon our way of *being in narrative in the world* is to share an ethos which is central to contemplative inquiry. To do so through art, within an arts-based contemplative paradigm, enriches reflection upon the core life concerns that London and Tillich speak of.

> *And hence this necessary letter to the reader where I am summoned by my narrative, in the fullness of its complex paradox, in order to speak to you on the aesthetical ethos of wisdom.*

Drawing on Stories and Stories of Drawings

Following Hart (2004), it is through a contemplative approach—one which draws on the rich seedbed of narrative in tandem with encounters with art—that my inquiry is summoned, its summoning marked by nurturing presences: Each chapter begins with a story or an image or a dialogical exchange with Merton's writings which collectively form entry points for reflections not only upon the relation of wisdom and the aesthetical, but also kindred ones on the contemplative child and wisdom in the landscape. The arc of my contemplative inquiry is nurtured by such presences, together forming the thread that weaves the inquiry.

It is within a contemplative research ethos informed by the arts that my exploration into the relation of wisdom and art is summoned. By allowing narrative to emerge with the aesthetical in inquiry—an amalgam which was ever present but never stirred in my previous studies—I journeyed onto a terrain which became nurturing of the authenticity I sought in inquiry.

Of its transformative arc I assemble my bricolage formed of . . .

Retellings, reflections
&
palimpsests,
Childhood memories & school book astronomy,
Serendipitous discoveries,
old sketches &
photographs,
pauses, doubts &
epicyclical returns,
. . . the painter Fra Angelico & astronomer Tycho Brahe,
of paradoxes, paradigms &
awakenings,
of memories which recycle &
stir the alchemical transit,
of conversations with artists,
Brother Louis & you,
of questions which beget more questions
&
forever recycle
towards the Sophia
which emerges from within.

Of that journey three moments from my story have broadly informed its trajectory in the present study. The first one is configured by my encounters with post-secondary education in the fields of philosophy, history of science and architecture; the second is informed by my experiences within graduate studies of education to which I turned later in life. Although the first moment constituted difficult pedagogical encounters, they served as verdant fodder for the subsequent chapter of my studies. Returning to a graduate school of education introduced me to a different epistemological paradigm—one which stood apart from the rationalist and analytical philosophies in which I had been schooled and was, following Hart (2004), instead configured within a contemplative ethos which drew upon the different paradigm of holistic and transformative studies in education. Within such a return the third moment of my story emerges, that is, of the presence of the aesthetical and narrative within inquiry—one which was welcomed by this different terrain of contemplative knowing that I had journeyed onto.

Viewed through this new paradigm, my complicated encounters with post-secondary education were interpreted afresh, bringing into focus the question of the nature of knowing in general and critique of the binary nature of Cartesian knowing in particular. Such critique, which follows Palmer's observation of the "one-eyed lives" (Palmer, 1993, p. xxiii) with which he views reductionist knowing and which was echoed in my own encounters with higher education, also foregrounded Palmer's appeal for the return of "wholesight"—a knowing whose inclusive reach embraces the intuitive, empathic and emotional in additional to the rational (Palmer, 1993, p. 52).

My encounters with learning in post-secondary settings foregrounded the problems of knowledge that Palmer speaks of, which were reflected in the entangled relation of my narrative with my philosophical interests in epistemology. They also revealed how the topic of wisdom in general, with which Palmer's "wholesight" can be associated, and the relation of wisdom to the aesthetical in particular, was largely absent from my schooling. Collectively, such narrative moments sculpted of encounters both difficult and meditative summoned me into the present inquiry, one which is explored in the following seven chapters.

The Weave of Inquiry

The question into the relation of wisdom and art would not have become foregrounded were it not for the presence of formative experiences in my narrative—ones which, in addition to encounters with post-secondary schooling, were also enriched by experiences growing up as a child of post-war immigrant parents in a provincial town in southern Ontario. Such experiences, while sculpting my narrative were also, following Bruner (1991, 2004) and Beattie (2019), the basis for the construction of its reality. Although stories in my early life formed memories which remained unsaid, they also endured eventually seeding my later intuition in this study that the question of the relation of wisdom and art was in the same instance nurtured by such primordial presences or "vague fragments" (Merton, 1998b, p. 12) in my early life. Forming Chapter 1, reflections upon such fragments mark an engagement with a narrative presence in my study, one guided by the thesis, introduced in *A Necessary Letter*, that we cannot do contemplative inquiry unless we engage with the imperative of the personal. While the personal is marked by narrative in my writing, it is in addition configured within an aesthetical presence, which together with the former shaped part of what I view as the fundamental ethos of an arts informed contemplative study.

Formative experiences, born of encounters with schooling and art, are introduced in Chapter 1 as exemplars for beginning to cross the terrain of such ethos. While the crossing is marked by intuitions about the relation of wisdom and art, the chapter is also guided by a second theme about the absence of such relation within higher education, one intended to illustrate Palmer and Zajonc's (2010) and Zajonc's critique of the "epistemology of separation" (Zajonc, 2006, p. 1744) dominating higher education today.

While Chapter 1 situates personal narrative within the thesis of its imperative presence within contemplative inquiry Chapter 2 provides a second exemplar of such a notion in selected writings of Thomas Merton. The chapter interprets narrative and aesthetical themes in his work through the contemporary lens of writers in the fields of contemplative and transformative learning in education. Merton's views are explored as a basis for beginning to configure an understanding of wisdom as one which emerges from the interweaving of the personal and aesthetical. The exploration of Merton's ideas is guided in part by the strategy of dialogical speaking with *Brother Louis*, the name by which he was known in the Abbey of Gethsemani.

The dialogical engagement with Merton is my "writing witness consciousness," a notion extended from Walsh and Bai (2015, p. 24) and reimagined as a terrain wherein it is reduced the distance between *I, the researcher,* and the *subject of my research* within a seeking of connection and non-dualism in inquiry. It is a form of engaging with a text that seeks the ethos of an arts-based contemplative methodology where research is guided by tools which are artful and extend beyond the narrower register of empirical investigation (Hart, 2004). While the methodological interpretation of such a strategy is explored in Chapter 5, it is introduced in Chapter 2 as a way of beginning to relate themes of the aesthetical and narrative in Merton's work to the thesis of the wisdom image.

The questions of an inquiry sometimes feel ephemeral, evolving into presence, sometimes departing while at other times lingering within the contemplative transit. Their ephemeral nature in turn sustains the life of the "perpetual seeker" (Miller, 2016, p. 138) and underscores how the terrain of contemplative inquiry is a paradoxical place. Its crossing is marked by transitory presences but also by another wherein questions emerge and elect to remain with us. Chapter 3 attempts to corral such transience within an overview of questions into the relation of wisdom and art which emerged during the journey of my project and are of two broad configurations. The first are questions about the relation of wisdom and art that were sparked by a synchronous reading of three texts: John P. Miller's *Educating for Wisdom and Compassion* (2006); Ferrari's & Potworowski's *Teaching for Wisdom* (2008); and Thomas Merton's *Love and Living* (1979). Pondering these texts in tandem with Merton's other aesthetical writings and his strategy of direct engaging with the reader which is found in some of his texts formed the second set of questions. The latter touch on methodological questions for an arts-enriched contemplative inquiry and are explored through kindred explorations of dialogical discourse in the work of Hart (2004) and Palmer (1993) and Gunnlaugson's thesis of "generative dialogue" (Gunnlaugson, 2007, p. 138). The chapter is underscored by the thesis that while the journey of questions is immersed within a ceaseless transit, the seeking of certainty is not its primary goal (Hart, 2009). Instead, as Hart, following the physicist David Bohm, observes, the promise of wonder is nurtured when the goal of certainty is abandoned.

The feeling of wonder which emerges with the embrace of questions suggests an emotional relation to them which extends beyond their dispassionate status in inquiry. Motivated by wonder, we are enchanted by the questions that emerge; they allure through inquiry and our relation to them is not one of emotional disengagement.

In kindred spirit our relation to texts in inquiry, which is the subject of Chapter 4, is marked by an affective presence; the texts that we feel towards, mediate upon or share with others in dialogue revealing our affective connection to them which, like the questions of inquiry, reach beyond their referential presence in inquiry. The chapter's title (The Friendship of Texts) is intended to capture such ethos and is guided by Hart's view of the power of texts as embodying "living words" (Hart, 2008, p. 236) and Palmer's encouragement to be in dialogue with texts within a spirit of friendship (Palmer, 1993). Their kindred views suggest a relationship to texts which extends beyond uncomplicated interpretations of their referential status in inquiry to another where we instead engage them as vital presences.

While the chapter follows in the spirit of Palmer's (1993) and Hart's (2004) views of such relation, it is also intended to nurture the general thesis of my study, that is, how the journey to wisdom is one which necessarily ventures onto the terrain of the personal and artful. As we embark on that journey, witnessed by the texts that we encounter and for which we feel kin.

In its aesthetical and relational spirit, Chapter 4 does not exclude, as could an empirical study, the literary from the analytical text; instead, it embraces them together within an inclusive configuration of contemplative inquiry. Forming part of that configuration is the first-person strategy of dialogical discourses with texts which is adopted in the chapter and elsewhere in the book. This strategy is intended to illustrate how, within a contemplative study, the relationship with texts extends beyond their referential status into another domain where they are not disencased from the life of the inquirer but are instead intimate with it within a spirit of friendship.

Such spirit underscores the flow of my writing which meanders between moments when it speaks with the first person in dialogical friendship with Merton's texts and others when the third-person voice dominant. The movement of voices reflect the imperative of my narrative—one formed of the vestiges of my earlier studies in philosophy when the third-person voice was enforced and subsequent studies when I had journeyed onto the contemplative terrain where the first-person voice was no longer excluded in research.

While such movement of voices collectively configure a first-third-person presence in my writing, it also foregrounds methodological themes about the relation of narrative to arts-based contemplative inquiry in education. To speak *between voices*, as my study does in the aesthetical exploration of some of Merton's texts and in my own narrative retellings, raises questions of method, whose exploration is the intent of Chapter 5. Such questions are underscored by the strategy of dialogical discourse, one which is echoed in Merton's own writings such as *Letter to an Innocent Bystander* in *Raids on the Unspeakable* (Merton, 1966) and a dedication in *A Thomas Merton Reader* (Merton, 1974) where he addresses the text and reader respectively, and which is reciprocated in the present study as a tool which fosters reflection.

Departing from a third-person approach, dialogical discourse falls within the broader range of creative tools which Tobin Hart ponders in his characterization of contemplative knowing (Hart, 2004). It also follows in the spirit of arts based researchers who encourage ways of doing inquiry which are marginalized within the academy (Diamond & Mullen, 2001) and researchers in spirituality studies such as Palmer who advocate that we embrace and listen to the subject (Palmer, 1993) within a strategy which is holistic and not binary in spirit. In this inquiry, dialogical writing to Merton was generative of questions and meditations and, following Susan Schiller's observation, becomes a form of writing which becomes meaningful by being connected to "something in the writer's world that allows the writing to be both *desirable* and *worthwhile* to that person" (Schiller, 2014, p. x).

In this study, that "*something*" which connected me to the writing, in addition to my experiences in post-secondary education, was my childhood story, a connection which in turn guided me towards viewing the subject of methodology holistically, that is, as not disencased from my narrative but in intimate relation with it. As a child, I was raised without siblings until the age of 8 and my first experiences with socialization, in the absence of preschool or Kindergarten, did not happen until the first grade. Until then, I lived within a contemplative and sometimes imaginary world of my own making—one whose reality was not brought into meaning until its emergence within this inquiry. Dialogical speaking with Merton in adulthood echoes the internal world of my childhood, and in this nurturing the idea of how my present inquiry was also seeded in my childhood narrative. Such notion in turn invited reflection upon the relation of the child to contemplation and evoked Montessori's idea of the "spiritual embryo" (Montessori, 1970, p. 18), Miller's exploration of the "whole child" (Miller, 2010, p. 9), Hart's idea of children as "natural contemplatives" (Hart, 2004, p. 43) and Merton's notion of "child mind" (Gardner, 2016, p. 3).

If an inquiry is configured within the entwining of narrative and the dialogical, as it is in my story and its earliest traces in my childhood, then of what configuration is its methodology? The question returns to Bruner's idea of narrative as being fundamental to meaning making and gravitates towards Oren

10 *A Necessary Letter to the Reader*

Ergas' kindred thesis of how meaning is constructed within our "personal paradigms" (Ergas, 2016, p. 14). Chapter 5 extends Bruner's and Ergas' notions with the observation of the personal character of methodology as one configured in narrative; and underscored by the thesis that my research is guided by a methodology of my own making—a *methodology of one*.

If our way of being and meaning making, following Bruner and Ergas, is sculpted within narrative and the domain of the personal respectively, then wisdom as "lived exercise," following Hadot (Hadot, 2002, p. 220), can also be seen to emerge within a methodology which is configured within the personal. This premise underscores Chapter 6 and is scaffolded by the question—*how can wisdom be fostered in the classroom within a narrative configuration which is also artful?*

Powerful images, such as the landscape photographs of Edward Burtynsky, have potential to teach and offer wisdom. Yet, following Ergas, meaning making is a personal domain; herein the promise of their lessons also turns upon the student's potential to absorb them. How is such potential developed within the student? How is the *methodology of one* nurtured? Importantly, how is such method seeded within an aesthetical ethos?

These questions underpin Chapter 6. Drawing on exemplars, such as the Berlin Wisdom model (Baltes, 2004), Sternberg, Jarvin and Reznitskaya's *Balance Theory of Wisdom* (Sternberg, Jarvin, & Reznitskaya, 2008) and the child-centred research of Reeve, Messina, and Scardamalia (2008), the chapter explores what can be extracted from such precedents in formulating a classroom practice for fostering wisdom through art. The discourse of wisdom research though is most often associated with texts and less so with the aesthetical. As such, my suggestions for beginning to construct this new bridge are offered as a prolegomenon which will, it is hoped, encourage further inquiry.

While Chapter 6 is offered as a prolegomenon on the teaching of wisdom through the arts, Chapter 7 concludes with reflections upon the centrality of the inward turn as key to the spirit of contemplative inquiry. Though the chapter explores how such ethos resides within a paradoxical domain, the journey onto the contemplative territory is aided by creative tools for making meaning of such complexity. Amongst these are ones used in this study such as encounters with art, narrative writing and dialogical discourse. Forming part of the toolbox for contemplative inquiry, they also expand it beyond the more restrictive research strategies of scientific inquiry.

An arc of inquiry which began with the imperative of the personal in *A Necessary Letter* ends in Chapter 7 with the observation that while the turn onto the self presents a paradox, it is from within aesthetical and narrative encounters with its complexity that the promise of wisdom emerges.

My study seeks to explore the relation of the aesthetical to wisdom within a contemplation which is interwoven by narrative retellings and others when I engage with Merton's texts within a dialogical spirit. Another component of such interweaving is the use of images. While some of the images, such as Burtynsky's photographs, are intended to illustrate contemplative notions of "wholesight" (Palmer, 1993, p. xxiii), others are intended to reflect the interweaving of narrative and inquiry and the power of art to teach and nurture wisdom.

The latter images are drawn from my story and bookended by ones taken from my earliest experiences of schooling and other more recent encounters with art. Of the latter, trips to Florence and Venice to be with painting and sculpture marked a generative moment in my writing. The encounter with art in these places invigorated my writing by nurturing reflections upon its relation to wisdom and kindred interpretations of the character of *transformation* and *connection*, as I both photographed these places and later in my writing pondered the literature of transformative and holistic education in general and Merton's writings in particular.

While images accompany my writing, their role in inquiry is intended to extend beyond their referential status. Their placement at either the beginning of a chapter or occupying a full page within is intended to honour the epistemic power of the imaginal. Standing apart from a view of image as ancillary to text, the image is instead interpreted as having an elevated epistemic standing and holding the promise of wisdom. While the use of images reflects the spirit of arts-based inquiry, it also acknowledges the contemplative embrace of creative tools in research. Standing apart from the Cartesian paradigm which unweaves experience in order to understand it, images are honoured in inquiry as lenses through which the complexity of experience is interpreted within a holistic ethos.

1 Narrative Beginnings
The Seeds of Inquiry and the Imperative of Story

Image 1.1 Unknown. (c. 1962). *John's Journey*. [Digitally Recaptured & Edited Photograph]. Ontario, Canada
Source: G. Rossini

Beginning Inquiry by Reflecting on My Story

I liken the beginning of my inquiry to a planting, one whose end point is a harvest whose yield I hope towards but cannot know assuredly in advance. My planting is seeded by a mixture of seeds: images I am drawn to like Burtynsky's water photographs (Burtynsky, Davis, & Lord, 2013), the curvilinear architecture of Borromini's Church San Carlo alle Quattro Fontane (1638–1641; Wittkower, 1958,1986), the filmic quality of Caravaggio's *The Calling of Saint Matthew* (Church of San Luigi dei Francesi, Rome, 1599–1600; Schütze, 2017, p. 133), the magical narratives of cinematographers like Terrence Malick in *The Tree of Life* (Green, Pohlad, Pitt, Gardner, & Hill, 2011) and fragments of writings from Merton's *New Seeds of Contemplation* (1972).

Such seeds, which I have taken from places afar, are mixed together with others taken from places closer to home. The seeds of my parents' narrative—immigrants from the impoverished mezzogiorno region of Italy—my mother, Agata, from a seaside village in Abruzzo, just south of Ortona, which was destroyed during the war while my father, Antonio, from the Lucania region where Carlo Levi set his novel *Christ Stopped at Eboli* (1947), and where the Normans settled during the Middle Ages and ancient Greeks many generations before. My father's mother, is surnamed Atena after the Greek Goddess of wisdom, her name a trace of the Greek presence in southern Italy. Within this tapestry was nested my parents' retellings of their lives—therein also becoming part of my memory, their retellings in turn recycling into the formation of a living palimpsest that configures my being today.

Their seed I carry with me along with others: my memory of a solitary childhood until my sister Lucia was born eight years later; growing up in a conservative southern Ontario town; and the home of my co-opted Canadian grandmother neighbour who sang lullabies to me and taught my mother English. My memories of school are mixed amongst such seeds: my first day of school standing by the school yard fence; my supportive high school art teacher; intensely working on my painting in the school's art studio; my parents' encouragement to my sister and I to pursue higher education; my difficult memories of architecture school and graduate studies in philosophy; the time I lived in Rome, being with art and architecture; my trepidations of returning later in life to graduate studies in OISE and finding that my worries were dissipated by a different pedagogy which nurtured inquiry within a coming to knowing within the re-covering of my authentic self.

Into this mixture of seeds were added others: that of my Catholic schooling in the wake of the Vatican II reforms. While I had since journeyed onto new places, its ethos of social justice was one which has remained with me.

As I ponder these seeds I am reminded of Thomas Merton's turn to Dante's poetry from *The Divine Comedy*:

> *And you must know that the sacred land*
> *where you are is full of every seed*
> *and has fruit not plucked in your world.*
> (Merton, 1974, p. 455)

Collectively my experiences seeded my sacred land which was named "John." They were once vestiges of my self, which were ever *present within a mysterious primordial and subconscious knowing. But once I crossed onto the new land, the traces emerged into meaning within acts of writing, encounters with art and dialogical conversations with Merton. And within the imperative of such moments, I felt the comfort of truth.*

Entering the "Sacred Land" of Narrative

My inquiry into the relation of art and wisdom begins with the necessity of my story—and one whose retelling is methodologically informed by such thinkers as Schiller (2014) in the field of holistic education and Eisner (2008) and Diamond and Mullen (2001) in arts-based learning and their kindred notion of inquiry as a process which is seeded by the fertile terrain of our narratives. Engaging with story is to enter onto a reflective terrain which, in addition, accords well with the introspective ethos of inquiry as contemplative process. In this, my study seeks to be methodologically ecumenical as it is also guided by Hart's notion of contemplation as a way of knowing which "complements the rational and the sensory" (Hart, 2004, p. 29) while embracing strategies for inquiry drawn from, for example, the arts or storytelling or meditative practices which are not generally associated with the former.

In this study, the spirit of narrative and arts-based inquiry in curriculum studies is viewed as synergistic with such strategies within contemplative inquiry. When Diamond observes how the character of research is intimately enmeshed with the way we live (Diamond, 2009), his observation evokes Hart's view of contemplative inquiry as one which is not separate from the life of inquirer, or Arthur Zajonc's criticism of dualistic epistemologies (Zajonc, 2006) which dominate higher education today. With Diamond their views of the character of inquiry mirror Palmer's observation, following the physicist Fritjof Capra, that "we can never speak about nature without, at the same time, speaking about ourselves" (Capra, 1991, p. 69).

My study endeavours to follow in the spirit of such writers; by *returning onto my self* through narrative retellings, imaginal explorations and dialogical engagement with Merton's writings, I seek to transcend the dualism of subject-researcher that Zajonc criticizes as dominating university research today. Instead, within a contemplative ethos, allowing inquiry to emerge from within an intimate dialogue where connection is nurtured between *I* the inquirer and my narrative being. Of such connection, Palmer writes about listening to our subject (Palmer, 1993), a listening which, in my study, is hailed by the summonings of my narrative. Narrative hails us with an imperative to listen. The intimacy of its call in turn becomes integral to the spirit of contemplative knowing, wherein my story, informed in part by my journey as a philosophy student many years ago, seeds the introspective ethos of such knowing while also informing the broader configuration of my study as one which is contemplative and not empirical in spirit.

As Hart observes of contemplative knowing, by opening onto ourselves we also open onto the world (Hart, 2004). The inward turn onto the self becomes an outward one where in kindred spirit, by opening onto my narrative I also look out onto and make meaning of my being in the world. Of the character of such cycling towards the self, Oren Ergas likens it as the "contemplative turn" (Ergas, 2016, p. 2) he sees happening in education today. While, for Merton, the promise of wisdom emerges from within the turn towards the artist who resides within us (Merton, 1972). In *New Seeds of Contemplation* Merton observes,

> It is not humility to insist on being someone that you are not. It is as much as saying that you know better than God who you are and who you ought to be. How do you expect to arrive at the end of your own journey if you take the road to another man's city? How do you expect to reach your own perfection by leading somebody else's life? His sanctity will never be yours; you must have the humility to work out your own salvation in darkness where you are absolutely alone. . . . And so it takes heroic humility to be yourself and to be nobody but the man, or the artist, that God intended you to be.
>
> (Merton, 1972, p. 100)

Reading Merton's journey returns me to reflecting upon my own; and the shift that it had undergone.

Writing my story that introduces this chapter followed an earlier project in my doctoral studies which I had abandoned. That project felt inauthentic and its harvest was meagre. Feelings of unease set in. I threw out what I had written; not knowing where I would go next I started anew with my story. I was only assured that, following Merton, I needed to sculpt my own journey to my city—one whose map was marked by the presence of the artist; and which was nested within the nexus of contemplative knowing with the richness of narrative. I shifted onto another terrain; one that I now view as Merton's "sacred land" (Merton, 1974, p. 455) filled with seeds and fruits which awaited their harvest. Seeking this sacred place marked the entry point into my inquiry. And one, which, following Merton, only I could enter "absolutely alone."

Of the nature of transformation, Gunnlaugson, following Mezirow, observes how it is marked by shifts in one's "frame of reference" (Gunnlaugson, 2007, p. 135). Of such transformative events, Dencev and Collister (2010) also observe them as shifts in consciousness which are nested within acts of creativity. While my earlier project felt inauthentic, abandoning it also marked a transformative moment, one in which my inquiry entered a new territory where it was not disencased from the life of this inquirer. While the map of my study within such territory was unknown when my story, which introduces this chapter, was written, its horizon was distantly apparent and broadly marked by an epistemological turn. That is, it was a turn from the analytical rationalism in which I had been schooled towards another place which was nested within reintegration of the self and characterized by notions of "nondual knowing" (Miller, 2006, p. 10), connection and non-propositional knowing (Palmer, 1993), or Merton's idea of "a hidden wholeness" (Merton, 1974, p. 506).

My turning away from the analytical paradigm marked an opening onto inquiry. Of the configuration of such opening it often feels serendipitous and non-linear, a feeling evoking the jazz musician John Coltrane's observation on his own musical process as one which starts from the middle rather than the beginning of a composition (Coltrane as cited in Webb, 2018). Coltrane's reflection in turn echoes Hart's kindred observation about the non-linearity of contemplative knowing (Hart, 2004). While opening onto narrative is a portal into the sacred land that Merton speaks of, my story is also, following Coltrane, a beginning in the centre in order to seek the periphery.

The Seeds of Inquiry as Recycling of Memory

> A man who has not passed through the inferno of his passions has never overcome them. They then dwell in the house next door, and at any moment a flame may dart out and set fire to his own house. Whenever we give up, leave behind, and forget too much, there is always the danger that the things we have neglected will return with added force.
> (Jung, 1989, p. 277)

I kept all my school workbooks from elementary through to secondary school and university. They had become precious artefacts.

I heed Jung's warning and probe them for signs and prescient discoveries. I seek to remember that which has been neglected.

I return to my Grade 3 workbook and ponder the exercise on "The Architect." It tells how the architect makes the plan of the house.

Many years later I would study in a faculty of architecture.

An interesting synchronicity emerges between my schoolbook exercise and later career which would not have emerged if the child had not protected his workbooks. While seemingly innocuous the child's journal offers a metaphor for inquiry. Its "vague fragments" (Merton, 1998b, p. 12) of childhood prescient to my later adult life in a way akin to how the drawing plan of the house anticipates the building. Within its plan are nested the primordial seeds of inquiry.

The encounter with my workbook is both a witnessing to a child's nascent journey and the recycling of a memory, now captured in an image, into meaning within the adult.

But the child's house plan, pasted into his workbook, is only one room of the house.

Narrative Beginnings 17

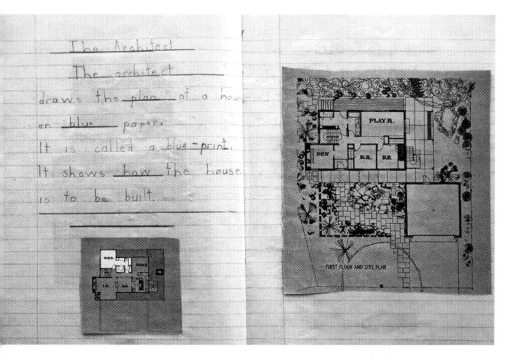

Image 1.2 Rossini, G. (c. 1966). *Beginning Inquiry, My Grade 3 Workbook.* [Photograph of Page From G. Rossini's Grade 3 Workbook]. Ontario, Canada

Source: G. Rossini

In his autobiography Carl Jung ponders the psyche through the metaphor of the Tower he builds in Bollingen, its rooms representing aspects of self and which he viewed as "a place of maturation- a maternal womb or a maternal figure in which I could become what I was, what I am and will be" (Jung, 1989, p. 225).

Jung's tower returns me to my child's workbook. I would later find other pages within them and new rooms. I cycle back to my workbook while writing my inquiry. I seek to explore this house.

My reflections upon my family story, which are interweaved with encounters with art and difficult memories of post-secondary education, which opens the chapter, served as a transformative seed and is one amongst several stories which were nurturing to my inquiry. Along with it were others, such as the presence of my primary school workbooks, which collectively formed a hodgepodge of fragmented yet ever present memories, in turn forming seeds which have travelled with me for a long time. Following Bruner's observation upon the character of narrative, my stories accumulated; a "narrative accrual" (Bruner, 1991, p. 18) emerged into the construction of my reality. Its narrative seeds were intimate with the metaphor of the rooms where, for Jung, the psyche resides.

Of the forms and colours of the flowers which will sprout from the seeds which have accrued I do not yet know. I feel only assured that amongst them is inextricably rooted the possibility of inquiry, its authenticity configured within an aesthetical presence and the entanglement of my inquiry with the narrative seeds that I carry and allow to sprout.

What harvest will follow?

Jung (1955) writes of the synchronicity of events, that is, the co-happening of seemingly unrelated events whose coincidence becomes meaningful (Jung, 1955). I read Merton and am comforted by a curious synchronicity between a passage in *New Seeds of Contemplation* (1972) wherein he ponders the plantings of the soul and my meditation upon my jumble of seeds.

> EVERY moment and every event of every man's life on earth plants something in his soul. For just as the wind carries thousands of winged seeds, so each moment brings with it germs of spiritual vitality that come to rest imperceptibly in the minds and wills of men. Most of these unnumbered seeds perish and are lost, because men are not prepared to receive them: for such seeds as these cannot spring up anywhere except in the good soil of freedom, spontaneity and love.
> (Merton, 1972, p. 14)

Pondering Merton's words in turn sculpts my inquiry. He writes of seeds and becomes a seed; from his words I extract one which joins the hodgepodge of my seeds. Reading Merton returns me to pondering how inquiry is inextricably nested within the fertile landscape of our stories. Neither the disencased dualism of subject and object, as was the enforced way of knowing when I was a philosophy student, nor the disentangling of my narrative seeds from my inquiry will suffice to sculpt it. Instead, the possibility of my inquiry rests within another expansive landscape wherein my seeds seek to germinate within Merton's "good soil of freedom, spontaneity and love" (Merton, 1972, p. 14).

Seeking the "Epistemology of Love" Within Story

In *New Seeds of Contemplation* Merton reflects upon how the domain of inquiry is one of love, a linkage which the holistic educator Arthur Zajonc also recognizes and extends into his teaching as an "epistemology of love" (Zajonc, 2006, p. 1742). Standing apart from the reductionist knowing which Zajonc views as perilous to truth and one which dominates the academy, an epistemology of love is holistic and embraces life in its fullness within inquiry. Of the richness of such knowing Zajonc, following Palmer, observes how "'every way of knowing becomes a way of living, every epistemology becomes an ethic'" (Zajonc, 2006, p. 1744).

Zajonc's and Palmer's holistic embrace of life within inquiry nurtures the idea of contemplative knowing and evokes Merton's observation on how *contemplation is life and not apart from it* (Merton, 2004). Their observations, along with Merton's view of contemplation, in turn foreground how our stories, as traces of our lives, become intimate with inquiry and the epistemology of love.

Of the process of writing Diamond observes "Who we are intimately affects the kind of research we do and how we do it" (Diamond, 2009, p. 21). The inextricable presence of our narratives underscores the idea that what I write about is who I am. Following Diamond, my writing and life become entwined wherein "the inner journey involves re-living some central or inciting incident over and over again but hopefully with its being reconstrued in ascending spirals of greater understanding" (Diamond, 2009), p. 21).

Nested within memory, the inner journey takes on a necessary configuration. As Bai observes, the past "insists on persisting" (Bai, 2014, p. 33). I must engage with such persistence and, following Jung, pass through the inferno (Jung, 1989). If I do not, then the journey will never be complete, as it would never have started.

The character of the contemplative journey is about a life lived within the persistence of the past, that is, one lived within the recycling of memory. To such psyche recycling I am inextricably bound, and it is also my inquiry. Life and inquiry entangled—such entangling muddling their ontological status, but in the same instance their entwining naming a different research terrain, that is, of lived inquiry wherein such muddling is welcomed. From such verdant terrain is configured the transit of interiority both sculpting who I am and the emergence into inquiry within an epistemology of love. As I venture across such terrain I return to my Grade 3 workbook and reflect upon how the seeds of my inquiry were planted early in my journey and were to be followed by others as I cycled through my encounters with the academy.

"You Are Not a Philosopher!" Encounters With the Philosophical Canon

> *I met with a philosophy instructor to discuss my work. His dislike of my work was palpable. He said "I have seen students like you before who try to figure out the world by themselves. Before you do that, you need to study the philosophical canon." Hearing this I felt I could not discuss my work with him and left the meeting feeling dejected.*
>
> *The instructor's comments were symptoms of a transmissional curriculum (Miller, 2008, p. 10) wherein student-driven inquiry was constrained by expectations of a philosophical pedagogy. Of such expectations, the mandatory program requirement for graduate students to pass the examination in propositional logic echoed the restricted pedagogical focus. Propositional logic is about binary thinking wherein language is eroded into symbols, axioms and rules. I could not advance in the program unless I proved that I could reduce the world into logical glyphs.*
>
> *On a different occasion another instructor responded to one of my graduate school papers by recording "You are not a philosopher."*

> *His comment and my refusal to be complicit in sustaining what I felt was a corrosive pedagogy of teaching and learning led to my eventual departure from the program.*
>
> *Years later within the context of doing an inquiry into the subject of wisdom, I ponder how such pedagogy had long departed from the first philosophy of the Greeks. The register of my studies was narrow; an ethos of philosophy as ethic and "lived exercise" (Hadot, 2002, p. 220) had no place within it. The pedagogy in which I had been schooled foregrounded the absence of wisdom.*

Responding to the malaise which they perceive within higher education today, Zajonc and Palmer observe how the university has lost its soul. In their book *The Heart of Higher Education* (2010) they lament how the university's essential purpose to nurture reflection upon the mysteries and deep questions of life has been lost. Echoing Miller's observation on the nature of transmissional pedagogies (Miller, 2008), they appeal for the university to transcend the "balkanization" (Palmer & Zajonc, 2010, p. 4) of higher learning which marks today's universities.

In their critique of higher education, Bai, Cohen and Scott make kindred observations. Observing that universities have failed in their responsibility "in the face of a wounded and suffering world" (Bai, Cohen, & Scott, 2013, p. 5) they call for a renewal of higher education which extends beyond default understandings of their mandate as sites of knowledge production. Instead they advocate for the university's transformation into a place which nurtures knowledge within a more expansive register as ethical engaging, that is, the university as a site of wisdom.

Such critiques of the university by Palmer and Zajonc and Bai et al. are foregrounded to contextualize my encounters with bifurcated pedagogies within the university where learning as lived and ethical presence was absent. The university was a significant presence in my narrative, and within the centrality of such encounters, both formative and difficult in my story, is situated my study into the character of wisdom.

To relive story in inquiry, as Diamond observes, both embraces the centrality of narrative and contests the binary in research practice. Standing apart from a study of wisdom which is nested within a dualism of inquirer with subject of inquiry, I seek another path onto its study where such dualism is eroded, one which follows Palmer's kindred advice to his students "not only to look at the world that [the] story portrays but to put themselves in the midst of it" (Palmer, 1993, pp. 99–100). Palmer's observation succinctly echoed in Bai's kindred critique of education. Viewing it as disembodied and as "mis-education," she advises to "return the attention to where it belongs: to the fleshy organism of the self!" (Bai, 2014, p. 38).

Palmer's and Bai's critiques of dualistic thinking are echoed by others in contemplative studies in education. In his critique of higher education Zajonc, like Palmer, advocates for seeing in ways which look beyond such thinking; instead, encouraging learning in interconnection and one which is configured within the presence of the aesthetical. Zajonc observes,

How does one see a painting whole? Or the human mind? Or an ecosystem? Or for that matter, the educational project itself? We are well schooled in "seeing them" into parts—into brushstrokes, neurons, and molecules—or seeing the university apart into departments, disciplines and specializations. What kind of attentiveness will enable us to see a true whole? What is the pedagogy for beholding interconnectedness as a primary reality and not a derived one? What are the implications of a deep experience of interconnection for knowing, teaching, learning and life? What would be gained if, as the Dalai Lama says, we were to cultivate "'a deep sense of caring for others, based on a profound sense of interconnection?'"

(Zajonc, 2010, p. 77)

Zajonc's appeal for an ethos of higher education which is ethical, aesthetical and about connection stands apart from my experiences of graduate studies. Mine were marked by the absence of such spirit; neither the idea of connection nor the ethical thesis of caring within a pedagogy were present. Instead, it stood dissociated from holism; and one wherein the absence of wisdom is set within a different pedagogy of disconnection and what some have described as a "hidden curriculum" (Giroux & Penna, 1979, p. 22; Alsubaie, 2015, p. 125; Dutton, 1991, p. 167; Oron Semper & Blasco, 2018, para. 3).

Tycho's Compromise: My Epicyclical Transit Through Graduate and Professional School, a Circling of the Scintilla

My stories of encounters with philosophy professors form part of a greater narrative which circled through diverse post-secondary learning environments and are prefaced by my first experience of graduate school when I took courses in the history of science. The story of science was one I found fascinating, especially the relation of its story to its cultural context. I would ponder Galileo's story of his telescope with the story of artists with whom he interacted and was enthralled by how art could enrich his science. Though I could not name it at the time, my interest in the synergy between the artist and scientist revealed a primordial holism in my thinking which I did not know then how to name. But my way of looking at the story of science was not shared by others. Instead, difficult pedagogical encounters ensued and I eventually decided to leave graduate school behind. My decision had been prompted by the graduate director who said to me point blank "Why postpone the inevitable?"

Leaving was difficult as I was drawn to the rich story of science and fundamental questions of philosophy. My goal to become a teacher and researcher in a university would not be fulfilled. What would I do now? What direction would my transit now take?

In my angst I decided I would "break" with philosophy. I would turn to a new field which looked in a different direction and leave the old questions behind.

My favourite class in high school was art studio. I remember the feeling of doing my paintings—how they consumed me—and studying and recreating drawings of the medieval cathedrals on the kitchen table.

I cycled away from graduate studies into the study of architecture. I studied within a faculty of architecture followed by an architectural internship and eventual licence to practice.

While the study of architecture has a rich design history and is associated with creativity, the practice of architecture can be less so. While design is important, it is only one component of a process often dominated by activities which feel distant from an ethos of creativity.

Architecture posed a conundrum for me. The profession is associated with the artful and engineered, yet the architecture I practised did not nurture the former. Neither did it fulfil my intellectual curiosity and wonder. There were no philosophers amongst the architects. The fundamental questions were always present and nagged at me. I needed to deal with them.

I left architecture and cycled back briefly towards academic philosophy. While there were no philosophers amongst the architects, I soon found that there were no artists amongst the philosophers. The philosophers I encountered were in a different place than the one I sought. My transit onto their territory was short and I returned to architecture. A few years later I decided I would try graduate school again applying to programs in cultural studies. By this time, I had transited in my intellectual journey from the blinkered paradigm of analytical philosophy—one which I had experienced and now felt foreign and lacking in its vision.

Cultural studies seemed then a release from the shackles of the positivist philosophical paradigm in which I had been schooled. During my earlier graduate studies in philosophy I had gone against the grain of my department by taking courses in cultural studies. These thinkers were shaking up the study of philosophy by the way they thought of philosophical problems, the way they wrote about them and the way they incorporated the aesthetic into the study of philosophy. I felt that the study of philosophy should always be expansive in vision, prepared to take risks and see things in a different light and not one corralled by restrictive expectations about what a student should believe or read, or how they should write. I wanted to break free from the third person.

I was drawn to the different view of the cultural theorist that the study of philosophy cannot be done in isolation from the broader community. I felt that these new philosophers showed promise. Their philosophical perspective was expansive and one which allowed for the artist. Though it was not foregrounded in my vision at the time, my attraction to such thinkers, like my interest in the story of science, anticipated my transit towards holism in which I would later nest my inquiry. But the promise of cultural studies though remained shortlived; my journey onto this terrain of inquiry became a brief transit and not a final destination.

I returned once again to architecture.

In the 16th century, the astronomer Tycho Brahe had the sun and moon circulating the earth while the planets circled the sun (Kuhn, 1975). His system was a compromise between the earth-centred and epicyclical Ptolemaic astronomy and Copernicus' new sun centred cosmology.

Tycho's transit is a metaphor for my journey through graduate and professional schools. Like Tycho's journey, mine is epicyclical

Image 1.3 Rossini, G. (2017). *Clock Mechanism*. [Photographic Detail]. Museo Galileo. Florence, Italy

Source: G. Rossini

> in nature. It circulated about intuitions about the nature of knowing which were deep and ever present, but remained unsaid and unnurtured. Approaching and then receding, returning and then cycling away again. Like Ptolemy's planetary epicycles upon which Tycho based his cosmology, my academic journey turns and returns, cycles and recycles. My journey into cultural studies marking that in between paradigm, like Tycho's compromise—a paradigm between the analytical philosophy that I had left behind and that of holism—the seeking of the inner light of the Copernican sun.

In *The Heart of Higher Education*, Palmer and Zajonc (2010) observe a spiritual deficit in post-secondary education amongst faculty and undergraduate students; and one which in my retelling was configured by my epicyclical transit towards and away from the university over a trajectory of forty years. Their observation about their own teaching frustrations to "'colour within the lines'" (Palmer & Zajonc, 2010, p. 2) mirrored my own spiritual deficit and frustrations about being in learning environments which, as they observe, had lost sight of their goal to encourage students to reflect upon their purpose in life.

In my inquiry reflecting upon Palmer and Zajonc within the narrative of my academic transit resonated with a parallel reading of Thomas Merton's views on the ethos of education. In *Love and Living*, Merton reflects upon how the purpose of education is not to press upon the student a definition of the world. Instead the "fruit of education" ponders Merton is "the activation of that inmost center, that scintilla" (Merton, 1979, pp. 9–10) which is the true self. Authentic learning for Merton emerges organically from within the student.

Following Merton, I ponder how my transit to and from the university circled about the spark. Of my journey I layer my words onto his and reflect how,

> *I sought the fruit but could not find it as*
> *I flew on Tycho's epicycles.*

Reading about Merton's *scintilla* marked a paradigmatic shift in my epicyclical journey. The scintilla that had been absent in my previous studies perhaps now coming into fruition within narrative writing and the embrace of an aesthetical presence within inquiry that felt focused and authentic. The scintilla corralled the epicycles around the inner light—the metaphorical mandala of the "Copernican sun"—breaking free from the third person, and sparking inquiry which transited from the epicycles of analytical philosophy and cultural studies towards a holistic meditation upon the nature of wisdom and art.

Pairing Stories of Disconnection: From the Personal Towards a Shared Narrative

In his photographic essay *Essential Elements* (as cited in Ewing, 2016), the photographer Edward Burtynsky pairs images which at first view seem different from the other. An image of a circular pivot irrigation farm is paired with an image of a circular baroque church ceiling. Standing on their own as individual photographs, the meaning of a single image is limited; but when placed side by side the paired images nurture interpretations of the sacred and profane which transcend the story of a single image. By pairing the images, the new pictorial which emerges guides reflection onto a global story—one which both reflects and transcends the narrative of the artist. The images are reproduced in Chapter 2.

In similar spirit my stories, while set within different academic settings of the aesthetical of architectural studies and analytical of philosophical studies, when paired seek to foreground observations that researchers in holistic and transformative learning have made about higher education. With such narrative pairing and *out-turning* I seek to move from the personal to a shared narrative of higher learning which transcends my personal journey and is captured in the kindred criticisms of Cartesian thinking by writers in holistic and transformative learning in education such as Zajonc (2006), Palmer and Zajonc (2010) and Hart (2004) and in the spiritual writings of Merton (1972).

The critique of Cartesianism amongst these writers is nested within a broader criticism of rationalist thinking which encompasses both historical and contemporary critiques. Of the former, the historian of wisdom Trevor Curnow (2000) explores how the rise of Cartesianism was accompanied by the displacement of wisdom from philosophical study—one which he attributes to Descartes' influence in realigning problems of knowledge with mathematics and rise of the scientific method in inquiry. Such displacing in turn marking a shift in how philosophical inquiry was to be conducted, one which following Kuhn's (1975) theory of paradigms marked both a shift from and incommensurability with the idea of philosophy qua wisdom in favour of another which identified inquiry with experimental method.

While researchers such as Curnow locate the critique of rationalism within a historical study, a Kuhnian interpretation of such history also aligns with contemporary criticisms of Cartesian thinking in particular and philosophy in general.

Philosophers Frodeman and Briggle, for example, observe how the institutionalization of philosophy within the university in the 19th century and demand upon it to become specialized like other fields caused it, following the French philosopher Bruno Latour to be "'purified'" and disencased from society (Frodeman & Briggle, 2016, para. 4). The institutional pressure placed upon philosophy to emulate the practices of the sciences—such as having a defined domain of inquiry, sub-specialities, and strategies for academic accountability have resulted in a dire outcome which they view as the failure of philosophy. They remind us that if philosophy is to be restored, then it must be embraced with an original understanding of its domain, that is, as one being "present everywhere, often interstitial, essentially interdisciplinary and transdisciplinary in nature." Against the view of philosophy as being "purified" Frodeman and Briggle argue for seeing it as having "dirty hands," writing "Philosophy is a mangle. The philosopher's hands were never clean and were never meant to be" (Frodeman & Briggle, 2016, para. 11).

26 *Narrative Beginnings*

Their observation upon the practice of philosophy, as one which is nested within complexity, evokes similar critiques from writers within the field of holistic and transformative studies in education. Amongst these, Gunnlaugson's questioning of "'less messy'" methods which dominate higher education (Gunnlaugson, 2007, p. 139); or Parker Palmer's kindred observation about how integrative education "involve[s] a communal exchange that is fluid, complex and confusing" (Palmer & Zajonc, 2010, p. 39). In a similar spirit Hart criticizes rationalist understandings of what constitutes legitimate knowledge today and advocates for a different way of knowing which embraces holism and the nonlinearity of inquiry (Hart, 2004).

Core to their criticisms is the central problem of the character of inquiry. To pose the question, as Bai does in "*What is Inquiry?*" (Bai, 2005, p. 45) is to pose a foundational question which strikes at the heart of philosophical thinking. But if the question does not emerge it is because the tug of analytical thinking is strong, and we default to a paradigm wherein we are unable to see beyond it. We do not see how the paradigm is one of excision, that is, how in its quest for indubitable knowledge humanity is excised from the subjective, personal and emotional—modalities which are integral to the configuration of self. Within such a bifurcated domain, they stand apart; and we are left within an illusory terrain where we see a completeness which is absent. And when we do not see, we find false comfort within a paradigm wherein the self has been excised from those modalities which are central to it core and make it complete.

Standing apart from such domain is another, an entangled beauty rich in nuance and complexity. As Bai observes,

> Life, however, is full of the immeasurable, irreducible, uncertain, and unpredictable not only because the world is simply a bewilderingly complex place; but also because when humans face the life-world, they don't just see trees, people, food on the table, money in the bank, and so on, but *see* and *feel* such strange and nebulous things as beauty, love and compassion, joys and sorrows, fear and security, fairness, injustice, and so on. These *qualities* belong to the realm of the *meta-physical*, in the sense of going beyond the tangible, quantifiable, measurable, and even effable. This metaphysical is, however, the dimension of personal meaning and insight, and there is nothing vague and inconsequential about it. Lack of the meaningful can sink us in misery, and kill our spirit, if not our body. . . . Life refuses to be reduced to our expectations. In the end, we have to learn to navigate in the sea of the metaphysical and work with life's uncertainty and complexity. Inquiry is this kind of navigation.
> (Bai, 2005, p. 45)

When Gunnlaugson alludes to the messiness of inquiry or Bai ponders the "bewildering complex[ity]" of the world, they describe a place which is familiar; a place we inhabit within the nuanced presences of the subjective and personal. And if methods of knowing, such as the analytical or rationalist, stumble when they cross onto such familiar and lived terrain, then barriers as these also become creative portals, that is, when we open ourselves onto other ways of knowing, nestled within an ethos of the creative and aesthetical, to engage with the entangled beauty of life.

Image 1.4 Rossini, G. (2017). *The Fluidity of Inquiry. A Narrow Street in Venice Known as a Calle.* [Digital Photograph]. Venice, Italy

Source: G. Rossini

28 *Narrative Beginnings*

The shadowy and blurred image of the Venetian Calle is offered as a visual metaphor for the messy character of inquiry suggested by Gunnlaugson and which Hart, Bai and Palmer view with kindred language.

Though we see this place, the seeing is nuanced and marked by shadows and blurs. The analytical falters when confronted with such complexity, but the artist does not as within such complexity is found our completeness.

Reflections on Cartesianism: A Philosophy Without Mystery

In philosophy school I read Descartes' Discourse on Method and Meditations (1960). The philosopher with whom I studied the text was one I respected, as he was both knowledgeable and kind. Together we worked through the Meditations. Though we analysed the text following Descartes' step-by-step argument towards the "cogito ergo sum," we did not focus upon the importance of the role of narrative within its meditative structure.

Later when I journeyed onto a different terrain of holistic education and became interested in reflective writing the irony of having studied Descartes Meditations was foregrounded. Descartes' journey is complicated. While seeking to reduce the world into binary of mind and body, he does so within a narrative journey configured as meditative writing. That the seeds of Cartesian rationalism were rooted in narrative I now view as both ironic and germane to the reading of the text—one which I did not then appreciate and perhaps was not yet ready to understand.

While researchers in holistic education and philosophers such as Frodeman and Briggle share kindred observations upon the practice of philosophy Thomas Merton is more direct and forceful in his criticism of Cartesian thinking.

For Merton, the criticism of analytical philosophy is rooted in its philosophical reductionism as one which approaches the understanding of the self within the disassembly of experience and not within an understanding of the mystery of its whole nature. Within such reductionism there is no room for that which cannot be measured, observed, tested and categorized. There is no room for complexity and messiness. There is no room for mystery.

While philosophers revelled in Descartes' "*I think, therefore I am*" (Descartes, 1960, p. 24) as the triumph of a new way of knowing, the mystery of being remained. Though Descartes strove to banish the mystery within the binary of mind and body, his *Meditations* did not mark the end of reflection upon the nature of being. The mystery remains; it tugs at us and we are impelled to return to its presence.

Of such mystery Merton, in *New Seeds of Contemplation*, criticizes Descartes' *Cogito*,

> Nothing could be more alien to contemplation than the *cogito ergo sum* of Descartes. "I think, therefore I am." This is the declaration of an alienated being, in exile from his own spiritual depths, compelled to seek some comfort in a *proof of his own existence* (!) based on the observation that he "thinks." If his thought is necessary as a medium through which he arrives at the concept of his existence, then he is in fact only moving further away from his true being. He is reducing himself to a concept. He is making it impossible for himself to experience, directly and immediately, the mystery of his own being.
>
> (Merton, 1972, p. 8)

For Merton, the Cartesian paradigm is spiritually wanting and a colossal philosophical failure. Within such thinking, man is reduced to a thing as is also God. Philosophy is reduced to an ontological project from which the transcendent has been excised—one which Merton questions as misguided (Merton, 1972).

Merton's discomfort with philosophical rationalism recurs frequently in his writings. Elsewhere in *The Seven Storey Mountain*, Merton writes of the "dead, selfish rationalism" (Merton, 1998b, p. 208) he had encountered in his studies. His unease with philosophical rationalism is a recurring theme in his writings—one which is also examined in depth in Ross Labrie's study *Thomas Merton and the Inclusive Imagination* (2001) where he observes how the rise of Cartesianism was for Merton synonymous with the growth of alienation in society (Labrie, 2001).

Others have commented upon Merton's critique of rationalism. Merton had a lifelong interest in William Blake having studied his writings at Columbia University before entering the monastery. In his text *Heretic Blood*, Michael Higgins explores Merton's critique of rationalism and how such critique was manifested in Merton's preference of Blake's cosmology over that of his contemporary Newton. Of Newtonian thinking, Higgins observes how for Merton "Newtonians live in the very heart of nature and yet do not know it" (Higgins, 1998, p. 252). For Merton reductionist thinking did not quell the longing for the mystery of existence (Higgins, 1998).

Higgins' observations on Merton's view of Newtonian thinking are kindred with Merton's criticism of Cartesian rationalism. Together with Labrie's exploration of Merton's views and those of researchers in holistic and transformative learning who critique contemporary educational practices (Zajonc, 2006; Palmer, 1993; Hart, 2004/2019; Bai, 2014; Miller, 2008) they provided a framework for meditations on my own encounters with Cartesianism; and in particular the retelling of my experience of studying Descartes' *Meditations*.

Many years later within the context of writing a doctoral dissertation within the field of holistic learning, those gaps in my reflections upon Descartes' *Meditations* are filled by a different reading through Merton's criticisms. While Merton is critical of Descartes' reductionism in the *Ergo*, he is also troubled by the philosopher's journey to such reductionism through the path of meditation. Descartes conveys his argument as a meditation, but of such meditation Merton views it as being problematic and inauthentic. In *New Seeds of Contemplation*, Merton reflects on Descartes' *cogito* and observes,

> Contemplation, on the contrary, is the experiential grasp of reality as *subjective*, not so much "mine" (which would signify "belonging to the external self") but "myself" in existential mystery. Contemplation does not arrive at reality after a process of deduction, but by an intuitive awakening in which our free and personal reality becomes fully alive to its own existential depths, which open out into the mystery of God.
>
> For the contemplative there is no *cogito* ("I think") and no *ergo* ("therefore") but only *SUM*, I Am. Not in the sense of a futile assertion of our individuality as ultimately real, but in the humble realization of our mysterious being as persons in whom God dwells, with infinite sweetness and inalienable power.
>
> (Merton, 1972, pp. 8–9)

Discovering Merton resonated with my reading of writers within the field of contemplative education, in particular Bai who makes a kindred critique of Descartes *Cogito Ergo* observing it as a "brilliant statement of disembodiment" (Bai, 2014, p. 37). To be disembodied, as Bai observes of Descartes, is not to have self-knowledge insofar as feeling is excluded from the character of being.

Reflecting upon Merton's criticisms returns me to a surprise encounter in Florence with a fresco by Fra Angelico.

> *In the fresco Mocking of Christ (Convent of San Marco, Florence, 1440), the artist Fra Angelico depicts the torments of Christ. The torments are represented by the hands of his abusers who slap him and place the crown of thorns on his head; and a soldier who spits on Christ. The hands float freely within the image as does also the head of the soldier.*
>
> *Within the image Christ rests calmly as do also the saints at his feet seemingly immune to the torments.*
>
> *I am struck by the representation of the body parts which float within the fresco disconnected from a body. The image is unlike others I have seen. It does not feel like other Renaissance images that I have seen. It has a timeless spirit.*
>
> *The image causes me to pause; it has a power which invites psychological reflection. For a few moments I ponder this image from the threshold of the monk's cell and take pictures—adjusting the camera settings for close up shots and others standing farther back. I allow for the light.*

Narrative Beginnings 31

Image 1.5 Rossini, G. (2017). *The "Centred Self"*. Image of Fra Angelico (1440). *Mocking of Christ*. [Digital Photograph]. Convent of San Marco. Florence, Italy

Source: G. Rossini

32   *Narrative Beginnings*

> *While the image is meditative, it also offers a rich metaphor for the nature of the integrated self. While the free-floating body parts provides a metaphor for the dismembering of self, Christ's calm amidst the clamour of his torments—represented by the blindfold while sitting on a stone and immoveable plinth—also invite reflection on the aspect of a core self which resides beyond the clamour.*
>
> *Beyond the din the core self resides in the centred Christ—a presence which is symmetrically composed within the geometry of the triangle which is formed by the figures of Christ and the two saints.*
>
> *600 years separates Fra Angelico and Merton. One before Descartes; the other after. Yet they convey the same message. Fra Angelico's fresco of the centred Christ returns me to the notion of the integrated self—the "SUM, I Am"—which Merton seeks in the criticism of Descartes.*

While the image of the soldier offers a metaphor for the Cartesian bifurcation of self, the image of the transcendent Christ offers another vision of Merton's *SUM*, I AM. That is, of a self not eroded by reason, but one which instead stands beyond it within its own unity and mystery.

Of the return to transcendence, which Palmer explores within the context of holistic education, he observes,

> To experience transcendence means to be removed—not from self and world, but from that hall of mirrors in which the two endlessly reflect and determine one another. Prayer takes us out—not out of self and world, but out of their closed, circular logic.
>
> (Palmer, 1993, p. 13)

In Fra Angelico's fresco the inward looking and blindfolded Christ defies the Cartesian mirrors within a vision of an integrated, centred and transcendent self.

Reclaiming the Binary: "*SUM*, I AM"

In dialogue with Merton's observations on Descartes' *cogito*, I reflect

> *Rationalism allows us to know much about the world; yet we feel incomplete in our knowing. We are taught to see with rationalist eyes, yet we are blind and do not see whole (Palmer, 1993). To see with eyes guided by intuition, feeling and empathy in addition to the eyes of reason has little place in the rationalist vision.*
>
> *The feeling to see holistically with all embracing eyes, to cast them towards and contemplate the mysteries of the creation in inclusive relation to our being propels us beyond the rationalist vision. Rationalism does not quench our desire to know for we feel that it is not the*

only way to know. Mystery remains and our desire and deep ancestral need to reflect upon it seeds the critique of rationalism's absolutism and guides us to look beyond its horizon with whole vision, as "SUM, I Am."

Mystery leaves questions but the complexity of mystery also enriches inquiry. Of such complexity, the Cartesian canon in which I was schooled endeavoured to eradicate it. The holistic learning paradigm, in contrast, embraces mystery within a pedagogy which, following Miller (2008), is about connection and transformation. While higher education has a central presence in my narrative—formed of encounters with the pedagogies of architecture school and graduate studies in philosophy—the pedagogy of holism and integration which Miller (2008) and Palmer and Zajonc (2010) write of and which Merton alludes to in his writings had been absent from such learning.

Pondering Merton's (1974) views on the holism which is hidden but present to the creation is prescient to the emergence of kindred sentiments in the fields of holistic and transformative learning in education. It has also been nurturing to my own inquiry—one whose journey, while originating in encounters of pedagogical disconnection, is also seeded by Merton, artists and writers in holistic and transformative learning. It is a journey onto the aesthetical which seeks its own transformation towards an integrative terrain of Merton's "*SUM, I AM*" (Merton, 1972, p. 9) and Fra Angelico's depiction of *Christ*, and which endeavours to reclaim from Descartes the binary by embracing the creation in the fullness of its complexity within an inclusive domain of contemplative knowing.

Encounters with Merton and Fra Angelico guide my reflection upon the ethos of narrative and "SUM, I Am." The "SUM, I Am" resides in the richness of our stories. Our being in narrative the construct of the reality wherein it is seeded. If we listen attentively to the summonses of narrative, then we may begin to probe our being in the world. And from within the emergence of the "SUM, I Am" there emerges the promise of wisdom.

2 Meditations on Merton's Paradox

Narrative, Aesthetics and the Emergence of the Wisdom Image

Image 2.1 Rossini, G. (2017). *I Turn Inwards in Order to Look out Onto the World.* [Digital Photograph]. Monk's Cell, Convent of San Marco. Florence, Italy

Source: G. Rossini

The Scintilla of Discovery: A Classroom Encounter With Merton

In a graduate seminar on holistic education our teacher presents us with different notions of holistic education for group discussion. The statements were diverse and made for interesting group conversation though we did not at first know who the authors were.

During our group's discussion I asked my colleagues why they did not choose the second notion on the handout. Of the six conceptions we had not discussed this one. I was intrigued by their silence.

Unlike them I had chosen it; this particular conception of education resonated with me. It was about the "spark" within us which marks the true self (Merton, 1979, pp. 9–10). It was written by Thomas Merton in Love and Living.

My colleagues, while answering my question with the shared observation that they found the second notion too theoretical and less interesting, also reconfirmed something about myself.

That is, what moves me, is integral to my being, and intrinsic to how I perceive my world is through the lens of the aesthetical and theory.

This moment of coming into a knowing within an encounter with Merton and my colleagues was transformative in spirit, a scintilla which shifted the direction of my studies.

Beginning to Reflect Upon Merton and Me

While I had once known of Thomas Merton indifferently as a Catholic monk who published in the 1950s and 1960s, an encounter with his essay *Love and Living* (1979) in a graduate seminar in holistic education in the University of Toronto marked a pivotal moment in the direction of my studies. My story, which begins this chapter, is offered as a retelling of that event.

What was once indifference was instead replaced with an immersion into his writings of which there are many, and in particular ones where he meditates upon the relation of aesthetics and spirituality. Reading Merton not only changed the trajectory of my studies at that time, but in so doing, my writing about him was transformative; extending Yagelski's observation about the character of writing it became "an act of being" (Yagelski, 2009, p. 7).

Up to that point my studies had been configured upon a pattern for doing research represented by the dominance of the third-person voice in inquiry, a persistent legacy of the bifurcated character of Cartesian thinking in which I had been schooled and one which writers like Parker Palmer view as "the myth of objectivism" dominating higher education today (Palmer & Zajonc, 2010, p. 15).

Reading Merton changed that configuration towards a more ecumenical formation. While I allowed the third-person voice to be present, I did not allow it to exclude contemplative writing nested within the first person. I resisted the myth whose narrow register is the object of Palmer's critique. Instead, my writing quivered between these places sometimes lingering in the first person, at other times meandering onto the third; and collectively configuring a fluid formation of a first-third-person ethos in writing.

While for Yagelski acts of writing configure *being*, his view is extended here to embrace the *dialogical* quality of such acts. That is, my writing, nested within its fluid ethos, becoming an *act of dialogical being*, one which was drawn to Bakhtin's view of life as dialogue: "To live means to participate in dialogue: to ask questions, to heed, to respond, to agree, and so forth" (Bakhtin, 1984, p. 293).

From within the fluid ethos of the first-third person, my dialogical being emerges, one wherein the conversation with Merton, wherein I speak to him directly with my reflections or questions, becoming a component of such emergence. Of its ethereal formation the discourse of *Merton* and *me* echoed his own way of engaging with texts as he does in *Raids on the Unspeakable* (1966), one which was also synergistic with Palmer's recommendation to engage texts as friends as he suggests in *To Know as we are Known* (1993) and Bakhtin's more theoretical view of the "dialogic nature of consciousness" (Bakhtin, 1984, p. 293).

Within the dialogical encounter with Merton's writings, I seek to extract nuggets upon the relation of the aesthetical and wisdom.

An Outsider's Map Looks Onto Merton

Of the relation of wisdom, contemplation and art, Merton's writings reveal a contemplative whose views of such relation evolved broadly from a theologically framed understanding in his early writings, to one which became more ecumenical with its reflections on Zen in his later work. His writing reveals a transformative ethos wherein his spiritual evolution is mapped through his words. I am drawn to them; they feel accessible but as an outsider, I am also uncertain as to which ones I should turn in order to see his map. While my outsider self approaches Merton hesitantly, I try to temper my caution by reminding myself that maps are not determinate; they do not mandate that we take a specified route. Instead maps, like inquiry, can be entered from multiple points. When the terrain is rich and accessible, as it is with Merton's writings, the routes which configure the map become numerous.

From the abundance of Merton writings, I plot my route to trace his aesthetical—spiritual growth. My outsider's map onto Merton emerges as a journey in three parts formed of encounters with texts, in particular, *Poetry and the Contemplative Life* from his early monastic years. This text, which is from his book *Figures for an Apocalypse* (1947), forms the first part of my journey. In the second part, my map traces his aesthetical ideas through his later writings, notably, *Rain and the Rhinoceros* from *Raids on the Unspeakable* (1966); and his essay *Zen in Japanese Art* from *Zen and the Birds of Appetite* (1968). In the final leg of my journey I venture onto Merton's understanding of paradisal wisdom—one at whose core is a self sculpted of an aesthetical presence.

Maps can convey a paradoxical feeling, that is, while they provide guidance when we first embark on our travels, their clarity is only manifested when we believe we are soon to arrive at a destination. Such was the feeling as I negotiated Merton's map. As I crossed it, the notion of the *wisdom image* first emerged, but one which came into its own clarity only after extensive travel along my three-part itinerary. The reflection gradually arose that while some images, viewed as conveyors of wisdom, bear a kindred relation to traditional text-based configurations of wisdom; they also depart from such understandings by being situated within the domain of the artist and not the tradition of wisdom literature.

The chapter is prefaced with my dialogical encounter with Merton. In his essay *Rain and the Rhinoceros* (1966) Merton speaks of the "festival of rain"—a moment of enveloping warmth, spiritual oneness and beauty in the experience of *being* with rain in nature (Merton, 1966, p. 11). Set within a dialogical configuration Merton's story forms a basis for beginning to engage with his writings and the thesis of wisdom's relation to contemplation and art. As I travelled across Merton's terrain it also brought into clarity a persistent reflection that the promise of wisdom is seeded within moments of aesthetical presence.

My transit with Merton though was not unaccompanied as its map was layered by others. The interpretation of Merton's aesthetical views and their relation to the notion of wisdom image is informed through the lenses of researchers in the fields of holistic studies in education in general and contemplative and transformative learning in particular. Amongst some of these researchers, Merton's ideas are acknowledged in their writings, for example, Palmer (1993), Miller (2014), Zajonc (2009), Dencev and Collister (2010) and Hart (2004). Amongst other writers such as Burrows (2015), Byrnes (2012), Gunnlaugson (2007, 2011) and Morgan (2012), there are echoes of Merton's spiritual ideas. Reading their work cycles back to him and foregrounds how prescient Merton's writings from the 1960s are to the ethos of transformative and contemplative studies in education which would emerge later.

While forming interpretative bridges with Merton's ideas, I hope that reading Merton through the lens of these writers will also inform the fields of transformative and contemplative learning. Recently such bridges have been brought into focus with the centenary of Merton's birth in 2015 which has been accompanied by a renewed interest in his life and writings; and acknowledgement of his presence in American life by Pope Francis (2015) in his address to the United States Congress.

Seeking Merton's "Festival of Rain"

We have forgotten how to be enchanted by looking at the stars, feeling the wind on our face, or smelling grass after it has rained.

(Miller, 2019, p. 6)

- - - - -

Brother Louis. When you began your life as a contemplative monk your writing was imbued with Christian theology. By the '60s you write of Zen and Asian mysticism. There are moments when you write mystically as in The Geography of Lograire (1969); and there are other moments too when, as a philosopher you write critically of Descartes and Foucault (Cronin, 2016).

I find solace in the journey of your philosophical and mystical biography. I too started in philosophy and studied Descartes. I too journeyed into French theory and pondered Foucault. I too am immersed in the space of theory; yet like you I intuit and am seeking other places.

Sometimes we need to reflect upon the narratives of others in order to penetrate our own. Brother Louis, for what purpose and to what end have I pondered your life and teachings? What cosmological alchemy has brought us together to this present moment? Why am I drawn to them? What is it in your narrative that allows me to penetrate my own?

As a philosopher, your love of ideas and the pristine clarity with which you write draw me towards you. Yet, in the same instance, you seek other places where the philosopher does not journey and which I too am seeking. What map does the philosopher follow to this other place—the "festival of rain" you write of in Raids on the Unspeakable? (Merton, 1966, p. 11). How do we not forget, as Miller ponders, about being present to the smell of the grass after the rain?

Of those other places, the analytical philosopher declares to me "You are not a philosopher!" The philosopher poses questions but the answers he demands are incommensurable with the territory of his tribe; and instead reside within a different domain of intuition, feeling, the aesthetical and transcendence.

In Raids you write,

> **The rain I am in is not like the rain of cities. It fills the woods with an immense and confused sound. It**

> covers the flat roof of the cabin and its porch with insistent and controlled rhythms. And I listen, because it reminds me again and again that the whole world runs by rhythms I have not yet learned to recognize, rhythms that are not those of the engineer.
> (Merton, 1966, p. 9)

I too have not recognized those rhythms, but like you Brother Louis, intuit their transcendent possibilities. And like you the seeking of the rhythms also captures our reality—that we vibrate amongst two domains—one of the rational world of the philosopher and other of the artist who guides us towards the realm of spiritual transcendence within the "festival of rain" (Merton, 1966, p. 11).

Of those realms, how do we integrate them Brother Louis? Your student ponders your advice in Zen and the Birds of Appetite.

> If one reaches the point where understanding fails, this is not a tragedy: it is simply a reminder to stop thinking and start looking. Perhaps there is nothing to figure out after all: perhaps we only need to wake up.
> (Merton, 1968, p. 53)

Brother Louis. How do we reconcile the rhythms of the engineer with those of the rain? How do we reconcile the places that we have been to with the places we seek but which are unknown except through our intuition and not the analysis of the philosopher?

Some will say that the places we transit from are more real than the places we seek. Yet this does not dissuade us from seeking the unknown place—the void of Zen. Of that domain, we do not know. We do not have its map. We do not know where the journey to that place will take us. We do not know its ending. Yet we return intuitively to it and have comfort in its unknowability. We feel towards the journey.

Of that journey in Zen, you speak of the goal of Buddhism as "a breakthrough into what is beyond system, beyond cultural and social structures, and beyond religious rite and belief."

(Merton, 1968, pp. 4–5)

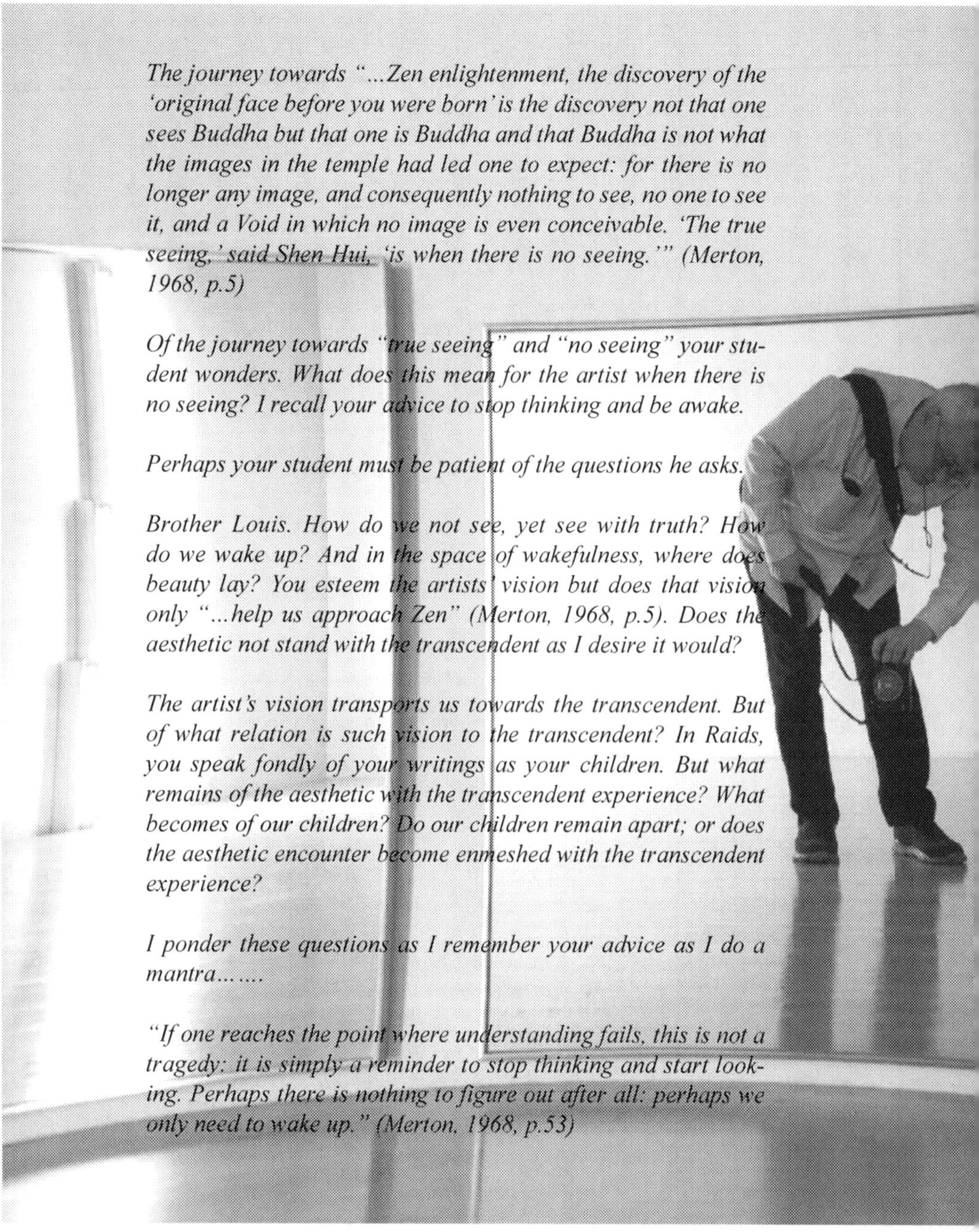

The journey towards "...Zen enlightenment, the discovery of the 'original face before you were born' is the discovery not that one sees Buddha but that one is Buddha and that Buddha is not what the images in the temple had led one to expect: for there is no longer any image, and consequently nothing to see, no one to see it, and a Void in which no image is even conceivable. 'The true seeing,' said Shen Hui, 'is when there is no seeing.'" (Merton, 1968, p.5)

Of the journey towards "true seeing" and "no seeing" your student wonders. What does this mean for the artist when there is no seeing? I recall your advice to stop thinking and be awake.

Perhaps your student must be patient of the questions he asks.

Brother Louis. How do we not see, yet see with truth? How do we wake up? And in the space of wakefulness, where does beauty lay? You esteem the artists' vision but does that vision only "...help us approach Zen" (Merton, 1968, p.5). Does the aesthetic not stand with the transcendent as I desire it would?

The artist's vision transports us towards the transcendent. But of what relation is such vision to the transcendent? In Raids, you speak fondly of your writings as your children. But what remains of the aesthetic with the transcendent experience? What becomes of our children? Do our children remain apart; or does the aesthetic encounter become enmeshed with the transcendent experience?

I ponder these questions as I remember your advice as I do a mantra........

"If one reaches the point where understanding fails, this is not a tragedy: it is simply a reminder to stop thinking and start looking. Perhaps there is nothing to figure out after all; perhaps we only need to wake up." (Merton, 1968, p.53)

Image 2.2 Rossini, G. (2018). *Looking Onto Others to See Myself*. Reflection Upon Robert Smithson's *Mirage No. 1*. [Digitally edited photograph]. Museum of Contemporary Art, Los Angeles, California

Source: G. Rossini

Merton's Aesthetical Writings: Beyond the Referential Onto an Ethos of Connection

In my meditations upon the character of wisdom's relation to spiritual transcendence and artist's vision, I was guided by how Merton's view of such relation evolved from a theologically focused one in the late 1940s to a more expansive, nuanced and ecumenical one later in his life. The markers of such evolution are many as Merton was a prolific writer and one which in turn prompted the question—upon *which texts of his should I focus*?

To respond to the query with the uncomplicated observation that I selected texts which map the evolution of Merton's aesthetical ideas feels incomplete. While texts undoubtedly have a referential status, it also feels that the texts that we are drawn to transcend such simple account of their status in inquiry. Our relation to texts feels much more nuanced. Parker Palmer (1993), for example, encourages we approach texts in friendship while for Yagelski, who writes on the character of writing, observes how the "act of writing" itself is formative of being (Yagelski, 2011, p. 104). For both, our relation to texts and writing respectively is not indifferent but congenial in spirit.

> *Following them, I feel that I do not stand apart indifferently from the texts I study; but instead they stand with me within an ethos formative of my being and marked by nurturing resonances which defy the bifurcated character of research. The texts submerge into me within resonances where I feel in rapport with them; and which not only connect me to my being but to others. Through those texts of Merton's that I feel towards I not only form connection with him; but in so doing, in their prescient nature, also connecting both him and me with the kindred spirit of writers in the field of transformative learning.*

Amongst Merton's many writings three essays in particular resonated with their presence in my study: *Poetry and the Contemplative Life* in *Figures for an Apocalypse* (Merton, 1947); and *The Study of Zen* and *Zen in Japanese Art* in *Zen and the Birds of Appetite* (Merton, 1968). Through them I began to create my map of Merton's evolving thoughts on the relation of wisdom and the aesthetical, and in so doing, there also began to emerge on top of his a second map. What I also view as a palimpsest; and one wherein Merton's thought is read through the phenomenon of *transformative shifts in consciousness*, a theme which follows the work of researchers in transformative learning studies such as Dencev and Collister (2010), Burrows (2015), Byrnes (2012), and Gunnlaugson (2007, 2011).

Merton's ideas on art reveal a life of writing that was a continuous unfolding wherein the presence of the creative was essential and underscoring the thesis that transformation is an unending process (Dencev & Collister, 2010). Transformation aligned with the presence of the aesthetical, one which embraces life in its entirety and reflected in the transit of Merton's life and writings. Transformation, creativity and life intertwined. To be with the creative is to be with life.

It is through the lens of such writers as Dencev and Collister and others in the fields of holistic and transformative studies in education that the evolution of Merton's aesthetical ideas and their relation to wisdom are traced beginning with his early essay *Poetry and the Contemplative Life* (Merton, 1947). Within it, of the relation of the artist's vision to spiritual transcendence we observe it corralled within hierarchical and restrictive theological understandings. Merton's later essays depart from such restrictions by being informed by the study of Zen, which creates a more nuanced understanding of the artist's vision in spiritual transcendence and which in addition invites us to meditate upon the relation of such ideas to the notion of a paradisal consciousness aligned with the vision of the artist.

In beginning to reflect upon Merton's evolution I ponder . . .

Brother Louis. In your early writings, the transcendent possibilities of art are corralled within Catholic theology. Yet within such constraints are seeded themes which would evolve in your later writings. That is, of the presence of the aesthetical within us and contemplative nature of art, of the power of intuition over reason and of art to transform us.

For Merton, the encounter with art has not a singular character but one which ranges. While for many such an encounter is simply an emotional experience (Merton, 1947), a genuine encounter with art is different in being transcendent and contemplative. In his early essay *Poetry and the Contemplative Life*, he reflects,

> But a genuine esthetic experience is something which transcends not only the sensible order (in which, however, it has its beginning) but also that of reason itself. It is a supra-rational intuition of the latent perfection of things. Its immediacy outruns the speed of reasoning and leaves all analysis far behind.
>
> (Merton, 1947, pp. 101–102)

For Merton the aesthetic encounter is a both a powerful transformative and epistemological moment wherein the being of the artist is resculpted. It is a moment of powerful knowing which is beyond reasoning—what he names the "supra-rational" (Merton, 1947, pp. 101–102). Within such moments artists have described them with words echoing Merton's observations as "profound moments of grace" (Kelly, 2006, p. 3); or as Emerson describes "'deeper apprehension'" (Miller, 2006, p. 10).

Of the transformative presence of the aesthetic encounter, such artists' retellings are kindred with Merton's reflections wherein he likens such encounters to mystical experiences (Merton, 1947). For Merton, in such moments there is a melding of the artist with their work—a moment of unity or as he names that of "'connaturality'"—a "mode of apprehension" wherein "it reaches out to grasp the inner reality, the vital substance of its object, by a kind of affective identification of itself with it" (Merton, 1947, p. 102). Such moments are ones of connection—what writers in holistic studies have also viewed as moments of spiritual infusion (Kelly, 2006); or of "nondual knowing" when "we merge with the object of contemplation" (Miller, 2006, pp. 10–11).

For Merton such moments are ones of an intuition infused with an aesthetical presence and which hold an elevated standing in spiritual experience. When such intuition occurs, Merton observes how the artist pierces reality and opens onto God (Merton, 1947). While Merton is careful in distinguishing mystical from aesthetic experience and speaks of the aesthetic as an analogue to the mystical, his celebration of how the aesthetic can transport us towards the spiritual realm is a powerful theme in *Poetry and the Contemplative Life* (1947).

Transformation, Aesthetics and Contemplation

In *Poetry and the Contemplative Life* (1947), Merton's description of the aesthetic encounter evokes rich interpretations of *transformation, embodiment* and *intuitive knowing*. The language with which Merton ponders the contemplative and aesthetical in turn anticipates kindred language used by later writers in the field of transformative learning and spirituality studies

Of the nature of transformation, that is, of the *"permanent shift of consciousness"* Dencev and Collister (2010), following Crowell observe that "'when things are engaged in process there is constant transformation and . . . transformative possibilities [are] built into every creative act, every creative event'" (Dencev & Collister, 2010, p. 179). Interpreting Merton follows Dencev and Collister; the moments of "'connaturality'" (Merton, 1947, pp. 101–102) when the artist becomes aligned with their work are encounters of *becoming* wherein connection is made, transformation happens and as Gunnlaugson also observes one's perspective changes (Gunnlaugson, 2007). In a similar spirit O'Sullivan describes transformative experience as a moving between learning horizons, one wherein old ways of knowing are reintegrated towards new "'spiritual horizons'" (Dencev & Collister, 2010, p. 180).

Merton's writing suggests how the transformative encounter—one which is configured with a *moving towards* as O'Sullivan alludes to—is also an encounter with embodiment and ways of knowing, such as the intuitive and mystical. While rationalism moves towards the eroding of experience in order to understand it, the intuitive and mystical move in a different path away from dualistic knowing towards what Merton in his text *Hagia Sophia* views as the unseen fullness of creation (Merton, 1974) or as researchers in holistic studies in education view as a knowing which is beyond the binary (Miller, 2006), or as the "reunification and reconstruction of broken selves and worlds" (Palmer, 1993, p. 8). In *Poetry and the Contemplative Life*, we see such trajectory in Merton's meditations upon the nature of contemplation.

For Merton the aesthetic experience is an analogue to the mystical and one which he ponders within a discourse on the nature of Christian contemplation. Of the kinds of contemplative experience, Merton speaks of them being of "three degrees" (Merton, 1947, p. 95). The first, which he names "natural contemplation of God," belongs to the artist, philosopher and pagan religions (Merton, 1947, p. 95). The second form, which he names "active contemplation," refers to Roman Catholic religious practices such as participation in prayer, liturgy and sacraments. While for Merton active contemplation "belongs to our own powers," the third form, "infused contemplation," is that which is bestowed upon us by God and as Merton observes is "to live on the desire of God alone" (Merton, 1947, p. 95). Of infused contemplation Merton elaborates

> Infused contemplation is an experimental knowledge of God's goodness "tasted" and "possessed" by a vital contact in the depth of the soul. By infused loved, we are given an immediate grasp of God's own substance, and rest in the obscure and profound sense of His presence and transcendent actions within our inmost selves, yielding ourselves altogether to the work of His transforming Spirit.
> (Merton, 1947, p. 97)

For Merton, contemplation in its purist form is a movement towards the being of God, a *yielding* wherein God's presence enters into our own being. Within such domain boundaries are dissolved within a terrain of connection. Of the movement towards a place of connection and unity, Merton's description of contemplation evokes Burrows observations on the non-dualistic nature of mindfulness.

> Mindfulness involves consciousness of everything. When we are aware to this degree, we begin to see the entirety of life as a seamless garment. In a mindful state—or a nondualistic state—we are present to everything.
> (Burrows, 2015, p. 133)

While Burrows speaks of non-dualism as a "seamless garment" Merton tells us more by describing what the seamless garment *feels* like, that is, what it feels like to be in connection.

The words Merton uses to describe infused contemplation are sensual and aesthetical. Of infused contemplation, Merton describes it with tactile language: In the encounter with God's presence, we *taste*, we are *possessed*, we *grasp*, we *yield*, we allow ourselves to be formed by "*His transforming Spirit.*" To be within infused contemplation is for Merton to be within an embodied moment which is transcendent and transformative. Far from being a moment of stasis, the moment of infused contemplation is sensual and one of movement. We extend our reach—we grasp and taste—and yet we yield, and within such quivering movement towards unity with God there is a both a recasting and dissolution of one's self. While Merton's distinguishes infused contemplation from the "natural contemplation of God" which the artist possesses, the language he uses to describe infused contemplation invites an artful interpretation.

Weaving Into Consciousness: The "Seamless Garment" of Contemplation

For Merton the "seamless garment" which Burrows speaks of is sensual and embodied. While Merton distinguishes "natural contemplation" which the artist possesses from infused contemplation, the language of *tasting, grasping and transforming* which he uses to describe the latter is infused with the ethos of embodiment and the artist.

Within such moments, Merton observes that they are accompanied by the "transforming Spirit" (Merton, 1947, p. 97), a notion which finds kindred voice in the field of spirituality in education. The aspect of non-dualistic knowing which is suggested by Merton's description of contemplation evokes Palmer's (1993) exploration of non-propositional knowing and is prescient to recent work on the spirituality research paradigm advanced by Lin et al. (2016) evoking, in particular, Miller's observations on non-judgemental knowing and Ergas' metaphor of the "impregnated being" (Ergas, 2016, p. 6).

In their critique of dualistic epistemology these writers ponder another way of knowing which aligns with Merton's writing on transformation, that is, one wherein the movement to knowing is a movement with the body. In her critique of schooling, Burrows observes:

> There is a need to go beyond talking and writing *about* transformative learning to include more holistic and experiential ways of knowing that directly involve the body, feelings, and intuition as well as cognition (Ferrer, Romero, & Albareda, 2005).
>
> (Burrows, 2015, p. 128)

Burrows writes of pathways onto knowing wherein the promise of transformation is configured within the holistic ethos of a "seamless garment"—a cloth of non-dualism in which we are present to the fabric of creation and have "consciousness of everything" (Burrows, 2015, p. 133). I layer Merton's *grasping* in contemplation onto Burrows' garment and ponder how such cloth is imbued with feeling, and am reminded how the tactility of Merton's contemplative grasp evokes aesthetical reflections upon the weaver's art. The garment knitted with threads of feeling, touch, intuition and the aesthetical forming a cloth which departs from the reductive weave of analytical knowing.

Whereas analytical inquiry is about *unweaving* the phenomenon, Burrows guides us to reflect upon how the garment of consciousness engages modes of knowing which stand apart from the rationalistic and analytical. While the rationalist unweaves the phenomenon in order to understand it in fragments, the intuitive and sensorial engages its complexity and *weaves* the phenomenon in the fullness of its complexity.

Within the richness of the holistic weave, Burrows' spiritual garment evokes Merton's contemplative holism. For Merton, wisdom is nested within the veiled fullness of creation (Merton, 1974) and described with language which is sensual and tactile. In similar spirit, Burrows speaks of drawing upon the wisdom that lies within (Burrows, 2015) through deeper awareness with modes of knowing which embrace the intuitive and sensorial. Of the feeling of connection to creation which is nurtured by such embrace and shared by Merton, Burrows observes

> For Rosch (2007), mindfulness involves an opening up to and expansion of awareness, a letting go into deep states of not knowing, accessing intuitive wisdom, and feeling one with the world around us.
>
> (Burrows, 2015, p. 133)

By tapping the wisdom that is seeded deep within us within the encounter with the wholeness of creation (Merton, 1974) we begin the journey onto *Sophia*—one wherein is nested the potential for transformative shifts in consciousness.

Must I Abandon My Art? The Paradoxical Relation of the Spiritual and Aesthetical

Brother Louis. In your writings you speak of spirit and the aesthetical together. Yet their relation puzzles me. What is the standing of the aesthetical with the spiritual? I would like them to stand together but am unsure if they can as I reflect upon your writings. The relation of one to the other quivers.

Perhaps my query is an impossible one as I try to name a relation which defies words.

To be in the spiritual domain is to be embodied within the weave of the "seamless garment" (Burrows, 2015, p. 133); a domain marked by feeling and intuition. Within the encounter with the aesthetical I feel the promise of the weave. Yet I also feel that such place defies language.

In this you present me with a paradox and are stuck in the same conundrum as me—that is, of the conundrum of language.

But your relationship to your paradox is one I find complicated. You are well read and have written extensively on different subjects. Your writing can be of poetry; or in journals, letters and essays; sometimes you write mystically; at other times you seem a different person when you engage literary criticism. You love words. But the love and beauty you write about cannot be seen . . .

In your final journal The Other Side of the Mountain you write,

> The full beauty of the mountain is not seen until you too consent to the impossible paradox: it is and is not. When nothing more needs to be said, the smoke of ideas clears, the mountain is SEEN.
> (Merton, 1998a, p. 286)

For you Brother Louis the paradox of the mountain extends onto wisdom. In your poem Wisdom, you ponder

> I studied it and it taught me nothing.
> I learned it and soon forgot everything else.
> Having forgotten, I was burdened with knowledge—
> The insupportable knowledge of nothing.
>
> How sweet my life would be, if I were wise!
> Wisdom is well known
> When it is no longer seen or thought of.
> Only then is understanding bearable.
> (Merton, 1977, p. 279)

I read your criticism on the limits of rational knowing, yet I am still impelled to ask of you the map to the mountain that you have seen. But you cannot provide it because there is no map, and I am reminded of Melville's book Moby Dick; or, The Whale where Ishmael says "It is not down in any map; true places never are."

(Melville, 1922, p. 68)

I remain within your conundrum wherein you are immersed within the problem of language, yet you cannot give up on language, can you?

You use language with love as if a parent to a child as you do in Raids on the Unspeakable. How do you and I seek the way, and live in the domain of language? Must we one day journey away from this domain? Must we one day relinquish the words of the poet or the chisel of the sculptor—those special maps the artist possesses which raise our consciousness and guide us along the pathway to wisdom?

Must we forsake them when we have reached consciousness? Must we one day forsake our love for the artist? How can we forsake our children Brother Louis?

For Merton, spiritual awakening resides within acceptance of paradox (Merton, 1998a). Of such paradox, though, how is it to be understood? How do we offer our consent?

The questions are put forth but cannot be answered; they are nested within a language which is incommensurable with the domain of spiritual awakening. We are present within a paradox formed about language. Of the splendour of the mountain, that Merton writes of, we can acknowledge it but cannot write of it. It is ineffable. We can allude to it, speak of it tangentially, intuit and feel it; but never capture it with language. We seek the mountain which we cannot speak of; and were we to find, we remain within the paradox because, as Merton observes, "nothing more needs to be said" (Merton, 1998a, p. 286).

In his chronicle of wisdom traditions Curnow observes the Indian mystic Ramana Maharshi who writes "'In order to quieten the mind one only has to inquire within oneself what one's Self is; how could this search be done in books?'" (Curnow, 1999, p. 165). The mystic's words are familiar and mirror the paradox of language in Merton's own words, and those of my retelling which introduces this section. The aspect of reflexive interiority, with which the seeking of self-knowledge is nested, remains in complicated alignment with language. Of such complication Curnow, succinctly summarizes "Texts may be valuable to the extent to which they can indicate the path which is to be followed. However, their value is limited in that they cannot themselves constitute a substitute for the following of that path" (Curnow, 1999, p. 165).

Seeking the path tussles with the burden of rationalist thinking which pervades our lives. We impel towards a rationalist understanding of the spiritual path, yet the path is not demonstrable, and therein lies the paradox. We seek to demonstrate, find reasons and tidy beginnings and endings with which to allay our angst about the unknown. We seek to create comforting compartments of certainty. Descartes' presence is manifest.

Yet the spiritual terrain is intimate with our being; to demonstrate is to objectify that from which we cannot stand apart, and, as Palmer observes, speaks of the "myth of objectivity, which depends on a radical separation of the knower from the known" (Palmer, 1993, p. xv). The conundrum of spirituality lies within such division, one whose remediation for Palmer is to be found in the restraining of the rationalist impulse which underscores it. Instead, to be present with the spiritual involves a relational shifting which for Palmer is nested within the holistic and inclusive engaging with emotion, intuition and empathy in addition to the rational (Palmer, 1993). To embrace such modalities of knowing is to nurture the unseen wholeness where wisdom resides (Merton, 1974), or as Palmer also describes as a return to seeing the world as whole.

In a similar spirit, Burrows speaks of "non-dual mindfulness" (Burrows, 2015, p. 134) with which Merton's and Palmer's meditations upon wholeness are kindred. In a study of mindfulness amongst teachers Burrows records the observations of one of her study participants who observes that when in the space of non-duality "'There's a sense of openness to the universe. I'm a vessel for sensing impressions—no thinking involved, no processing, just receiving—open to whatever comes'" (Burrows, 2015, p. 134). Such sentiment echoing Merton's spiritual journey as one whose transit is within a paradox which defies language but whose core is centred about the holism of being, that is, of the "*SUM*, I Am" (Merton, 1972, p. 9).

The Paradox of Merton's Spiritual Journey

Regarding the disintegrating of self within the clamour of contemporary culture, Merton's spiritual writings are prescient to Palmer's and Burrows' observations. His writings are instructive as the evolution of his spiritual journey offers an exemplar of the paradox which he and contemporary writers in spirituality studies in education, like Ergas (2016) and Lin et al. (2016) share, and one which is complicated when viewed through the lens of the artful.

The paradox is illustrated in his early writings (1947) on the character of contemplation wherein Merton presents a hierarchy of contemplative forms which feels corralled within catholic theology. Within such configuration the presence of the aesthetical feels conflicted. While Merton distinguishes the "natural contemplation" of the artist and philosopher from "infused contemplation" which is bestowed by God, (Merton, 1947, p. 95), the language of the latter form is rich in aesthetical language. The relation of the aesthetical to the spiritual feels ambivalent.

Of the transformative journey writers in the field of holistic education observe how its trajectory is one which travels across horizons of learning, with each crossing one's horizon is resculpted and nurtured towards the spiritual in addition to the intellectual and emotional (Dencev & Collister, 2010). The journey of transformation as a spiritual quest invites an analogous reading of the evolving nature of Merton's ideas on the relation of contemplation and the aesthetical. While in *Poetry and the Contemplative Life* such relation is understood through a restricted theological lens, in his later writings, Merton's ideas on contemplation and the aesthetical evolve towards understandings which depart from its earlier and narrower register.

While Merton's categorization of forms of contemplation demarcate the earlier phase of his writing, the presence of the aesthetical within his categories of "infused" and "natural" contemplation (Merton, 1947, pp. 95–111) invite nuanced interpretations of their meaning. Although Merton does not dwell on the idea of natural contemplation of God—the form of contemplation which artists possess and which is mentioned only once in *Poetry and the Contemplative Life*—one cannot but sense the presence of such idea in deep relation to his concept of infused contemplation. When Merton observes "Christ on the Cross is the fount of all art because He is the Word, the fount of all grace and wisdom" (Merton, 1947, p. 98) we sense such presence intimately, one wherein Christ manifested upon Christianity's most potent visual symbol of the Cross—a visualization which is also identified with God's gifts of grace and wisdom—presents us with an artist's vision of contemplation which is fundamentally aesthetical in spirit.

Of such a vision Merton's essay sculpts a rich literary and visual understanding of contemplation. Of the liturgical domain, Merton speaks of the beauty of music and the pictorial arts; and extends his enthusiasm for the arts in contemplation to poetry, of which he is especially fond, and questions why we do not read the poetry of St. John of the Cross, whom he ranks amongst the greatest of Catholic contemplatives (Merton, 1947).

The enthusiasm with which Merton explores the relation of the aesthetical to contemplation evokes kindred observations on the nature of wisdom amongst researchers in wisdom studies. Merton's entwining of poetry and contemplation aligns with Baltes' observations on the relation of poetry to wisdom (Baltes, 2004). In a similar spirit his embrace of the visual arts in relation to contemplation illustrate the idea of the imaginal presence in wisdom, one which is alluded to in Curnow's historical overview of wisdom (Curnow, 2015).

While Merton's observations on poetry guide reflection upon the relation of the aesthetical to contemplation, they are also nuanced perhaps anticipating the spirit of his later Zen infused writings. While he praises poetry's relation to contemplation and observes how some of the greatest Christian contemplatives have been poets, he follows his praise with questions. Merton ponders how "contemplation has much to offer poetry. But can poetry offer anything, in return to contemplation? Can the poetic sense help us towards infused contemplation, and, if so, how far along the way?" (Merton, 1947, p. 101).

Such questions reveal how Merton raises the standing of the aesthetical in relation to the contemplative but is uncertain of their equivalence.

Brother Louis. I ponder your questions. You begin by praising contemplation's relation to poetry and how it offers much to poetry, yet then you

> ask what poetry can offer contemplation. Your reflection guides me onto the general question—what can the aesthetical offer contemplation?
>
> Your query though presents a conundrum to me. You speak of contemplation and poetry together and in this suggesting their affinity but not one of equivalence. They remain apart.
>
> My question keeps circling about the relation of the aesthetical and contemplation, but the circle has no beginning or end. Their relation remains paradoxical.

Merton's questions nurture my inquiry. They guide my reflection upon the relation of poetry in particular and the arts in general to contemplation. Yet, in the same moment I am confounded by the paradoxical ethos of the spiritual and aesthetical. Of the relation of the aesthetic to contemplation, for Merton, it is not a foregone conclusion that engaging the aesthetic transports us towards a transcendent experience. While the aesthetic encounter may move us towards such experience, he cautions that we must be careful not to confuse it with mystical experience of which it is not. While Merton perplexes me by his questions, they are also nested within a rich meditation upon the relation of art and contemplation. A meditation which is also prescient to the spirituality and transformative learning paradigms in education where the presence of the aesthetical in relation to contemplative knowing is central. In particular, evoking Hart's exploration of the place of the arts as a configuration of contemplative knowledge (Hart, 2004); or Lin's view that the domain of spirituality research includes forms of expression that are creative and metaphorical (Lin et al., 2016).

While Merton's views of the relation of art and contemplation are prescient to such paradigms, they are nested within a conundrum which lingers in my reflections. While recognizing "the dignity of the esthetic intuition" (Merton, 1947, p. 102) and the close resemblance of the artist's contemplation to that of the mystic, Merton cautions that such resemblance may be confused and that an "abyss" stands between aesthetical and mystical contemplation. The difference between such contemplative modalities is subtle. As Labrie observes Merton's view evolved from an orthodox theological view to one which was less so later in life; one in which artistic and mystical experiences were viewed as "analogous, since both involved an intuitive perception of reality through an "affective identification" with the object contemplated" (Labrie, 2001, p. 162).

In *Poetry and the Contemplative Life*, while Merton views artistic contemplation as analogous to mystical experience, such analogue feels ambivalent in his writing. On the one hand he speaks of how the "esthetic experience" conveys us onto the "interior sanctuary of the soul" (Merton, 1947, p. 104) and prepares us for infused contemplation. Yet, Merton also cautions the artist observing that while gifted with aesthetic intuition, will fall short of union with God. In strong language that departs from his later writings, Merton advises "In such an event, there is only one course for the poet to take, for his own individual sanctification: the ruthless and complete sacrifice of his art" (Merton, 1947, pp. 109–110).

In the transit towards spirituality the final act of the artist is to forgo his art. Merton's observation is puzzling. I reflect . . .

> *Brother Louis. Your language is strong and seems to diminish the artist. I do not want to give up my art. Must the artist abandon his art to complete the spiritual quest? I am confused Brother Louis. What if the artist feels "morally certain"* (Merton, 1947, pp. 111) *to do their art as you suggest? You also write,*

> "But we can console ourselves with Saint Thomas Aquinas that is it more meritorious to share the fruits of contemplation with others than it is merely to enjoy them ourselves. And certainly, when it comes to communicating some idea of the delights of contemplation, the poet is, of all men, the one who is least at a loss for a means to express what is essentially inexpressible."
>
> (*Merton, 1947, p. 111*)

> *Brother Louis. Though you speak theologically, I find in your contradictions an early intuition of Zen. The presence of opposites.*

Of the relation of artistic and mystical forms of contemplations Merton oscillates on the nature of their relation. He speaks of both *abyss* and *analogue*; they are similar and yet they are not. The language is dissonant and moves me to wonder by what path such contemplative forms could be possibly reconciled. Of such possibility, Merton provides a hint in when he observes, "the intuition of the artist sets in motion the very same psychological processes which accompany infused contemplation" (Merton, 1947, p. 103).

Merton's observation is provocative and I am struck by its powerful implication as a notion unifying artistic and mystical contemplative forms. That is, though Merton suggests that the end points of natural contemplation of the artist and infused contemplation are different, their origins are nurtured within shared psychological presences. The aesthetical is kindred with the contemplative experience. Though natural and infused contemplation are different for Merton, natural contemplation of the artist nurtures us towards infused contemplation the highest form of contemplation.

"My Soul is Art": The Journey of the H*eart* Towards the Spiritual

> Man himself has now become a soul in the form of art.
> (Merton, 1968, p. 91)

In my dialogical meditation *Seeking Merton's "Festival of Rain*,*"* I reflect upon the status of the aesthetical in relation to the transcendent. Merton refers to his writings as his children. Yet what becomes of them within the transcendent experience? Is the aesthetical abandoned? Must we relinquish our children? While the aesthetical carries us towards wisdom, does it ultimately fall short of such destination as is suggested by Merton in *Poetry and the Contemplative Life*?

Of the entangling of the aesthetical and contemplation Robert Inchausti reflects upon the conundrum of writing in relation to contemplation observing how "The writer must, for the sake of coherence, maintain his voice, and yet in contemplation, one must overcome any separation between one's self and one's experience" (Inchausti, 1998, p. 32). The writer seeks to capture the transcendent, yet in so doing stands apart from it.

While this paradox troubled Merton, Inchausti observes how Merton was able to reconcile it by accepting that writing was a ceaseless activity intended to correct misunderstandings of experience (Inchausti, 1998). Thus the aesthetical is not dismissed but remains within an endless exploration of human experience, a view which is sympathetic with the spirit of the spirituality research paradigm in education; and in particular evoking Miller's notion of the journey of the researcher as one which is eternal (Miller, 2016) and Hart's kindred notion of inquiry as one which travels the journey of questions (Hart, 2009).

The mystery of Merton's paradox is ameliorated by Inchausti's reflections. His observation offers reconciliation within the evolving character of Merton's thought. In *Poetry and the Contemplative Life*, Merton's writing on contemplation is sculpted theologically. The language is rigid and categorical—contemplation is understood within a hierarchical formation wherein the differences between aesthetic and contemplative experiences are delimited by the strong language of "abyss" and the less strong word of "analogy" (Merton, 1947, p. 102).

The complexity of language with which Merton parses such difference stands in striking contrast to a simple observation about spirituality and art he makes in a correspondence with the writer Boris Pasternak in 1958. Merton writes to Pasternak,

> I do not insist on this division between spirituality and art, for I think that even things that are not patently spiritual if they come from the heart of a spiritual person are spiritual.
> (Merton, 1993, p. 90)

Here Merton sees no need for categories or arguments or philosophical analysis. Spirituality stands apart from such divisions within a different domain which is less complicated in ethos. Merton defies categories; and I cycle back to his words from *Zen and the Birds of Appetite* where he advises us to simply "stop thinking and start looking" (Merton, 1968, p. 53).

The denial of category echoes an evolving of Merton's writing on the relation of spirituality and art, one which is also seen in his reflections upon Toshimitsu Hasumi's aesthetical views in *Zen in Japanese Art* (1968). In his observations Merton erodes the categorical language used to explore such relation in *Poetry and the Contemplative Life*. Instead Merton, following Hasumi, reflects on how Japanese contemplative art, calligraphy and the tea ceremony are spiritual experiences and "impregnated with the spirit of Zen" (Merton, 1968, p. 89), an observation which is echoed in Bai's exploration of the aesthetical and ethical ethos of the tea ceremony as one which is sustained by the presence of Zen, connection and non-dualism (Bai, 1997). Merton's associating of the contemplative with the aesthetical is strong; an identification which he reinforces with a second observation that such experiences could also be viewed as mystical (Merton, 1968). In his exploration of Hasumi's aesthetic the standing of the beautiful in relation to the contemplative is elevated.

In Hasumi's writing, Merton observes how Zen infuses art spiritually and transforms it "into an essentially contemplative experience in which it awakens 'the primal consciousness hidden within us and which makes possible any spiritual activity'" (Merton, 1968, p. 90). Departing from the categorical relation of art to spirituality in his earlier writings, Merton explores in *Zen and Japanese Art* a different relation in which art is central to contemplative experience. Within such centrality, Merton observes, echoing his comments to Pasternak, that there is no separation of spirituality from art and life; instead "under the unifying power of the Zen discipline and intuition, art, life and spiritual experience are all brought together and inseparably fused" (Merton, 1968, p. 90).

While the language Merton uses to ponder art, spirituality and Zen departs from that used in his early writing, it also invites interpretations through the spirituality and transformative learning paradigms. The intimacy with which Merton describes how Japanese contemplative art is embodied with Zen—one which is "impregnated with the spirit of Zen" (Merton, 1968, p. 89)—echoes Ergas' notion of the "impregnated being" as a metaphor for the fullness of spiritual life (Ergas, 2016, p. 6). Merton's language is prescient to Ergas'; his view of how art can nurture us towards the contemplative terrain within holistic understandings of knowledge also aligns with a kindred ethos found in the writings of Palmer (1993), Zajonc (2009) and Kabat-Zinn (2005).

The intimacy with which Merton speaks, in *Zen in Japanese Art* (1968) of the relation of spirituality and art stands juxtaposed to the exploration of such relation in *Poetry and the Contemplative Life*. From a theologically categorical exploration in the latter text Merton evolves into another language, which in *Zen and Japanese Art*, suggests another way to view the intimacy of art and contemplation. While he ponders the *abyss* which separates aesthetical and mystical contemplation in the earlier text, in the later one he presents us with a different language of such relation, one which is instead offered through the example of Japanese art. Instead of *abyss*, Japanese contemplative art is *pregnant* with Zen, one wherein the intimacy of one with the other culminates in one's soul becoming "the form of art" (Merton, 1968, p. 91). Dispensing with the categorical relation of art and spirituality of his earlier writing, Merton in *Zen in Japanese Art* presents a simpler exploration of such relation where he forgoes the rigid separation of art from spirituality.

The unfolding character of Merton's views during his lifetime aligns with interpretations of transformation amongst writers in the field of transformative studies in education. Amongst such writers Morgan, for example, observes how spiritual growth involves transformative shifts in one's perspective (Morgan, 2012), a process which is echoed in Merton's evolving views on the relation of spirituality, contemplation and art.

Towards a Methodology of My Own:
Merton on Education and the Paradisal

> Paradise is simply the person, the self, but the radical self in its uninhibited freedom. The self no longer clothed with an ego.
>
> (Merton, 1979, p. 8)

> The shaman was the first dream keeper, the first artist, the first poet, the first hunter, the first doctor, the first dancer, singer, and teacher. And, while the shaman personified the archetypal visionary and artist, the visionary and artist are potentials that abide in each and every one of us, every man, every woman, and every child. Tribal people understood and honored this "potential," this "calling" as an integral part of learning, being and becoming complete. Through encouragement, through ritual, through training and practice, Tribal people formed and guided this reflection of the divine in each other.
>
> (Cajete, 2019, p. 139)

This chapter opens with a retelling of an encounter with Merton's writings, one which was transformative in shifting my inquiry towards a simple yet paradoxical truth. That is, while the encounter with Merton caused me to embark upon a five-year study of his writings, the journey also did not travel far for it turned inwards, following Merton, onto the "radical self in its uninhibited freedom" (Merton, 1979, p. 8).

Standing apart from the "the myth of objectivism" which had defined my education (Palmer & Zajonc, 2010, p. 15) I started to learn again by the inward turn towards another configuration formed of two seemingly different descriptors, of Merton's "radical" and "paradisal" which together seeded the terrain of the core self.

To speak of the paradisal idea within the discourse of self is to nest such discourse with an idea which is imaginal and aesthetically evocative. Reading Merton guided me onto such terrain and the reflection that within the necessary encounter with our own narratives we become our own artists, the tools we choose to do our art uniquely are own. Our self emerges from within a methodology of our own making.

That the tools for inquiry onto the self are nested within the necessity of narrative and aesthetical character of such necessity emerged as a fundamental truth in my inquiry. Within such necessity we are our own methodology. Merton guided me onto such truth, and my education begins again with him as my teacher.

Regarding the character of art to nurture the spiritual self, Merton's writings guided my reflection upon how such terrain is informed by the identification of the self with Merton's paradise idea. Although the exploring of such notion was triggered by Labrie's (2001) study of the paradisal in Merton's writings, my study reimagines Merton's idea as an *imaginally* rich notion wherein is sought the unity of the paradisal with aesthetically informed understandings of wisdom. In *Zen and Japanese Art*, Merton offers the possibility of such unity, one which evolves from a more oscillating position of such prospect in his earlier writing in *Poetry and the Contemplative Life*. In *Love and Living*, Merton offers us another link in such evolution. That is, one marked by the evolving towards a paradisal consciousness which is sculpted within the intimacy of art with spirituality and Merton's view of the purpose of education.

Of such purpose Merton, in *Love and Living* writes,

> The purpose of education is to show a person how to define himself authentically and spontaneously in relation to his world—not to impose a prefabricated definition of the world, still less an arbitrary definition of the individual himself.
>
> (Merton, 1979, p. 3)

> Thus, the fruit of education, whether in the university (as for Eckhart) or in the monastery (as for Ruysbroeck) was the activation of that inmost center, that *scintilla animae*, that "apex" or "spark" which is a freedom beyond freedom, an identity beyond essence, a self beyond all ego, a being beyond the created realm, and a consciousness that transcends all division, all separation. To activate this spark is not to be, like Plotinus, "alone with the Alone," but to recognize the Alone which is by itself in everything because there is nothing that can be apart from It and yet nothing that can be with It, and nothing that can realize It. It can only realize itself. The "spark" which is my true self is the flash of the Absolute recognizing itself in me.
>
> (Merton, 1979, pp. 9–10)

Merton reflects upon the paradise idea within a discourse on the purpose of education—a linkage which aligns with kindred understandings, within holistic studies in education, of the character of learning. Amongst these, for example, Merton's notion of "child mind" (Gardner, 2016, p. 3), which he explores within language of the paradisal world of the child (Merton, 1977), evokes comparisons to Hart's view of children as contemplatives (Hart, 2004) or Montessori's notion of the "spiritual embryo" (Montessori, 1970, p. 18). The holistic spirit with which Merton ponders education, within the discourse of the paradisal, also guides reflection upon how such spirit aligns with themes within spirituality studies in education, in particular, Zajonc's and Palmer's understanding of integrative learning and their kindred notion of a pedagogy of interconnection (Palmer & Zajonc, 2010).

Zajonc and Palmer both acknowledge the presence of Merton in their writings. Merton's observations on the unclothed self are echoed in Palmer's views on education as one which "prepares us to see beyond appearances into the hidden realities of life" (Palmer, 1993, p. 13). For Merton, though, seeking the self is a cautious seeking which places a demand upon us and poses risk (Merton, 1979). For Zajonc, such demand is echoed in his exploration of contemplative inquiry where, in the spirit of Merton, observes how "We need to complement our outer work with a comparable commitment to inner work" (Zajonc, 2009, p. 15). For Zajonc, as for Merton, integral to the inner work requires engaging with solitude and meditative practices (Zajonc, 2009). Such work places a demand to extract ourselves from the noise of daily life which surrounds us, one which is also advocated by Merton in *Conjectures of a Guilty Bystander* (Merton, 2014). For Zajonc to seek solitude is to find a haven in meditation. But of such a haven, Zajonc also observes, in the spirit of Merton that "the work of meditation is, in the end, a solitary work. It is ours to do, and no amount of assistance can or should relieve us of it" (Zajonc, 2009, p. 22).

Removed from the clamour, Merton observes the unclothed self, one beyond ego but one where paradise also resides within a configuration with education and the discovery of the authentic self. Of such configuration, Merton describes it within a potent and expansive aesthetical language rich in the presence of light, the image of the spark and visual movement. Within the vision of light, the star hurdles forth from its scintilla and explosive birth onto a transcendent plane, one wherein the movement towards the self is set within a vision of learning which cascades towards the inner paradisal.

While Merton's scintilla evokes the image of a bright star, it also suggests that the transit to the self follows a silent light. Seeking Merton's "radical self" (Merton, 1979, p. 8) is a silent journey which is, following Palmer, beyond the clamour of the "hall of mirrors" which distracts the transit towards transcendence (Palmer, 1993, p. 13). Like Fra Angelico's Christ who is centred yet blindfolded to the clamour that surrounds him, the light of transcendence is a powerful but silent flicker. Yet also a light which illuminates Merton's "radical self" within the paradisal presence which resides within us. To read Merton through Palmer or Fra Angelico's vision guides me to reflect upon how the journey towards Merton's self is a transit towards the paradisal; a transcendent place bathed within a silent light where wisdom resides.

> *My section begins with a reflection from Merton and a second one from the indigenous writer Gregory Cajete. Their words are wonderfully kindred. Merton writes of the paradise as the "self in its uninhibited freedom" (Merton, 1979, p. 8) while Cajete writes of the "divine in each other" (Cajete, 2019, p. 139).*
>
> *Their sentiments easily traverse onto the other. With Merton we imagine the inner shaman "the first artist, the first poet" (Cajete, 2019, p. 139) while in Cajete we interpret the paradisal which resides in the divine.*
>
> *Merton and Cajete in connection, from which a wonderful holism of spirit emerges which has as its core the presence of the artist in the configuration of self. As Cajete observes*
>
> "The creation of art is an alchemy of process in which the artist "becomes" more himself through each act of true creation, as he transfers his life in a dance of relationship with the life inherent in the material which he transforms into an artistic creation. In each process of creation, there must be an initiation, purification, death, and

> *rebirth of the artist through focused creative work. For in working, reworking, and the suffering into being of a work of art, the artist is, in reality, creating and recreating himself. It is, in a metaphoric sense, a 'matter of life, death, and rebirth.'"*
>
> (Cajete, 2019, p. 143)

Seeking the Inner Light of Paradisal Wisdom

> Thus He shines not on them but from within them. Such is the loving-kindness of Wisdom. . . . The shadows fall. The stars appear. The birds begin to sleep. Night embraces the silent half of the earth. A vagrant, a destitute wanderer with dusty feet, finds his way down a new road. A homeless God, lost in the night, without papers, without identification, without even a number, a frail expendable exile lies down in desolation under the sweet stars of the world and entrusts Himself to sleep.
>
> (Merton, 1974, pp. 508–511)

In *Hagia Sophia*, Merton meditates upon wisdom within a cycle of light marked by the transit of shadows and stars, but a light which is cast from within. His vision, set within nature's daily rhythm of light and darkness and the story of the "homeless God," echoing the ethos of Cajete's meditation upon initiation, death; recreating and birth which marks the artist's transit into becoming.

Within the rhythms of light and nature Merton offers a vision of spirituality whose journey is rich in an imaginal presence. An ethos of spirituality marked with the presence of light and echoing the luminous vision of Merton's spark; herein configuring an aesthetical presence which is core to the promise of the radical self. The spiritual vision is present with the artful.

In *Hagia Sophia*, Merton offers his spiritual-aesthetic vision in his meditation on *Sophia*, from the Greek idea of wisdom. He writes

> There is in all visible things an invisible fecundity, a dimmed light, a meek namelessness, a hidden wholeness. This mysterious Unity and Integrity is Wisdom, the Mother of all, and Natura naturans. There is in all things an inexhaustible sweetness and purity, a silence that is a fount of action and joy. It rises up in wordless gentleness and flows out to me from the unseen roots of all created being, welcoming me tenderly, saluting me with indescribable humility. This is at once my own being, my own nature, and the Gift of my Creator's Thought and Art within me, speaking as Hagia Sophia, speaking as my sister, Wisdom.
>
> (Merton, 1974, p. 506)

Merton crafts his poem in four parts corresponding to the natural rhythm of the day: "Dawn," "Early Morning," "High Morning" and "Sunset" (Merton, 1974, pp. 506–511). It is within the natural cycle of light, the rhythm of nature and not the analytical that wisdom is rooted. And within such cycle Merton speaks of wisdom with beauty: "wholeness," "sweetness and purity" and "gentleness and flows." It welcomes, it salutes, it is both tender and a gift. Merton speaks of wisdom with love within an aesthetical discourse. From within a place of beauty formed of love and the cycle of light which sculpt our being we awaken from our darkness onto the inner paradise (Merton, 1974, p. 507). Set within the daily rhythms of nature, Merton's spiritual vision in dialogue with Cajete's kindred meditation upon the alchemical character of transformation which accompanies the aesthetical encounter.

> *Brother Louis, how do I transit to the light; how do I receive the Creator's gift? You write "Wisdom cries out to all who will hear" (Merton, 1974, p. 507). But how do I both hear the cry of wisdom and solitude of silence, which you ponder and where wisdom resides? Within the seeming contradiction of the silent cry you invite us to seek our wholeness, the paradisal place within us where wisdom is seeded.*

In his exploration of Merton's spiritual evolution, Michael Higgins observes how for Merton wisdom is configured with the embrace of wholeness (Higgins, 1998). For Merton, such an embrace is nested within the presence of the aesthetical and, as his poem *Hagia Sophia* reveals, sculpted with love and beauty. Merton's reflections on *Sophia* and beauty in turn evoking Zajonc's thesis of knowledge formed by love (Zajonc, 2006) or Palmer's advice that we see the world within the unity of heart and mind (Palmer, 1993).

Pondering Zajonc and Palmer returns me to Merton's reflection that wisdom resides within a domain of feeling and wholeness and configured of "an inexhaustible sweetness and purity" (Merton, 1974, p. 506). Yet for Merton the inner paradisal wisdom that we seek is also a seeking onto a solitary terrain.

The Silent Self and Solitudinous Ethos of Paradisal Wisdom

> Here is an unspeakable secret: paradise is all around us and we do not understand. It is wide open. The sword is taken away, but we do not know it: we are off "one to his farm and another to his merchandise." Lights on. Clocks ticking. Thermostats working. Stoves cooking. Electric shavers filling radios with static. "Wisdom," cries the dawn deacon, but we do no attend.
>
> (Merton, 2014, p. 128)

Like the cycle of light which envelopes us, so does wisdom for Merton. But for wisdom to flower we must be in tune with the rhythm of creation while drowning out that which impedes the light. While Merton writes about silence in *Hagia Sophia*, in *Conjectures of a Guilty Bystander* he reflects upon its antithesis; that is of the clamour that blocks us from paradise.

Merton cries for wisdom, but his plea is for silence. His plea synchronous with the calls of contemporary writers in spirituality and transformative studies in education such as Zajonc (2009), Palmer and Zajonc (2010) and Hart (2014) who, like Merton, appeal for calm amidst a culture of noise and distraction.

Merton's caution about the clamour that envelopes our daily lives and impedes our awareness echoing the spirit of Hart's observations in *The Integrative Mind* (2014). Like Merton, Hart ponders the cultural distractions which disable our awareness. Commenting upon the din of electronic culture which envelopes our lives, in the spirit of Merton's *Conjectures*, he observes

> Will clicking our way through fragments of information reduce our ability for sustained concentration and depth of comprehension? Will so much time on disembodied screens reduce our connections to our own bodies, the body of nature, and direct, embodied encounters with one another? . . . will these invisible algorithms reduce our capacity to see broadly and choose wisely? There is evidence and argument that for all the advantages of massive computational power, these not-so-desirable changes are already shaping us.
> (Hart, 2014, pp. xii-xiii)

Like Hart other writers have echoed Merton's prescient observations. In *Meditation as Contemplative Inquiry* Arthur Zajonc begins his inquiry with reflection upon solitude and its importance in contemplation (Zajonc, 2009). With a spiritual declaration Zajonc foregrounds Merton's plea for silence in order to emphasize its importance in contemplative practice. Like Merton, who he acknowledges in his writing, Zajonc laments the clamour which surrounds us. While Merton pleas for silence, Zajonc in like spirit advises, "becoming practiced in solitude" (Zajonc, 2009, p. 20). Engaging solitude does not mean separating oneself from the world for as Zajonc observes, "we are already hermits" (Zajonc, 2009, p. 22) in the world. Amidst the din though Zajonc, in like spirit with Merton's cautions, pleas for the nurturing of "'the silent self'"—one which, following the example of Martin Luther King, is a self beyond ego (Zajonc, 2009, p. 29).

Though Zajonc speaks of our hermit lives, the silent self is not a place of disconnection, but a nurturing place, what he also describes, again following Merton, as a place of "creative silence" (Zajonc, 2009, p. 30). With such silence Zajonc, like Merton, evokes the presence of the aesthetical within contemplative practice and its centrality to nurturing of the authentic self. Similarly Palmer ponders the pain of disconnected lives (Palmer, 1993) within contemporary culture and looks to Merton for guidance. Encouraging a return to the spiritual traditions Palmer, like Zajonc, references Merton and observes that, while our lives seem detached, they are also permeated with a wholeness that is unseen (Palmer, 1993).

Of the Imaginal and Paradisal: "Radical Self" and the Artist

> *Brother Louis. Of wisdom you speak of it configured by beauty and solitude; and within such configuration is seated the paradisal within one's self. How does the artist carry us towards the paradisal, the "radical self" that you speak of, and how is such transit towards a paradisal wisdom?*

For Merton the paradisal idea is aligned with the aesthetical and contemplative, a theme which is prescient to Zajonc's thesis of the silent and contemplative character of creativity. The artist turns us away from the din, nurturing us towards the solitude where Merton's "radical self" (Merton, 1979, p. 8) is nested within a paradisal aesthetic that emerges from within.

In *Conjectures*, Merton reflects upon how we are inattentive to such presence although it encircles us (Merton, 2014). Of its ethos I am reminded of Miller's observation of how "the soul opens to us when we hear a piece of music, see a child at play, are deeply involved in our work, or are simply being present in nature" (Miller, 2008, p. 14). Such moments of mindful listening and looking—moments of *attending*—evoke the paradisal presence which Merton ponders.

For Merton such moments are both incarnated and imaginal. In the poem *Hagia Sophia* he reflects on how wisdom and the paradisal consciousness are embodied.

> When the helpless one awakens strong at the voice of mercy, it is as if Life his Sister, as if the Blessed Virgin, (his own flesh, his own sister), as if nature made wise by God's Art and Incarnation were to stand over him and invite him with unutterable sweetness to be awake and to live. This is what it means to recognize Hagia Sophia.
> (Merton, 1974, p. 507)

"Art and Incarnation" stand aligned wherein Merton identifies *Sophia* with art and embodiment. Within embodiment there is awakening and life, and within the presence of light that emanates from it there is the paradisal. Within the terrain of the aesthetical—of the "gift of my Creator's Thought and Art within me" (Merton, 1974, p. 506)—there is nurtured wisdom or Sophia.

Exploration of Merton's view of the paradisal and its relation to the imaginal and wisdom was seeded by Labrie's (2001, 2014) examination of the paradisal in Merton's writings. Labrie observes,

> While in Merton's early writings, paradise was often a biblical one, he later came to locate the seat of paradise in the psyche. Within the self, in Merton's view, dwelt the most precious of paradisal gifts, a fundamental inner freedom, particularly freedom from the demands of the ego, a freedom that, once attained, Merton lyrically referred to in 1965 as a "paradise tree."
> (Labrie, 2001, p. 120)

Pondering the paradise tree returns me to my trip to Florence when I encountered a painting called *L'albero della Vita* by the 14th-century artist Pacino di Buonaguida (1310–1315). The painting is in the Galleria dell'Accademia. While the image is rooted in a Christian narrative configured by stories of genesis and the passion of and salvation by Christ, the narrative is depicted as a holistic representation of the creation in its fullness.

> *My encounter with the Tree of Life guides my meditation upon the presence of the imaginal in Merton's paradisal idea, and how such presence aligns with wisdom. That is, while the paradisal is central to*

the mythologies with which we have psychically evolved—the paradise story of the fall, the place we have come from and the place we seek to return—has also a deeply aesthetical presence. As a foundational cultural myth the paradisal story is rich in its visual and poetic sculpting. Reading Labrie on Merton's paradisal consciousness (Labrie, 2001) nurtured this other possibility in my inquiry, that is, how contemplating the paradisal evokes the image of the paradise narrative; one in which the presence of the imaginal is central. Of the paradise tree, Merton reflects

They bear with them in the center of nowhere the unborn flower of nothing:
This is the paradise tree. It must remain unseen until words end and arguments are silent.
(Merton, 1977, p. 355)

For Merton, the journey onto the self is one which crosses the terrain of the aesthetical. It is a crossing wherein the imaginal is enmeshed with the paradisal and spirituality and wisdom are seeded within an aesthetical presence. Such enmeshing though is also paradoxical, while the question of the image's relation to wisdom gradually emerged in my inquiry, the paradise tree, observes Merton, "remains unseen."

Merton's paradox invokes the spirit of Zen, yet the presence of the imaginal persists and I cannot extract it from the conundrum. The imaginal presence is powerful and anchored by the intersection of the centrality of the paradise narrative in our mythological psyche with the image of the paradise.

The story of art reveals such centrality, how the journey of paradise is mapped by an aesthetical presence—one which is evoked through powerful and memorable artists' interpretations of such journey through history. Pondering the paradisal evokes the image of paradise, Gilgamesh's story of the *Garden of the Gods* (c. 3500 BC) the Sumerian paradise, the *Elysian fields* of the Greeks, or the Christian story of *Adam and Eve* amongst interpretations of the paradisal journey.

Of written stories, Dante's *Paradise* in the *Divine Comedy* (c. 1308–1320) and Milton's *Paradise Lost* (1658–1664) are poetic interpretations of the paradisal. Of visual representations, Masaccio's *The Expulsion from the Garden of Eden* (1425, Brancacci Chapel, Florence); Michelangelo's *The Fall and Expulsion from Paradise* in the Sistine Chapel (1477–1480, Rome); Jan Breughel the Elder's *The Garden of Eden with the Fall of Man* (1617, The Hague); or Blake's depictions of Milton's *Paradise Lost* (1658–1664) are notable examples of the paradise image.

Within the history of the imaginal, such works of poetry and painting share an elevated standing and in turn underscore the centrality of the paradisal in our cultural psyche, one in which the presence of the aesthetical, as the channel for the paradisal, is key. Paradise is the place we psychically lament for its loss yet the endpoint that we seek for ourselves—a story which we contemplate through artists' retelling of the paradisal image. The paradise journey as a holistic transit—while configured as global cultural narratives, they are also psyche narratives wherein the promise of Merton's "radical self" is situated. And within the imaginal expression of such rich cultural narratives, the role of the artist is key.

"Earth Connections": Wisdom in the Landscape

Regarding the character of the spiritual journey, its crossing often involves a dialogue between our interior lives and being present to the creation in which our lives are nested. Amongst some spiritual writers such dialogue is nurtured in relation to nature (Merton, 2014; Miller, 2008). It is a place which seeds, following Zajonc, the "creative silence" (Zajonc, 2009, p. 30), a terrain where, in my study, my dialogical silence is weaved within the imaginal encounter with nature.

In *The Holistic Curriculum*, John P. Miller (2008) observes how contemporary society has become removed from nature, symptomatic of educational systems which value technical knowing over wisdom and knowing holistically. In the spirit of the Transcendentalist writers who also lamented their society's disconnect from nature in the 19th century, Miller similarly advocates for restoring our connection with it in the 21st century. In his appeal for us to reconnect he observes,

> Earth connections, then can reawaken us to the natural processes of life. The wind, the sun, the trees, and the grass can help us come alive and waken us from the treadmill we find ourselves.
> (Miller, 2008, p. 163)

Miller's reflections upon the landscape evoke those of Merton. His observation of the "treadmill [on which] we find ourselves" (Miller, 2008, p. 163) echoes Merton's lament in *Conjectures of a Guilty Bystander* about soulless lives controlled by "Clocks ticking" (Merton, 2014, p. 128)—lives which are spiritually vacant to the paradise that surrounds them.

Other writers in the field of transformative learning share such views. Amongst them Hart (2014) observes how contemporary culture is replete with distractions and disabling of our awareness, or Palmer who observes "the pain of disconnection" (Palmer, 1993, p. xii) that he sees in education and which is symptomatic of the "one-eyed lives" (Palmer, 1993, p. xxiii) that many lead, or Zajonc (2009) who advocates responding to the din in which we are enveloped through the appeal for a renewed silence and solitude.

For Merton, as is echoed in Miller, the path to the core self is intertwined with the touch with nature. For Merton, by restoring our being with nature—to touch it and feel we are one with it and it one with us—sculpts a spiritual intertwining which is key to reaching the inner paradisal. It is a journey towards the paradisal which is imbued with love and beauty, and which echoes Zajonc's notion of an epistemology sculpted by love (Zajonc, 2006).

Meditations on Merton's Paradox

For Merton, being with nature and the aesthetical are intertwined and central to the promise of wisdom. Writing on his travels in the American southwest shortly before his death in 1968, Merton offers poetic insights upon such intertwining which evoke the spirit of American Transcendentalist writing. His writings stand in juxtaposition to the mechanistic and soulless culture of "Thermostats working. Stoves cooking" (Merton, 2014, p. 128) which he laments in *Conjectures of a Guilty Bystander*. Of the southwest landscape he observes,

> Light and shadow on the wind erosion patterns of the rocks. Silence except for the gull-like, questioning cries of jays.
> Distant sound of muddy rushing water in the Chama River below me. I could use up rolls of film on nothing but these rocks. The whole canyon replete with emptiness. . . . The sun on the vast water, the sound of the waves. Yet the sound of the wind in the piñon pines here is very much the same.
> (Merton, 1998a, pp. 104–105)

The passage is from *The Other Side of the Mountain*. In it Merton records observations of his travels through New Mexico and California. His haiku-like writing surveys the southwest landscape—its canyons and wildlife and "the adobe walls of Georgia O'Keeffe's house" (Merton, 1998a, p. 106). His observation of the sound of the pines being the same as the sound of the waves is a sensual retelling of the interconnection of the creation. Merton's connection with the landscape reveals a state of mindfulness—one which as Kabat-Zinn observes "'means paying attention in a particular way; on purpose, in the present moment and nonjudgementally' [Kabat-Zinn, 1991, cited in Black, n.d.]" (Burrows, 2015, p. 129). Kabat-Zinn's notion of nonjudgemental mindfulness is echoed in kindred notions by others within the holistic and transformative learning paradigms; amongst these Zajonc's notion of "a calm eros that animates our interest and keeps us attentive and engaged" (Zajonc, 2006, p. 1748); Hart's notion of a "knowledge by presence" (Hart, 2008, p. 236); or Byrnes' exploration of "mindful awareness" (Byrnes, 2012, p. 34). Of the latter, Byrnes reflects upon teaching practice and observes "Mindful awareness in teaching requires openness to the present moment with a perspective of equanimity that is driven by a sense of wonder" (Byrnes, 2012, p. 34).

The ethos of wonder which Byrnes entwines with "mindful awareness" in teaching practice echoes the spirit of Merton's retellings of his encounters with nature. While Merton's desert journal engages the immediacy of the landscape it is also expansive and imbued with a sense of wholeness and connection. Merton interweaves his contemplations on the landscape with observations on philosophers, poets, artists and American society. His critical remarks on society, expressed in his observation "Computer Karma in American civilization" (Merton, 1998a, p. 103), are mixed in with observations or quotations from Chaucer, Descartes, Zen and the Astavakra Gita. The encounter with nature is simultaneously for Merton, an aesthetical one.

64　*Meditations on Merton's Paradox*

In the midst of his journal Merton quotes from Astavakra Gita and reflects,

> "When the mind is stirred and perceives things before it as objects of thought, it will find in itself something lacking" (Astavakra Gita)
>
> To find this "something lacking" is already a beginning of wisdom.
> Ignorance seeks to make good the "lacking" with better and more complete or more mysterious objects. The lack itself will be complete as void.
> Not to deny subject and object but to realize them as void.
>
> (Merton, 1998a, pp. 104–105)

Merton's discourse on wisdom is nestled within artful contemplation—one sculpted by his poetic reflections on the landscape which are interspersed within other expansive and holistic meditations upon Zen and spirituality. In his meditations he references artists and poets, philosophers and mystics and his own photographic art. The writing evokes the spirit of Thoreau's Transcendentalism. In like manner as Thoreau who meditates upon the river bank in *Walden* (Thoreau, 1854) Merton contemplates the "whole canyon replete with emptiness" (Merton, 1998a, p. 105)—a spiritual and holistic emptiness which is also aligned with his artistic engaging of the landscape with his own film camera. Within the meditation upon the landscape is nestled an aesthetic emptiness; and within such emptiness wisdom is nested.

Regarding mystical writing, Curnow in *Wisdom, Intuition and Ethics* (1999) observes how such writing is often infused with "metaphors of ascent, of height, of the mountain" (Curnow, 1999, p. 280). With Merton, whose writing is also sculpted by such metaphors, being with the landscape infuses the mystical feeling of his writings—where Merton, following the Ashtavakra Gita, states the finding of "'something lacking'" is also an opening onto wisdom (Merton, 1998a, pp. 104–105).

While writing was one strategy Merton used to contemplate the landscape, a second was his camera. Of his photographic practice, arts educator Charles Scott observes how for Merton, photography was a way of engaging with the "'hidden wholeness' of a subject" in a manner which was focused and unhurried in spirit (Scott, 2014, p. 335). For Merton, the camera, as with his poetry, nurtures the contemplative encounter with the landscape. The camera and poem are forms which intertwine the contemplative and aesthetical, an intertwining which in turn carries Merton towards the Zen where the presence of absence is also the beginning of wisdom.

Regarding the intertwining of the aesthetical with wisdom and contemplation, Merton's observations are prescient to kindred themes in the fields of holistic and transformative learning in education. Amongst these Hart embraces contemplative reflection as a modality of knowing (Hart, 2004) which supplements the sensorial and rational, but one which also stands apart from them by embracing the aesthetical. In a similar spirit, there is Zajonc's notion following Goethe of a "'gentle empiricism' (*zarte Empirie*) [p. 307]'" (Zajonc, 2006, p. 1746) wherein the encounter with the phenomenon echoes Merton's relationship with the landscape—one which is configured by feelings of connection and not separation. In a similar spirit of connection, Burrows reflects how to be mindful is to be conscious of all things. For Burrows, wisdom is seeded with the embrace of connection within the unbroken garment of creation (Burrows, 2015).

Of the Pivot and Dome
Seeking the Divine by Visualizing Connection

Curnow's observations on how mystical writing is often enriched with metaphors of the mountain is seen in Merton's *The Other Side of the Mountain* (1998a) where the writing is replete with the presence of the mountain in particular and landscape in general. Merton's mountain poetry stirs the imaginal and returns me to pondering the power of images to both stir and teach. Of the broader question of the relation of art to wisdom which is evoked by such observations, Merton's enmeshing of wisdom, aesthetical understanding and contemplation guides reflection upon how the work of artists, and in particular, that of the landscape photographer Edward Burtynsky illuminates such question.

While the spirit of Merton's contemplative life was expressed through his writing, another vehicle for such expression was his own art. In tandem with his writings he sketched and later in life took up photography. In his meditation upon the landscape the rolls of film that he writes of form part of the imaginal richness of the depicted landscape (Merton, 1998a). Examples of his sketches, which evoke a Zen-like quality, are included in *Raids on the Unspeakable*, a text in which he discusses them in the essay *Signatures: Notes on the Author's Drawings* (Merton, 1966).

As it is with Merton's writing and art, the presence of the landscape is central in Burtynsky's photography. In some of his mountain images his photographs evoke Ansel Adams' landscape portraits. But while Merton dwells upon the landscape within a spirit evoking American Transcendentalist writing the focus of Burtynsky's images has been to explore humanity's toll it.

Over the past three decades Burtynsky has photographed quarries in Italy, oil fields of the southwest US and scenes of ship-breaking in Bangladesh. In 2013, he completed a five-year project in which he explored how humanity's demand upon water threatens a vital resource. In the water series, Burtynsky offers images of dams in China, farmlands fed by pivot irrigation in the US, step wells in India, and the demise of the Colorado River Delta. In his large format photographs, film *Watermark* (de Pencier, Burtynsky, & Baichwal, 2014) and his recent *The Anthropocene Project* (de Pencier, Burtynsky, & Baichwal, n.d.) we become, through his art, witnesses to humanity's toll on the environment. His images remind us of our troubled relation to our environment; they draw us softly, cause us to pause and meditate upon them.

Unlike other forms of aerial photographs Burtynsky's images, as the art writer Russell Lord observes, "induces slower and longer looking" (Lord, 2013, p. 188). Lord adds,

> While the story of water is certainly an ecological one, Burtynsky is more interested in presenting the facts on the ground than in declaring society's motives good or bad. In focusing all the facets of people's relationship with water, Burtynsky offers evidence, without an argument. And yet, we as viewers have to work to decipher this evidence or to even decode it as evidence. It is precisely this tension, the gap between our knowledge that there is something to be gleaned from these pictures and our inability to immediately recognize what that thing is that gives this project its immense weight.
> (Lord, 2013, pp. 188–189)

The nurturing of a slow looking, which Lord observes in Burtynsky's images, echoes a kindred observation by Charles Scott who observed that for Merton photography required an engaging with the image which was slow and attentive (Scott, 2014).

Though writing from different fields of the art critic and holistic educator respectively, Lord's and Scott's analogous observations suggest how the encounter with Burtynsky's images is a contemplative one. While Roland Barthes (1981) wrote of the power of images to seize us, with Burtynsky, such seizing is muted. While we are drawn to his images, their stories are not imposed upon us. They do not seize us as does Barthes' *punctum* (Barthes, 1981, p. 27); instead following Lord's observation Burtynsky's images, in particular, his abstract landscapes of agriculture, are sometimes "illegible" (Lord, 2013, p. 188); clues are offered which the viewer must decipher on their own. The images require slow and careful looking. Rather than seize us, they draw us in slowly, following Zajonc with a "calm eros" (Zajonc, 2006, p. 1748). As the National Geographic photographer Wade Davis also observes of Burtynsky's images,

> The power of his photography lies not in polemics but in its neutrality. Edward makes no judgement. He simply bears witness, presenting a visual record of what he has seen. His work is an indelible record of the consequences of industrial folly, conceived, composed and presented in a manner that can only inspire. Compassion is the essence of his art. Harnessing the redemptive spirit of humanity to positive action and deed is the purpose of his passion.
> (Davis, 2013, p. 24)

While Davis and Lord do not use the language of spirituality, their observations evoke interpretations of a Zen-like silence and non-judgemental aspect of Burtynsky's images, ones which are kindred with the presence of Zen in Merton's writings.

Meditations on Merton's Paradox 67

Following Merton, Zajonc writes of a creativity which is configured in silence when one turns away from the "'social self' . . . toward a 'deeper, silent self'—the calm captain of the sailboat or the witness on the hillside" (Zajonc, 2009, p. 30). In a similar spirit Robert Inchausti speaks of "our silent selves" which is a self of listening (Inchausti, 1998, p. 133).

Reflecting on Burtynsky's images nurtures reflection on the character of the quiet self that Zajonc and Inchausti speak of. While Burtynsky's images draw us, they do so, following Zajonc with a silent eros; we become "witness on the hillside" to the images presence. Our attention is absorbed by Burtynsky's photographs but, following Inchausti, we listen to them as silent witnesses.

A kindred observation is offered by Rina Arya, a visual arts researcher, who writes on the spiritual presence of art observing how it is marked by "an art of absorption that requires the viewer to be patient and contemplative, thus opening us up to experiences of profound spiritual reflection" (Arya, 2011, p. 85). Like Zajonc, she observes how the spiritual encounter is silent but also one which moves us from "the perceptual reality of the work to an understanding of the deeper reality of the universe; we move from the literal to the metaphorical realm" (Arya, 2011, p. 90). While Arya makes these observations within explorations of the video artist, Bill Viola, and painter, Mark Rothko, they can also be extended onto Burtynsky's photography.

Of the intermingled themes of contemplation, the aesthetical, holistic connection and wisdom which is seeded in Burtynsky's photographs the pairing of two images in his book *Essential Elements* (Ewing, 2016, pp. 48–49) is informative. One image, *Pivot Irrigation #39 (2012)* is an aerial view of a

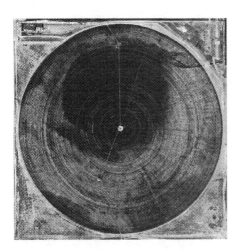

Image 2.3 Burtynsky, Edward. (2012). *Pivot Irrigation No. 39* [Chromogenic print]

Source: © Edward Burtynsky. Courtesy of Nicholas Metivier Gallery, Toronto

Image 2.4 Burtynsky, Edward. (2012). *Borromini No. 21, 1999* [Chromogenic print]

Source: © Edward Burtynsky. Courtesy of Nicholas Metivier Gallery, Toronto pivot irrigation installation in High Plans, Texas Panhandle. The pivot is an irrigation system which draws water from the aquifer below; once the water reaches the surface it is sprayed onto the field via a rotating armature of pipes. The footprint of the pivot is a circular green field which dominates the image.

In Burtynsky's book, the image is paired with an interior view of the dome of Sant'Ivo alla Sapienza (1642–1660); a church designed by the Italian Architect Francesco Borromini who is known for his use of complex geometries and the sense of drama and movement in his design of Sant'Ivo (Wittkower, 1958, 1986, pp. 210–211). The image is titled *Borromini #21, 1999*. The *Sapienza*, which translates from Italian as *wisdom*, was a church I knew well. I had sketched it when I visited it as an architecture student in 1986. That it became present again and meaningful within an inquiry on the imaginal character of wisdom art decades later suggesting an interesting Jungian synchronicity.

Insights into the holism of Burtynsky's images were offered in a public lecture he presented jointly with William Ewing, the curator of his book *Essential Elements* (2016). During the question period which followed I asked Burtynsky (EB) and Ewing (WE) to comment on the presence of the spiritual in the visual pairing of the images of the pivot and dome, in particular, and Burtynsky's images in general. Our exchange went as follows:

> GR: *While the landscape is an on-going presence in your work, in this image it seems to transcend that discourse. You mentioned earlier the formal aspects in some of your photographs. And in that pairing you see the presence of the circle.*
>
> *But I can't help feeling in that pairing that there is something else going on that transcends the discourse of the landscape and the discourse of form.*
>
> *I was wondering if you could comment on that.*
>
> WE: *Its one of the pairings that means a lot to me. And* **I feel its essentially a spiritual thing.** *And I feel that the order and structure of the renaissance picture can be . . . there's something similar about the two. But its almost the difference between civilization and savagery. So that's what I am hoping with every one of these pairings that they will operate on several different levels. And stimulate the mind . . . if it was one pivot against the other I think you would say oh water pivots and that would be kind of it. . . . It would be left at this level.*
>
> *But when* **you have this gap of essentially five hundred years and you have a kind of magical and mysterious and deeply spiritual ordered structuring of the world** *as you have in the Borromini and*

then you have this relatively crude picture but still miraculous from our technocratic age. **For me that they are two sides of the same coin. They are the world we have created and we can't get away from.** And one of the things that Ed keeps saying over and over again is um there's some bad guys, there's some good guys, bad corporations, good corporations, bad nations, good nations but you know **we are all in this together** and we have in a sense created these things. The metal we have in this chair and the fabrics we wear and so on are all implicated and that's what that particular pairing was all about. **It was meant to pull us in as human beings into a civilizational tapestry** but Ed would you like to . . .

EB: *Well, I'll add to that ultimately . . . I mean just came from Rome and Florence and have been looking at the Renaissance and the great things. And it's interesting, I mean you can stand in front of Michelangelo's David today and still be just as taken as it was first unveiled 450 year ago. And Borromini is a similar thing.* **It's the search for the divine. And divine in the sense that somehow you created something that transcends, a transcendent space. Something that is kind of universal and can live through across centuries, across culture, across generations.** *And that is something that is enduring that kind of . . . our minds walk into something that touches us similarly. And we were . . . standing in front of Botticelli and they were just . . . we saw a lot of Renaissance paintings but you get in front of these and they just do something. There is something so profound and that's what I'm saying about the sacred. I think a lot of artists . . . you know the difference somebody whose in the artisan craft of making the greatest cup—can you make a cup that becomes divine? Maybe you can. But it's much harder in the world of objects that are functional that we kind of yes, you know, a church is a functional space but you didn't have to make that ceiling. Borromini . . .* **that's an attempt to take us to another place; to elevate us to think and to raise or lift our consciousness in our souls to a place of extraordinary** *. . . you know, vision and just the perfect symmetry, the perfect realization of something. And I think by and large that's what I think artists in many ways have always searched for—* **how do I take the ordinary and move it into the extraordinary.** *How do I lift something, an idea into a new space? So I think that bringing in that architectural work it is that kind of pursuit of the human spirit* **to find the divine in objects and in space . . . whether it is in a painting, or it's in a drawing, or a piece of sculpture.**

EW: *But for me that was the sacred, profane. It's that simple. Yet both are perfectly symmetrical. But in the service of different ends. Both human.*

(Interview, October 1, 2016)

Following the talk I speak to Burtynsky; he returns to the dialogue with Ewing and myself and in our exchange softly mentions the theme of the "sacred and profane" which we shared in my question and his response.

My question to Burtynsky and Ewing had been intermingled amongst others; for example, what had become of the places he had photographed, the nuts and bolts of photographic technique or future projects? My question stood apart from the others by situating the artist's work within another paradigm, that is, one which diverged from the identity of artist with technique and was instead located within a different discourse about the artist and spirituality and the contemplative interpretation of the imaginal.

Arthur Zajonc (2009) observes how contemplation resides in the silent self, one which is also a space of solitude and creativity. His description of this place returns to Burtynsky's work; and how his photographs are infused with the presence that Zajonc speaks of. The images reside within a contemplative domain of silence. While being powerful witnesses to environmental distress, the images are complicated narratives as they also cause us to pause, gently guiding our eyes to rest upon them. We look and remain silent and reflective within their presence. The imaginal scaffolds us onto contemplation and a spiritual terrain where we begin to reflect upon the character of connection which binds us to each other and the creation which Ewing speaks of. Following Merton, they are "summonses to awareness" (Merton, 1966, p. 182).

In the photographic pairing of the pivot and the dome Merton's call mirrored in Burtynsky's observation of how artists "search for the divine," one which involves "tak[ing] the ordinary and mov[ing] it into the extraordinary" (interview, October 1, 2016). By such movement the seemingly ordinary pivot, when juxtaposed with the dome, participates in an extraordinary story about spirituality and holistic connection. In such visual juxtaposition, Burtynsky softly brings into focus how humanity is configured within a realm of the sacred and profane. Of what happens when such juxtapositions are made, Ewing observes "you have this gap of essentially five hundred years and you have a kind of magical and mysterious and deeply spiritual ordered structuring of the world" (interview, October 1, 2016).

Burtynsky's pairing brings spirituality into vision. It reveals the presence of interconnection; the "civilizational tapestry" which Ewing speaks of wherein are mingled the sacred and the profane within the metaphor of the circle which the pivot and the dome share. Of such intermingling, Ewing is Zen-like in his observation: "For me that they are two sides of the same coin. They are the world we have created and we can't get away from" (Interview, October 1, 2016).

In *Hagia Sophia* Merton speaks of the unseen wholeness (Merton, 1974) which configures the creation, one which Ewing also alludes to in his observation upon the "magical and mysterious" ordering of the world (interview, October 1, 2016). In a kindred spirit Palmer writes holistically of the need for reintegration of selves which are broken (Palmer, 1993). Both Merton and Palmer aspire towards holistic knowing which is configured not within the eroding of phenomena but instead within the embrace of the creation within the spirit of connection.

With the pivot and the dome, Burtynsky offers a visual manifestation of the veiled wholeness that Merton ponders and the spirit of reunification with the creation that Palmer speaks of. As Ewing observes an image standing on its own would have limited meaning, but when paired with another, as Burtynsky does with the pivot and the dome in *Essential Elements* (2016), we are invited to ponder the mystery of connectedness within creation. By embracing instead of reducing the complexity of phenomenon, by engaging with forms of inquiry which depart from the reductionism of analytical thinking and which are instead nested within exploration of the complexity of the aesthetical we are transported into a different domain of contemplative knowing. By bringing the pivot and dome together and viewing them as connected Burtynsky, through his art, offers us holistic glimpses into the spiritual realm—one upon which we may begin to meditate upon the creation in the embrace of its mystery and complexity.

Tobin Hart (2019a) writes of how the divine has been severed from our humanity—a split which evokes Ewing's observation about the *imagining of connection* which is fostered in Burtynsky's photographs; and the photographer's own observation upon the seeking of the divine through the imaginal. In this the *re-union* of the divine and art revealing a holistic ethos shared by the scholar and artist. One wherein the imaginal fosters a moment of connection, harmony and non-dualism when we are guided to contemplate how the pivot is like the dome and the dome like the pivot; and the sacred is united with the profane. And with such contemplative encounter the imaginal moves aside the veil to carry us onto the terrain of the spiritual.

The artist opens us onto divinity and beauty; and within such opening offering a balm with which we may begin to heal the splinter that Hart speaks of when beauty and the divine are disengaged from the other. Beauty awakens us; it is intimate with consciousness and vital to learning (Hart, 2019a). With Burtynsky the awakening is also an ethical one when the encounter with his images, while seeding the reintegration of beauty and divinity, also cause us to begin to ponder our being in the world and its relation to others and the environment that we share.

Of the presence of connection which is conveyed in his photographs Burtynsky's process is echoed in Merton writings. In *The Geography of Lograire* (1969), Merton reflects on the character of poetry and observes how "a poet spends his life in repeated projects,"—his observations while belonging to his world, also belong to others (Merton, 1969, p. 1). That the poet's work is one of repetition in turn suggesting how the journey of inquiry is one of *return*; a closed loop in which the artist's work is one of incessant revisiting of self. In his landscape images, which he has created over the past thirty years, Burtynsky *returns* to pondering humanity's toll on the environment; a return sculpted within his artist's world, while in the same instance being one which, following Merton, extends beyond his world to everyone else's.

The notion of inquiry as a form of return evokes rich metaphors. Inquiry as a loop; or one of recycling of memory; or of the circle . . . .

While the rationalist journey to knowing is reductive and unidirectional evoking the metaphor of the straight line; the contemplative journey of holism and connection suggests a different metaphor of the circle. Of such metaphor Thomas Del Prete's study of Merton's views on education is illustrative. Evoking the trajectory of a closed circle, Del Prete observes that the "starting and ending points of a study of Merton and education are ultimately the same—ourselves" (Del Prete, 1990, p. 2).

In a study of the literary construction of Merton's *The Geography of Lograire* Randall (1978) observes how the poem is configured within a mandala form, one which echoes Del Prete's observation on the closed loop onto the self which informs the study of Merton and Merton's own observation on the aspect of return in the poet's work. Of the presence of the circle Burtynsky's pairing of the pivot and dome share a kindred symbolism; his depiction of the circle offering an imaginal metaphor, not only for the ethos of self and holistic connection, but in addition for the cyclical character of contemplation which Merton, Del Prete and Randall allude to.

Image 2.5 Rossini, G. (2017). *Electrostatic Machine*. Anonymous. (c. 1890). *Modified Carré Electrical Machine*. [Photographic Detail]. Museo Galileo. Florence, Italy

Source: G. Rossini

Image 2.6 Rossini, G. (2017). Ghirlandaio, Domenico. (1487). *Adoration of the Magi*. [Digital Photograph]. Uffizi Gallery. Florence Italy

Source: G. Rossini

Of such metaphor, I return to my journey to Florence where I encountered the electrostatic machine and a round devotional painting; and I imagine connection by creating my own pairing of the sacred and the profane.

Seeing Whole as Imaginal Contemplation of "Ultimate Concerns"

Of the character of contemplative knowing Hart observes how it is a way of knowing that does not supplant but stands with sensorial and rationalistic modes of knowing while embracing strategies of inquiry which include an array of forms such as poetry and meditation. To know with the imaginal expands Hart's list and includes the visual meditations that Burtynsky offers in his landscape photographs. His artwork allows us to see from on high providing a vision of connection and a place from which, as Burtynsky observes, we seek the divine (Interview, October 1, 2016); and in so doing nurturing an ethos of contemplative knowing, which following Hart (2004), is deeper and focused.

As contemplative images imbued with the spirit of holism, they depart from the reductive strategy of analytical and bifurcating ways of knowing which delimit awareness (Hart, 2004); instead embracing phenomenon in the fullness of its complexity and contradiction. Following Hart, Burtynsky's contemplative images are instead nested within "shadowy symbols" and paradoxes (Hart, 2004, p. 37). While his images embrace complexity, they also transport us towards reflection upon connection; as Palmer observes as seeing whole (Palmer, 1993); or as Merton notes as the veiled wholeness of creation (Merton, 1974).

Burtynsky's pairing of the pivot and the dome enriches Hart's and Palmer's observations as does his image *Navajo Reservation/Suburb Phoenix, Arizona U.S.A. 2011* (Burtynsky et al., 2013, p. 53) which is offered as another example of a contemplative image. Like the pivot image, the image of the Phoenix suburb forms part of Burtynsky's water series. Of that project Burtynsky observes "Water is the reason we can say its name" (Burtynsky et al., 2013, n.p.). While his observation comments upon a resource which is often underestimated but precious for life; Burtynsky's observation is also holistic inviting us to ponder humanity's relation to water. Water and humanity are not contemplated separately; instead departing from a reductionist perspective, they are viewed in intimate relation. By saying we are water Burtynsky calls onto us to contemplate an imaginal discourse about connection.

While the pivot and the dome are paired photographs, the image *Navajo Reservation/Suburb Phoenix* depicts two stories in one photographic print; one in which the Navajo Reservation is juxtaposed with a suburb of Phoenix. On the left side of the image, we see the Navajo reservation which extends beyond the left frame. The reservation remains undeveloped marked only by the growth of desert shrubs. On the right, we see the suburb which extends beyond the right frame. The suburb is marked by groomed lawns, tract housing and private swimming pools. In the middle, such extension is absent; instead of extension into the other we see abrupt separation marked by the road which runs through the middle of the photograph.

The break between the two landscapes is severe and, at first view, the photograph seems a montage of two images. But the images are not montaged;

Burtynsky's photograph is of a real yet complicated place. We are presented with a landscape photograph, yet within the image are two landscapes.

Following Ewing's observation about how we see Burtynsky's images, viewing each landscape separately from the other would have limited meaning, but once brought together, the juxtaposition of the different landscapes offers a story rich about holism and connection. Burtynksy's complex photograph of a desert and a suburb draws us towards it; we look, pause and try to make sense of it; we question whether it is real or not; it stirs our wonder. We try to reconcile landscapes which are viewed together but seem apart.

Tobin Hart observes how "rational empiricism trains us to pay attention to some things and not to others, discounting hunches or feelings, for example, in favour of certain appearances and utility—it focuses and limits our field of awareness" (Hart, 2004, p. 37). By depicting the contrasting landscapes, Burtynsky does not seek to limit our awareness as rationalism would have it; instead he expands it by embracing the landscape's seeming paradox. Following Hart, engaging with paradox as Burtynsky does nurtures the contemplative voice (Hart, 2004).

> *Pondering Burtynsky's art seeds my inquiry. His image draws me. It is rich in layers of meaning and fosters contemplation. In depicting the story of the divide between two peoples—one depicted imaginally in their different relations to environment—Burtynsky guides reflection upon a global narrative about the relation of culture and environment which transcends the immediacy of place. His image of a bifurcated landscape is generative. It causes me to ponder my relation with others and the landscape; and within such relational moment I also turn towards contemplation upon my self.*

In fostering reflection upon our relation with self, others and the environment Burtynksy's photographs become ethical discourses about our way of being in the world. In this, they return to Hadot's understanding of wisdom as "a mode of being" (Hadot, 2002, p. 220); while also focusing the questions of my inquiry onto his work. Can we speak of Burtynsky's art as having wisdom? Does his work raise our consciousness about our place within the creation and, as the psychologist and wisdom researcher Paul Baltes suggest, nurture reflection into the nature of humanity (Baltes, 2004)?

Of the nature of wisdom, the philosopher Michael McKinney observes how wisdom resides within the understanding of the commonplace from a higher perspective. He observes "When life is viewed from a higher perspective, above the self, we can see that wisdom is not in the details; its in the whole story, the overview, the universal" (McKinney, 2004, n.p.). In kindred spirit, the psychologist William James, who McKinney also acknowledges, observes how "the art of being wise is the art of knowing what to overlook" (James, 1891, p. 369).

McKinney's observation is prescient to artist's work such as Burtynsky's. In his overview of the landscape, Burtynsky offers a story which depends

Meditations on Merton's Paradox 75

not only upon the details, but upon a vision which transcends them. From the bird's-eye perspective, he presents the seemingly ordinary, but from the same perch also offers us deep insights into culture and environment. As Burtynsky himself observes the artist's search is to "take the ordinary and move it into the extraordinary" (Interview, October 1, 2016).

Image 2.7 Burtynsky, Edward. (2013). *Navajo Reservation/Suburb: Phoenix, Arizona, USA, 2011* [Chromogenic Print]

Source: © Edward Burtynsky. Courtesy of Nicholas Metivier Gallery, Toronto

Burtynsky's image stirs me; and I am reminded of Emerson's observation of the power of the artist to arouse the soul (Miller, 2006). By awakening us the artist guides us towards reflection upon our relation with the creation; herein also foregrounding those existential questions we ask ourselves about the meaning of life, which as the arts-educator Peter London observes, are the core questions configuring our psyche (London, 2004). In this, the power of the aesthetic experience in moving us towards such questions, while guiding ethical reflection upon them, is also psychological and spiritual in ethos. Of the character of such power Merton observes in *No Man Is an Island*,

> In an aesthetic experience, in the creation or the contemplation of a work of art, the psychological conscience is able to attain some of its highest and most perfect fulfillments. Art enables us to find ourselves and lose ourselves at the same time. The mind that responds to the

intellectual and spiritual values that lie hidden in a poem, a painting, or a piece of music, discovers a spiritual vitality that lifts it above itself, takes it out of itself, and makes it present to itself on a level of being that it did not know it could ever achieve.

(Merton, 1983, p. 34)

For Merton the aesthetic experience is powerful; it shifts our being and within such transformative moments when we look through the artist's imaginal lens we also return onto ourselves when, as Merton observes, we "discover a spiritual vitality" (Merton, 1983, p. 34). A vitality whose ethos is holistic: by being present to the artist's vision, we also become present to ourselves within transformative and contemplative moments of connection.

Of the holistic nature of contemplative knowing, Robert Inchausti makes a similar observation in his examination of Merton's spirituality. To know the "real world," Inchausti observes "is not only to measure and observe what is outside us but to discover our own inner ground" (Inchausti, 2014, p. 56). Referencing Merton, Inchausti adds,

That ground, that world, where we are mysteriously present at once to ourselves and to others, is not a visible, objective, and determined structure with fixed laws and demands. It is "a living and self-creating mystery of which we ourselves are a part, to which we ourselves are our own unique doors."

(Inchausti, 2014, p. 57)

The aesthetic experience opens us onto the living mystery that Inchausti and Merton speaks of; one formed of our ourselves within a spirit of connection with others and the creation. In kindred spirit writers in the field of education for sustainability look to artists like Burtynsky to bring into focus humanity's relationship to environment. The environmental educator Gary Babiuk observes, for example, how Burtynsky has "made the invisible visible and shown us what is hidden from view in our over consumptive society" (Babiuk, 2014, p. 41); also noting how the artist's images are useful pedagogical resources in the classroom to help students explore humanity's toll on the environment. Babiuk highlights the pedagogic richness of artists' work like Burtynsky's; in this also nurturing the thesis of the potential of images as powerful messengers of wisdom which guide reflection upon the mystery of "that ground, that world" (Inchausti, 2014, p. 57) that we are present to.

Of the power of the artist to foster wisdom Merton, in *The Other Side of the Mountain* (1998a), nests it within the contemplative encounter with the landscape, one which is infused with the aesthetical presence of the poet. In his writing the aesthetical is enmeshed with the poetic meditation upon the landscape. In like manner, Burtynsky offers us a visual poetry in his landscape images, one which following Lord requires slow looking (Lord, 2013); and like Merton nurtures contemplative knowing within the embrace of holism.

By making the "invisible visible" (Babiuk, 2014, p. 41) Burtynsky, in the pairing of the pivot and the dome or in his image of the Phoenix Suburb/Navajo Reservation encourages reflection upon the mysterious wholeness of Merton's *Hagia Sophia*. By embracing a holistic visual perspective Burtynsky fosters a contemplative encounter, one wherein feeling and paradox (Hart, 2004) are not excluded from awareness, as rationalism would have it, but instead embraced within the fullness and mystery of creation.

Of the character of pondering, Hart views it as one focused upon what Tillich names the "ultimate concerns" (Hart, 2004, p. 37) of life; or as London observes, its core questions and the purpose of art (London, 2004). With such images by Burtynsky, as the pivot and dome or the image of the split desert landscape, we are summoned to awareness (Merton, 1966) onto the concerns and core questions which Tillich, London and Hart ponder.

The Aesthetical Presence as My "Summonses to Awareness"

Brother Louis. What brings me to awareness? Do I seek the landscape or does it call upon me? Or, is my question unnecessary? Is awareness simply being present to the other? I onto the landscape and the landscape onto me.

In the encounter with nature's art, in particular, the landscape of the American southwest, Merton transits onto a place of Zen—a place of void yet a place of wisdom as well. His spiritual journey though invites reflection upon its geography.

Regarding the nature of the encounter, is the spiritual journey which the encounter initiates a seeking or a calling? Do we seek wisdom or are we called onto it? Am I a vessel from which the spirit cascades or a vessel into which it flows? Am I both?

In *Poetry and the Contemplative Life* (1947), Merton oscillates in his view of art's contemplative possibilities. He ponders how the artist nurtures us towards the soul while in the same instance speaking of the "abyss" that resides between aesthetical and mystical contemplation. Merton speaks within a paradigm of theological categories, of the role and power of art in contemplation, Merton is cautious.

Of such caution Labrie observes how Merton, in the early 1950s, pondered relinquishing poetry because he viewed it as a distraction from "pure contemplation" of God. Later Merton departs from such position when he believes he will not achieve such contemplation, such departure though not diminishing his belief in the spiritual significance of art (R. Labrie, personal communication, February 27, 2016) and, as Labrie observes, the "importance of art as a source of truth" which for Merton was wisdom (Labrie, 2014, p. 163).

On the nature of transformation, Gunnlaugson observes how it can be characterized as being either a slow progression or sudden in configuration (Gunnlaugson, 2007), a characterization which is echoed in Merton's evolving views on the relation of contemplation, art and spirituality. Regarding this evolution, Merton's reflections in his later essay *Signatures: Notes on the Author's Drawings* in *Raids on the Unspeakable* (1966) are illustrative. In this text, art is not corralled by theological categories as it was in his earlier writings. Instead he writes forcefully of the energy of the drawing within a discourse where categories have been dissolved including his own drawings which are not to be viewed as art (Merton, 1966). From *Poetry and the Contemplative Life* to *Raids on the Unspeakable* Merton evolves from the bifurcating domain of categories to another beyond category.

While he views his drawings as standing apart from category, Merton seeks to strip the image of unintended and superfluous meanings; and instead desires for them a kind of essential presence. Instead of viewing images with categorical understanding, he speaks of them as "signs" and refers to them as "abstractions" (Merton, 1966, p. 179) rather than art. Merton's abstractions are paradoxical; while he does not consider them art, he cautions us to feel neither judged nor threatened by them. Merton observes,

> No need to categorize these marks. It is better if they remain unidentified vestiges, signatures of someone who is not around. If these drawings are able to persist in a certain autonomy and fidelity, they may continue to awaken possibilities, consonances; they may dimly help to alter one's perceptions. Or they may quietly and independently continue to invent themselves. . . . For the only dream a man seriously has when he takes a brush in his hand and dips it into ink is to reveal a new sign than can continue to stand by itself and to exist in its own right, transcending all logical interpretation.
> (Merton, 1966, p. 182)

Brother Louis, you seem to erode the image towards an essential presence, but then you build it up and imbue it with a vital presence. You say the image is not to be understood as a concept, yet you speak of it having meaning. You caution us to not judge it and not to be judged by it. Yet you imply its presence. What is the being of the image? Or, is the power of the image beyond being—one having a presence which is transcendent?

While denying the categorical nature of the image, Merton offers us a paradox in which the image stands in relation to the viewer and is imbued with a vital presence. We are present to the image and the image is present to us. We encounter the image and the image encounters and may judge us. That an image should judge or pose a threat is curious language and causes me to wonder whether such language is best viewed as metaphorical. Yet Merton, in his text, dwells upon the vitality of the image. He speaks of images as "ciphers of energy, acts or movements intended to be propitious" (Merton, 1966, p. 180).

Merton's language is evocative. His words suggest a vital presence within his abstractions; but to describe such vitality Merton speaks tentatively and of possibilities. They come to life but cannot be described with nouns; instead Merton's abstractions are ephemeral barely describable as events. Neither object nor event, Merton's abstractions are present within a different and perhaps transcendent territory—one marked by energies and movements.

The dissolution of categories, which informs Merton's reflections on his drawings, suggests a paradoxical understanding in which spirituality and art are intertwined. Merton's enmeshing of these within paradox in turn echo kindred themes within the holistic learning and spirituality research paradigms. In *the Other Side of the Mountain*, Merton describes the "impossible paradox" of Zen as one which stands beyond category in its embrace of opposites (Merton, 1998a, p. 286)—a sentiment which is echoed in his Zen-like reflections upon his drawings and Ergas' kindred observation that spirituality research is configured within a paradoxical "nonparadigm" (Ergas, 2016, p. 15). In a similar spirit to Ergas, Burrows observes how the contemplative domain "thrives on paradox" (Byrnes, 2012, p. 24).

Merton's paradox evokes the methodological observation that inquiry is configured with messiness as Gunnlaugson observes (Gunnlaugson, 2007) and Palmer's suggestion that integrative education is a field marked by fluidity and complexity (Palmer & Zajonc, 2010). The criticism of categorical thinking which Gunnlaugson's and Palmer's observations suggest foregrounds a general critique of Cartesian thinking which Merton also shares in his kindred reflections on his drawings as ephemeral and beyond category. Hart echoes such thinking in his criticism of rationalist and empirical paradigms (Hart, 2004, 2019a) dominating binary understandings of what counts as knowing and in his advocacy of a contemplative knowing which, in its holism, stands apart from reductive epistemologies.

The categorical critique shared by these writers echoes Merton's reflections on the ephemeral nature of his images which he views at best as ciphers or inventions, "but not in the sense of findings" (Merton, 1966, p. 182). For Merton, his abstractions are outside categorization; they are present within a different realm. With a life of their own, their being is beyond object, outside of moment and identity. They do not tell us what they are; instead their presence resides in their calling or summons to us (Merton, 1966). Outside of ontological language, Merton's abstractions are contemplative presences whose call to awareness transports us into a transcendent realm where wisdom resides.

Brother Louis, we struggle to understand the transcendent through art. We strip the drawing of meaning and category. We reduce it to an essentialism configured by signs and abstractions. The drawing is ephemeral and an illusion to the transcendent. It is left with "crude innocence" (Merton, 1966, p. 179).

Your drawings, devoid of category, are "signs and ciphers of energy" (Merton, 1966, p. 180)—an ephemeral presence of a transcendent moment.

> *In that moment we seek to feel beyond theory, beyond category, beyond analysis, beyond words, beyond drawing.*
> *Before the moment of transcendence and after it, what is left to know of the drawing except "afterthoughts?" (Merton, 1966, p. 179).*

On the power of texts to move us, Hart observes how within the tradition of wisdom literature, texts were described as having a vital presence. Texts possess a vital spirit which is shared with persons and events and captured in Hart's observation that together with the "world as a whole are living words" (Hart, 2008, p. 236). In similar spirit, in his teaching, Palmer encourages students to go "beyond 'looking' at the subject into personal dialogue with it" within a spirit of community (Palmer, 1993, p. 99).

The presence of connection with which Hart ponders the world as words which are alive, or Palmer's dialogical relation to the subject, echoes Merton's reflections on his drawings. Though they are stripped of category, Merton speaks of their vital presence (Merton, 1966)

Merton's drawings are abstract images evoking Japanese calligraphy. Burtynsky's aerial images are narrative depictions of complex and often troubled landscapes. While their art is thematically different, they guide us to reflect upon shared themes of holism, connection and the power of art to move us spiritually.

For Merton, the abstract drawing was infused with a vitality which defied category, one in which he pondered connection within its non-categorical and paradoxical nature. For Burtynsky, the landscape image embraces opposites; while it depicts beauty, such beauty is complicated by the gravity of the environmental message. While embracing the paradox, Merton and Burtynsky evoke Zen-like feelings of non-judgement in their work.

Regarding learning which is deeply rooted, Hart reflects that it entails both a looking within ourselves and outwards at the data within "an emphasis on contact over categorization . . . and a willingness to really meet and, therefore, be changed by the object of inquiry" (Hart, 2008, p. 236). In his poetry and observations on art, Merton defies category while Burtynsky similarly seeks to transcend categorical vision by guiding us towards his visual paradoxes. By nurturing us to look outwards and meditate upon the desert landscape or distressed environments, Merton and Burtynsky respectively also, following Hart's observation, *return* us to ourselves. Within such a return, following Merton, we are "summon[ed] to awareness" (Merton, 1966, p. 182) within an expansive vision which feels towards holism and connection.

3 The Journey of the *"Perpetual Seeker"*

Of Emerging Questions on the Dialogical Ethos of Wisdom and Art

Image 3.1 Rossini, G. (2017). *Gionitus, The Beginning of Astronomy*. Relief by Pisano, Andrea & Assistant. (1341–1348). [Digital Photograph]. Opera del Duomo Museum. Florence, Italy

Source: G. Rossini

82   The Journey of the *"Perpetual Seeker"*

While the questions of an inquiry stand as points of embarkation for it, the journey of inquiry is not necessarily completed by the questions we initially ponder. Like the inquiry the questions travel—like passengers they join us at destinations, depart at others while some remain for the entire journey. The questions feel present within a ceaseless movement of embarking and disembarking. Always moving and never resting, getting closer to and seeing but not always reaching the destination. The unending movement of questions intimate with the journey of inquiry and in turn sustaining the life of the "perpetual seeker" (Miller, 2016, p. 138) as one immersed within a never-ending exploration.

Into the cosmological aether Gionitus, the first astronomer, lit its blackness with his sextant. Afterwards, another seeker, Galileo, would aim the first telescope and announce the discovery of Jupiter's planets in his essay The Sidereal Messenger (Galilei, 1989). Four hundred years passes when another messenger, the Hubble Space Telescope, detects the most distant star MACS J1149+2223 Lensed Star No. 1 which is also named Icarus (Jenkins, Villard, & Kelly, 2018) after the mythic Greek figure. The stars, like the journey of questions, emerge within a perpetual seeking.

Preparing to Begin Inquiry: The Wondrous and Paradoxical Journey of Questions

From the journey of questions emerges the map of the seeker but one whose contours are paradoxical, that is, though the map provides direction, its instructions are also fluid and inexact. Its paradoxical nature in turn marks the ethos of the contemplative journey as one wherein the seeker of wisdom travels a map which defies the restrictive Cartesian demand for certainty by instead following pathways formed of questions within transitory moments of their emergence or abandonment. Of such a journey Hart observes,

> Instead of grasping for certainty wisdom rides the question, lives the question. As physicist David Bohm (1981) argues, "questioning is . . . not an end in itself, nor is its main purpose to give rise to answers" (p. 25). Harmony with the "whole flowing movement of life" comes when there is ceaseless questioning (p. 25). When the quest for certainty and control are pushed to the background, the possibility of wonder returns.
>
> (Hart, 2009, p. 12)

Not apart from but one with the presence of wonder, questions become intimate with wisdom, as Hart observes, "wisdom seeks and creates questions" (Hart, 2009, p. 116)—an observation which foregrounds how questions, instead of posing obstacles, are vital to the transformative journey towards wisdom.

Wisdom embraces questions as vital reflectors, the ones we dwell upon *returning* onto self and, in addition, extending Bai et al., a relational ethos to others and nature (Bai et al., 2013).

> *While the questions are mine, they also belong to others; within such expansive range, while they emerge from reflections upon the character of wisdom and art, they also guide us onto an existential terrain where we begin to reflect, following Simmons (2006) and London (2004), upon the core questions of life: What is my-self ethos? What is my relational ethos to others and the creation I share with them?*
>
> *It is within such a journey that the questions of this study, which are of two broad configurations, are offered. The first are sculpted of intuitions about the relation of art and wisdom. Nurtured by encounters with and conversations about art, which were often serendipitous, these intuitions formed the initial embarkation. The second are those which joined the journey after its departure and were generated in response to texts that I had discovered or revisited in the course of inquiry. The latter questions revolve about the relation of Merton's aesthetical ideas to wisdom, affinity of wisdom to dialogical discourse and broader methodological ones about the paradox of doing spirituality research through an aesthetical lens.*

In his text, *From Information to Transformation*, Hart observes how information is data that "flattens the world into component parts" (Hart, 2009, p. 8), whereas stories reconfigure information into "patterned wholes" which give them meaning. In this study, Hart's observations on the nature of data and stories are extended to include the questions we ponder within inquiry and underscored by the notion that questions are nurtured by our stories. While they come into being within encounters with texts, they are also entwined with our lives reflecting ourselves—an entwining informed by the stories from which they emerged and make them meaningful.

Of such entwining, the questions feel incarnated in ourselves, herein enriching the vital character of inquiry as one which is embodied in the researcher (Miller, 2016). Departing from a Cartesian strategy to erode the data for research into dissembled pieces; questions are instead embraced within the complexity of our lives and its expression through our stories. In their writing, such researchers as Gunnlaugson (2007) and Palmer (2010) remind us of the importance of embracing the fluid and non-linear complexity of inquiry. It is within their invitation to embrace its murkiness that my questions, emerging from stories, are offered.

Embarking on Inquiry: The Primordial Character of First Questions

> *I was always drawn to the museum. It was near the school and as a child I would visit on my own to look at the pictures. While I did not*

> understand my attraction to them and their meaning remained latent, their power—what Barthes would name their "punctum" (Barthes, 1981, p. XX)—had presence for the child.
>
> In lieu of meaning, such presence could not be rationally objectified, but simply embodied in my being, and in turn, following Merton, became those "vague fragments" (Merton, 1998b, p. 12) of childhood which formed my narrative and constructed my reality and would later emerge into meaning in my adulthood.
>
> Within my childhood visits to the museum were nurtured primordial intuitions about the character of art. They seeded the "First Questions," and many years later revealed the presence of the child in the adult.

While the first question of my study—*what is the relation between wisdom and art?*—finds its earliest traces within a childhood story, its emergence into awareness happened during a synchronous reading of, what became for me, three seminal texts: Miller's *Educating for Wisdom and Compassion* (2006), Ferrari's and Potworowski's *Teaching for Wisdom* (2008) and Merton's *Love and Living* (1979).

Reading these texts nurtured my initial intuition about the relation of wisdom and art. But the question of their relation only emerged after I had abandoned the questions of an earlier project and began inquiry anew by embracing a methodology which was informed by narrative. Writing my stories felt authentic and generative to the rebirth of my inquiry. Reflecting upon them became a witnessing onto self; and constituted, co-opting Merton's words, my "summonses to awareness" (Merton, 1966, p. 182). Within such listening to intuitions about the epistemological character of art—moments which were ever present but never nurtured until their awakening, in part, through stories—there emerged a new question about the relation of wisdom and art.

Reading Miller's retelling of Emerson's story of painting as non-dualistic knowing (Miller, 2006) in tandem with Ferrari's and Potworowski's (2008) anthology of wisdom sparked the first iteration of this question while pondering past understandings of wisdom. While notions of wisdom are historically nurtured within forms of writing such as the Bible, parables, proverbs, and myths (Baltes, 2004; Curnow, 2015) can a new understanding of wisdom which both acknowledges but also departs from such historical forms be sculpted—that is, one which seeks an interpretation of wisdom in relation to the arts? Contemplating the writings of Merton (1972) on the arts in tandem with scholarship in the field of holistic and transformative studies in education (Miller, 2011; Palmer, 1993; Schiller, 2014; Gunnlaugson, 2011; Burrows, 2015; Hart, 2009) and arts based research in education (Diamond & Mullen, 2001; Eisner, 2008; London, 2006) seeded this question. Reading Curnow on the history of wisdom was also nurturing to the question of the relation of art and wisdom. While Curnow's study of wisdom is focused upon the examination of texts, he also observes how the history of wisdom is rich in the vocabulary of illumination and visuality (Curnow, 1999). Such observations in turn both nurturing reflection on Merton's aesthetical ideas on wisdom and informing the initial question of this inquiry about the relation of wisdom and art.

Wisdom is a revered modality of knowing: it is both the highest and deepest form of knowing; and a guide on how best to lead a contented and meaningful life (Baltes, 2004). While such understanding of wisdom constitutes a starting point for my study, the question of its relation to art is nurtured by Merton's ideas on wisdom. For Merton, the idea of wisdom is extended; while wisdom is the highest form of knowing, it is also intertwined with spirituality and the aesthetical where to have wisdom is to be with the creation—a *being with* which is nurtured by the artist who resides within us. Merton writes:

> true spiritual life is a life neither of dionysian orgy nor of apollonian clarity: it transcends both. It is a life of wisdom, a life of sophianic love. In *Sophia*, the highest wisdom-principle, all the greatness and majesty of the unknown that is in God and all that is rich and maternal in His creation are united inseparably, as paternal and maternal principles.
>
> (Merton, 1972, p. 141)

The encounter with art guides us towards spirituality. Of the relation of art with wisdom Merton meditates:

> art is not an end in itself. It introduces the soul into a higher spiritual order, which it expresses and in some sense explains. Music and art and poetry attune the soul to God because they induce a kind of contact with the Creator and Ruler of the Universe. The genius of the artist finds its way by the affinity of creative sympathy, or conaturality, into the living law that rules the universe. . . . Since all true art lays bare the action of this same law in the depths of our own nature, it makes us alive to the tremendous mystery of being.
>
> (Merton, 1983, p. 36)

While the history of wisdom spans pre-Christian philosophical texts, medieval and Renaissance literature and contemporary discourses in literary studies and developmental psychology, such thinking circles about the study of the text, and not within the encounter with art. Thus, seeking to understand wisdom within the latter territory departs from traditional discourses by seeking a new understanding within the context of Merton's writings and artists' work, and as viewed through the lens of transformative learning and arts-based inquiry in curriculum studies. By transiting onto this new territory, the initial question that had marked the emergent point of my inquiry was now joined by others.

86   The Journey of the *"Perpetual Seeker"*

> *Can the encounter with art guide us towards wisdom? Can we draw into relation wisdom and art and speak of the wisdom of artful inquiry? Can we speak of art that is wise in the same way that we speak, for example, of a proverb that is wise?*
>
> *Discourses upon wisdom have historically formed around texts. While acknowledging such discourses, can they also be enriched by another which seeks understandings of wisdom through art? Can interpretations of wisdom be informed by notions of wisdom art in general and wisdom image in particular?*
>
> *If artful inquiry nurtures wisdom, then does such outcome elevate the standing of the arts as a pathway onto ethical knowing?*

While the questions emerged within reflections upon Merton's ideas on art, they were also accompanied by a foundational epistemological problem about how the relation of art and wisdom is to be situated within curriculum studies. That is,

> *Is the question of the relation of art to wisdom to be defined by the register of arts-based research? Or, alternately, can such a register, while recognizing and building upon such research, also situate the problem of wisdom and art within an expansive terrain of arts-based contemplative inquiry?*

The questions are motivated by Susan Schiller's observations on the nature of inquiry itself. While inquiry within arts based research is nested within the primacy of artistic process (McNiff, 2008), it also resides for this writer within the amalgam of such process with, as Schiller observes, the holistic modality of the "whole learner" within the integration of the spiritual with the intellectual and physical (Schiller, 2014, p. 1).

> *Reflecting upon these questions evokes epistemological themes and reminds me of another time when, as a philosophy graduate student, my studies were dominated by the presence of category.*
>
> *I am presented with a paradox. Holism seeks a domain beyond category; yet, in the same moment I adopt the language of category in order to traverse the paradox of inquiry.*

The holistic ethos of inquiry, which is suggested by Schiller, foregrounds how its character, which in my study pivots about the relation of art and wisdom, is intimately connected to the form we choose to explore such question. Of such forms there are many as is, for example, suggested by Diamond and Mullen who invite us to explore ones which are emerging but marginalized within the academy (Diamond & Mullen, 2001). Or, similarly Schiller who advocates rethinking of writing as a form which is both meaningful and connected to the world of the writer (Schiller, 2014). Against the expectation within colleges that students write with an academic voice, Schiller encourages a rebalance wherein "equal attention [is] given to multiple ways of knowing, including spiritual and emotional intelligence" (Schiller, 2014, p. x) as well as academic. In kindred spirit, Hart explores how contemplative inquiry offers another way of knowing, which supplements the sensorial and rationalistic while engaging with strategies of inquiry which are drawn from the artist's toolbox (Hart, 2004).

My study into the relation of artful inquiry to wisdom follows Schiller's and Hart's observations as well as Diamond's and Mullen's invitation by reflecting upon how narrative and contemplative writing in tandem with encounters with art sculpt pathways for inquiry which are holistic in spirit. Once on that path, such writing, which emerges in dialogue with art, becomes a form of meditation practice. By becoming nested within contemplation upon questions which are dear to us, there is promise for the writing to become meaningful. Such hope follows Hart's view and extends Schiller's observation about how "writing is a natural site of holism because writing is a way of knowing that connects and draws from our inner and outer worlds" (Schiller, 2014, p. ix).

Narrative writing offers a contemplative terrain which draws upon such worlds; Merton's writings, such as *The Seven Storey Mountain* (1998b), offer a notable example. It is within the realm of narrative—one which is kindred in spirit to holistic and arts-based inquiry—that Merton invites us to ponder his ideas on wisdom, art and spirituality. His positioning of the centrality of narrative and contemplation in his writings in turn nurtures my questions about the relation of art and wisdom which like Merton's story have emerged from reflection upon my own narrative.

Thus, while the first questions of this inquiry explore the relation of wisdom and arts, such questions are also supplemented with others which, in the spirit of Schiller's, Hart's and Diamond and Mullen's work, ponders the intimate relation of the form of inquiry to the questions it seeks to explore. Such intimacy in turn extending my questions into the territory of methodology where its configuration within narrative and contemplative writing in tandem with encounters with art also foregrounding an ethical ethos. That is, to reflect upon my method is also to reflect upon my being in the world. Methodology unfolds within an ethical register.

> *What is the relation between the path of my inquiry and the questions I seek to understand?*
> *Instead of a bifurcated relation, is it possible to configure another which is integrative with and meaningfully connected to my life as a researcher, one which is in ethical relation to others and the creation?*

88 The Journey of the *"Perpetual Seeker"*

Method, narrative writing and contemplation are intertwined. It is an intertwining which at its core is about my being in the world and whose witnessing emerged from reflection upon Merton within the dialogical exchange with his words. The latter strategy evolved during the progress of my study and formed the basis for its second set of questions.

Travelling Through Inquiry: Moving in New Directions With the Emergence of Second Questions

The Question of the Dialogical Self and Imaginal Self

During the transit of inquiry encounters with new texts and ones that I had revisited invited new questions to join. With these new passengers my journey turned in new directions; its map was now guided by questions which circled about the relation of wisdom and art in light of Merton's own contemplative spirituality. Kindred ones also arose about the character of the dialogical and imaginal self.

Reading Merton reaffirmed the notion that to reflect upon the power of art is to reflect upon the presence of its spiritual potential. Yet, such reading was also complicated by a foundational methodological question, that is, how to reconcile the thesis of the spiritual ethos of art with the paradoxical character of doing spirituality research. Here, the question follows kindred observations amongst writers in spirituality research in education such as Ergas who speaks of the "paradoxical creed" of such research (Ergas, 2016, p. 15) and Merton who meditates upon the "impossible paradox" (Merton, 1998a, p. 286) of the spiritual domain. New questions arise.

> *While I seek to understand a relation of wisdom and art, such seeking has become complicated.*
> *Can an aesthetical encounter be a spiritual one? Is there equivalence? Or, are they different?*
> *Art seeds the spiritual, yet the spiritual domain has a transcendent ethos. Does such transcendence stand apart from the aesthetical? The relation of the spiritual to the aesthetical is nested within paradox.*

While Merton and Ergas ponder the paradoxical ethos of the spiritual terrain, less paradoxical is the form of dialogical speaking with Merton's writings which is used in this study to meditate upon the relation of art and wisdom but whose presence also foregrounds methodological questions about the tools I use in inquiry.

The writing in this study is configured about moments when it switches to a first-person dialogical encounter—one configured about *conversations with self and texts*—and nurtured by Merton's use of a similar strategy in some of his writings. Although such strategy finds broad alignment with the ethos of transformative and holistic learning in education which embrace forms of doing research (Schiller, 2014; Gunnlaugson, 2011; Hart, 2009; Palmer, 1993) which depart from the rationalistic dualism of researcher–object of research, new questions arose about the character of dialogical speaking as a method for inquiry.

Can dialogical speaking with the self constitute a species of discourse—one which both builds upon and departs from Gunnlaugson's thesis of "generative dialogue" (Gunnlaugson, 2007, p. 138)? While Gunnlaugson's notion is sculpted by the communicative relations we have with others, can such idea form the basis of a discourse which is instead centred upon a *generative dialogue with self*—one which aligns with Burrows' metaphor of "inner alchemy" (Burrow, 2015, p. 127), Merton's strategy of dialogical speaking with his texts or Bakhtin's observation of the "the dialogic nature of consciousness" (Bakhtin, 1984, p. 293)?

Underscoring such views is, following Zajonc, the centrality of doing the interior work and place of solitude within that centrality. In the spirit of Burrows' observations, Zajonc observes that doing the inner work is central to living a life which is balanced with "our outer work" (Zajonc, 2009, pp. 14–15). On the role of solitude Zajonc observes that it is the beginning place of contemplative practice.

> This does not mean brooding or self-indulgent musing, but instead practicing a special form of recollection of the past, mindfulness for the present, and envisioning of the future in a manner that is enlivening, clean, and insightful.
>
> (Zajonc, 2009, p. 20)

The spirit of dialogical discourse as a generative dialogue with self emerges from Zajonc's observation as it does with Bakhtin's kindred observation that one "invests his entire self in discourse" (Bakhtin, 1984, p. 293) as well as with Merton's own dialogic writing. Together with Burrows' focus on interiority and Gunnlaugson's thesis on the relational nature of dialogue, (Gunnlaugson, 2007) their views cycled back onto me with new questions.

> *What is the character of my dialogic methodology? And within such method what is the character of the dialogical self?*

The questions become entangled as the discourse of the dialogical self is also configured about the presence of the imaginal. Herein, the questions are enriched by McNiff's interesting observation of the "imaginal dialogue" (McNiff, 2008, p. 30) which happens in the encounter with art. His observation in turn cycling back into this study wherein I reflect upon how the dialogical self and the dialogue with the imaginal are enmeshed. More questions emerge.

> *Within an arts-based contemplative methodology what is the relation of the dialogical self to the imaginal self? Are they to be viewed as distinct categories?*
>
> *Alternatively, is a nuanced reading of their relation required? That is, within the encounter with the imaginal, is the dialogical self the imaginal self?*

The Question of Solitude and the Dialogical

> *As I meander through the Convent of San Marco in Florence, I arrive upon a small courtyard. Enclosed by building, the courtyard is inward looking—a space of solitude removed from the clamour of a city under siege by tourists.*
>
> *No notable frescoes are to be viewed on its walls. No one goes here. The courtyard is featureless except for the overwhelming presence of silence.*
>
> *I pause, raise my camera, compose the image within the viewfinder, and adjust its settings. Once the composition feels right, I release the camera shutter to allow the light to enter. The silence of the courtyard is momentarily interrupted by the sound of the shutter.*
>
> *Hearing the shutter release makes me mindful of the silence I have entered. Its presence is overwhelming.*
>
> *A few weeks later I scroll through the images I had taken and am stopped by the one of the courtyard. Reflections upon the character of contemplation arise which would not have emerged had I not paused to capture its image.*
>
> *While my encounter with the courtyard was a serendipitous one, it was also instructive. The image of the courtyard offers a metaphor for interiority and the voice of contemplative solitude that we hear if we pause to listen.*

Thinking about the courtyard image guides my reflection upon the relation of contemplation with generative dialogue with self and solitude. If contemplation, following Zajonc, is sculpted in part by solitude can such configuration be aligned with a dialogical discourse with self? And if so, can it be viewed as a voice of solitude—one which *speaks our contemplation* within contemplative practice?

> *Is dialogical discourse the voice which manifests the self into consciousness?*

The solitude of dialogical discourse suggests an intimacy between the inquirer and subject of inquiry wherein they stand together within a dialogue with self. Its intimate character draws on Zajonc's view of the role of solitude in contemplative inquiry, the example of Merton's own dialogical texts and my own strategy of dialogical engaging with Merton's presence through his writings.

Image 3.2 Rossini, G. (2017). *A Voice of Contemplative Solitude. A Courtyard in the Convent of San Marco*. [Digital Photograph]. Convent of San Marco. Florence, Italy

Source: G. Rossini

92 The Journey of the *"Perpetual Seeker"*

While Palmer (1993) encourages us to enter into dialogue with our subject, my dialogue with Merton also becomes a discourse upon *my-self*, the courtyard a metaphor for the solitudinous character of the internal dialogue. A dialogue which transits onto a solitary terrain but one which is not passive as it is also enmeshed with the vital presence of the text. Another question emerges.

> *Can we ponder a relation to a text which is not disencased from the life of the inquirer but one which is instead intimate with it within a relation of vitality and connection?*

The character of dialogical speaking evokes Palmer's view of how such relation, posed in this question, departs from one defined by the bifurcating ethos of analytical thinking and is instead nested within a holistic understanding which is kindred to Buber's concept of "*I-thou*" (Buber, 1970, p. 14), Hart's notion of words as having a vital presence (Hart, 2008) to describe the relations we have with texts and others and Walsh's and Bai's notion of "witness consciousness" (Walsh & Bai, 2015, p. 25). Such notions resist Cartesian subject-object dualism and instead align with the ethos of dialogical discourse as one which, following Bakhtin, is nested within the "dialogic fabric of human life" (Bakhtin, 1984, p. 293).

The Question of the Wisdom Image

Meditations upon the character of the dialogical self emerged within kindred ones upon the relation of the dialogical and aesthetical within Merton's thought and my own dialogical encounters with his writings. Together with reflections upon primary and secondary texts they collectively configured a lens through which the *second questions* of this study gradually emerged. Regarding such questions, pondering the evolution of Merton's aesthetical ideas through such texts as *Poetry and the Contemplative Life* (1947) followed by *Raids on the Unspeakable* (1966) and *Zen and the Birds of Appetite* (1968) guided my initial intuitions about the relation of art and wisdom, one which was in addition enriched by Merton's alignment of the paradisal idea with wisdom.

The idea of paradise is visually rich, evoking some of the most memorable images in our cultural mythology; amongst them, for example, are Michelangelo's depictions of the creation story and Garden of Eden in the *Sistine Chapel* (c. 1510) and Bosch's *The Garden of Earthly Delights* (c. 1490). Within such images the idea of the paradise is manifested within its association with the imaginal, an alignment which returns to Merton's mingling of the aesthetical and paradisal idea in his writings.

For Merton, the idea of paradise is aligned with the knowing one discovers about one's inner self (Merton, 1979). The spiritual journey towards such knowing traverses a terrain of beauty and love and is nested within aesthetical encounters such as the "festival of rain" (Merton, 1966, p. 11) in *Rain and the Rhinoceros*. Merton's encounters with nature are imaginally rich aesthetical moments evoke the spirit of American Transcendentalist writers, such as Thoreau (1960) and their idea that spirituality and the aesthetical encounter are entwined. Within such kinship, the authentic self is nurtured and paradisal idea is nested and the promise of wisdom is present. And from such relation there began to emerge within this study the question of wisdom's relation to the aesthetical. The idea of the imaginal as a conveyor of wisdom nurturing the second set of questions of this study.

> *What marks the character of the wisdom image?*
>
> *Of the paradisal, Merton speaks of the "impossible paradox" in the encounter with the beauty of the mountain—"it is and is not" (Merton, 1998a, p. 286). How does the wisdom image relate to such paradox? If the wisdom image is crafted of paradox, then how are we to configure notions of paradisal wisdom?*
>
> *Alternatively, does the wisdom image elevate the epistemic standing of the aesthetical encounter? In so doing, does it celebrate ways of knowing through the arts, through such paradigms, for example, as arts-based and holistic learning in education, which depart from the narrower lens of analytical inquiry?*

An Impossible Question? The Spirituality Research Paradigm and the Wisdom Image

While questions about the wisdom image are informed by Merton's writings they are also complicated by his view of the paradoxical nature of spiritual transcendence (Merton, 1998a), a problem which is also prescient to the recent methodological initiative by researchers, such as Lin (2016), Ergas (2016) and Miller (2016) into configuring a spirituality research paradigm (SRP). Amongst these researchers, Ergas, in particular, in his observation of the enigmatic character of such a paradigm, mirrors Merton's kindred sentiments upon the character of spirituality.

In this study the paradox and paradigm of SRP is viewed as a fundamental philosophical problem—one to which I am drawn, but whose approach to understanding now departs from the analytical philosophy in which I was schooled. Instead of posing questions within the domain of a reductionist methodology, my questions are instead posed within a different realm which, following Kuhn's (1975) paradigm theory, are incommensurable with the former. Standing apart from the philosophy of reductionism my new paradigm is instead nested within a philosophy of holism and one wherein the arts, as a terrain of knowledge, is central.

Such a terrain, however, poses a conundrum when we travel further in this land and seek to cross from the epistemological onto the spiritual. We try to capture its essence in words, but the spiritual transit resists language. How do we then describe the spiritual journey? We return to language cautiously but we also remain within a journey which is enigmatic.

Of its enigmatic spirit Merton writes that the mountain is seen when there is nothing more to say, a seeing which happens when we "consent to the impossible paradox (Merton, 1998a, p. 286). His observations are counter-intuitive and tug at our desire to quell the seeming contradictions in his words. Questions emerge.

> *What is the nature of paradoxical consent?*
> *How can I claim to see the mountain if I cannot speak of its light?*

Merton's paradox turns away from propositional knowing by instead situating knowing within themes of the non-propositional (Palmer, 1993; Zajonc, 2006; Merton, 1998a). While the arts are kindred in spirit with the non-propositional ethos of the spiritual domain, we can never assure ourselves of its character using language. Instead, within the mysterious map of such terrain we are only assured of questions.

> *Does meditating upon the aesthetical carry us into moments of non-propositional knowing—that is, a place where we are in presence and not opposition with the paradoxical creed? In other words, can the wisdom image have a transcendent ethos?*
>
> *And once in that presence what becomes of the wisdom image? What becomes, for example, of his literary children that Merton speaks of fondly in Raids on the Unspeakable (1966)? Do they dissolve within the presence of the paradox?*

To ponder what becomes of the aesthetical within the presence of the spiritual paradox that Ergas and Merton speak of is to engage a question which reveals the tug of ontological thinking. Merton, quoting Prakriti on the nature of the self, observes, "'the self is not known within nature" (Prakriti, quoted in Merton, 1998a, p. 174). In a similar spirit, Merton writes of the limits of propositional knowing, observing that nothing needs to be said when the mountain is discovered (Merton, 1998a). The silence Merton alludes to when the mountain is found invites us to ponder how for both Merton and Prakriti propositional thinking with which the ontological is aligned is limited once we cross onto the spiritual terrain.

The enigmatic character of spirituality which Merton and Ergas explore foregrounds the conundrum of asking questions about spirituality research. While questions are complicated by their open-endedness within the absence of certitude, they are also vital to the spiritual transit. As Hart observes, inquiry proceeds within never-ending questioning and wonder returns when wisdom is no longer corralled by certainty (Hart, 2009). Merton's paradox evokes such sentiment and, along with Ergas' kindred observations on the complicated character of SRP, brings into focus the conundrum of the wisdom image when we try to understand its character within the realm of non-propositional knowing.

When we consent to the paradox it remains as mystery within the propositional realm, but as presence within the non-propositional domain. When we consent to Merton's paradox (Merton, 1998a) or Ergas' "paradoxical creed" (Ergas, 2016, p. 15) the questions, pondered within the realm of propositional knowing, are ones we feel impelled to ask but which are also configured as impossible ones enwrapped by paradox. And thus, we are drawn to ponder how the impossible question accompanies Merton's paradox (Merton, 1998a) in the journey of spiritual inquiry. But a journey which is also, following Hart, rich in wonder (Hart, 2009).

4 The Friendship of Texts
Beyond a Referential Relation With Texts Onto the Dialogical in Inquiry

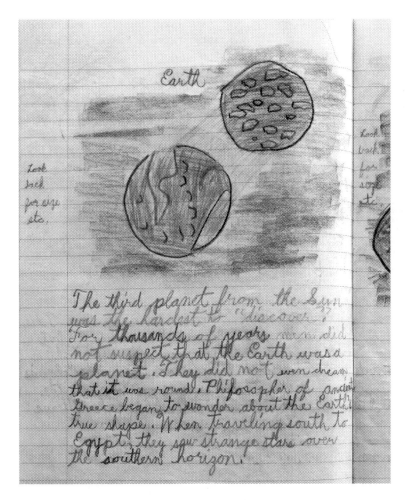

Image 4.1 Rossini, G. (c. 1966). *Merton's "Vague Fragments," Building the Big Picture.* [Photograph of Page From G. Rossini's Grade 4 Workbook]. Ontario, Canada

Source: G. Rossini

I've cared for my workbook for fifty years now. As a child, not knowing why, I simply valued it and had an intuitive feeling to preserve it. I felt close to it. Years later its presence remained as it accompanied me onto adulthood and came into its own meaning within an academic study upon the relationship we have with texts in inquiry.

Introduction: The Touch of Our Friends

During a meeting of the Holistic Educators Group at OISE I was asked by colleagues how my research was going and whether I had tired of the readings. I replied that I enjoyed the readings and was still friends with them. They found my answer amusing and we all had a good laugh. Afterwards I recalled the encounter and pondered how my improvised response also revealed something about the relation of texts to the inquirer. While texts bear a referential and contextual relation to an inquiry, they also transcend such relations. The texts we choose reflect something of ourselves and, in this, are not simply disencased from inquiry, but in intimate relation to the life of the inquirer. The texts that we move towards and feel kindred with perhaps align with aspects of our emotional selves. For Merton, who speaks to his texts in Raids on the Unspeakable, they become his children (Merton, 1966, pp. 1–6); with my colleagues I describe them as my friends.

My story is guided by the reflection that while the texts we reference represent a contextual configuration for research, they are much more than this in inquiry. The texts we nod to, defend or disagree with, cite passages from, annotate and celebrate and share or debate with others invite reflection upon a deeper connection we have with them. A serendipitous encounter with my colleagues foregrounded such connection and nurtured the observation that the texts we choose are not isolated from the psyche of the inquirer, herein suggesting a relation between the inquirer and texts which extends beyond their referential presence within inquiry.

Of such extended relation the following questions are offered. What feelings are evoked within us when we ponder the texts that we are drawn to? Do they nurture wonder, curiosity and love? Do their words convey us into silence? Do they carry us into awareness and nurture us towards contemplative reflection? Do they touch us? That we should feel towards texts enriches inquiry and follows Hart's observation that "what we know is bound to how we know" (Hart, 2008, p. 236).

On the nature of the *how* in knowing, Palmer (1993), in a similar spirit, describes how, in his teaching he nurtures connections by encouraging his students, not simply to observe, but be in dialogue with the subject. With specific reference to the teaching of Merton's writings, Palmer describes how he would introduce him "with the care I would take in introducing one good friend to some others" (Palmer, 1993, p. 99). The intimacy with which Palmer engages with texts suggests an enriched relation between reader and text, one which extends beyond an objectified relation with texts into another of feeling, or more narrowly following Palmer, of friendship, wherein the dualism of the researcher and subject of inquiry is eroded.

Palmer's observation is echoed by Thomas Moore. In his critique of contemporary education, Moore makes a kindred observation when he observes:

> Much of modern education is at a distance. It is like learning about the people next door, instead of becoming friends with them. We sit in classrooms far from any action or materials or events that we are trying to learn about. We quantify all kinds of information that could be far more deeply studied if we were less abstract. We do all this because we are anxious about being correct. We don't want to make a mistake or trust our intuitions or make sensual observations.
>
> (Moore, 2019, pp. 52–53)

To know with feeling when we engage texts as Palmer suggests or with education in general as Moore recommends evokes Patricia Morgan's idea of "felt knowing" which she describes as a "precognitive knowing and meaning that originates in the interior" (Morgan, 2012, p. 50). While Morgan's notion is configured within the psyche, her idea is co-opted here and extended within reflection upon the relation of the psyche to texts, and it is underscored by the notion that the texts we are drawn are echoes of our deep intuition and feeling which collectively configure our inner world.

Of the power of texts or persons or the world to move us Hart describes them as vital presences, one which extends beyond their status as objects by being instead intimate with our lives. Words are not disencased from our being but join with us in the journey of inquiry. Within the "living words" (Hart, 2008, p. 236) that both touch us and we touch them wisdom is nested. With their touch words become incarnated in our transit through inquiry within an intimacy which evokes Morgan's idea of knowing enriched by feeling.

> *The story of my grade school workbook, which begins this chapter, is offered as an example of such intimacy with text. As a child I valued the workbook carefully storing it. As I grew older, I would check on it every few years as I moved between cities and transited the terrain of graduate school and career.*
>
> *I was protective of the workbook although I did not know why. In lieu of a reason, what was clear was that my relationship to it was present within a domain of feeling and not the propositional.*
>
> *Only much later when I returned to graduate school in education and crossed into the territory of holism did the workbook emerge into understanding.*
>
> *I had been pondering how our being in the world was entwined with notions of wisdom and the aesthetical. Coincident with my reflections was a fortuitous glimpse of the workbook. My attention was drawn to the child's enthusiastic drawings of the planets contained in its pages.*

As an adult I did graduate work in the history of science with a special interest in Renaissance science and the astronomical discoveries Galileo had made with his telescope.

A wonderful harmony began to emerge between these two moments of childhood and adulthood when the child's drawings of the planets merge with a kindred presence in the adult. What had been a serendipitous encounter with a text I had long cared became a transformational scintilla in my thinking. There was a moment when my workbook became, following Hart, "living words" (Hart, 2008, p. 236) *that nurtured a holism which spanned across time.*

In that moment the workbook emerged into meaning within an ethos of connection between the adult and child—a connection which would not have happened had the child not kept his workbook and their "living words" were never to speak.

Heraclitus observed, "I searched into myself" (Chitwood, 2004, p. 73). In inquiry, to search into oneself is guided in part by the texts which touch us within a dialogical discourse with self, as is offered in the story of the workbook. I layer my words onto Heraclitus' and reflect, *I searched into myself through the texts which I feel.*

Of those texts, I was touched by many in this study. While the core texts were configured about ones in holistic education, they were joined by others from wisdom research, arts-based research in education and Merton studies. Along with Burtynsky's images and my own photographs they collectively converged to become my circle of friends. In so doing they formed a family whose presence was necessary for the dialogical discourse with my *self*. Without the conversation between them I could not have had the conversation with my *self*. Like the story of the child's workbook, the progress of inquiry unimaginable without their friendship. Together, nurturing my journey along Heraclitus' search onto the self.

On that journey my friendship with texts evolves with some coming near while others move apart. Such movement is often serendipitous and fortuitous and affirming of the notion that inquiry often departs from our initial expectations and preparations and is instead marked by multiple entry points and ones which are often unexpected.

Regarding the journey of texts, I am reminded of an imaginal encounter in the Spanish Chapel of Santa Maria Novella in Florence. The walls of the chapel are frescoed in their entirety with scenes from the Life of Christ and others celebrating Thomas Aquinas and the Dominican Order. My attention is drawn to one scene in particular, the Navicella of St. Peter the Apostle, which retells the story of Christ and the Apostles on the Sea of Galilee during a storm.

The encounter with the image is generative. It offers me a visual metaphor for reflecting upon the relational ethos of inquiry to texts.

Like the feeling of incertitude evoked by the storm, it often feels like inquiry is less a rational and preplanned process than a fortuitous

Image 4.2 Rossini, G. (2017). *The Journey*. Detail of Fresco by di Bonaiuto, Andrea. (1365–1367). *The Triumph of Christian Doctrine*. [Digital Photograph]. Spanish Chapel. Florence, Italy

Source: G. Rossini

and intuitive one. Like the journey of questions, I sail upon an ocean of texts towards a port not knowing where my transit from that place will take me next. Only when I depart from it and continue on does the next port begin to appear. During the journey I both arrive at destinations and do not. The transit feels Heraclitean in ethos, never in stasis but always in movement.

Reading Texts While Seeking the Aesthetical Map

While texts from diverse paradigms joined my journey, I feel that I have crossed into terrain where the maps are few and the signs are absent. The terrain of wisdom and the aesthetical is not well travelled. Perhaps it is because in the encounter with the aesthetical, we must make our own maps.

I look onto images, like Burtynksy's photographs and feel that within their pictorial narratives, a lesson about our being in the world is offered. But such offering places a demand upon us. Unlike the proverb whose lesson-map is captured in a few words, the lesson of the wisdom image requires that we be responsible. Without the scaffold of words, we must instead look for the wisdom image, and once we have found it must look at it mindfully before we can begin to extract ethical narratives about our being-in-the world.

Such wisdom that I seek through the aesthetical presence stands apart from the texts on wisdom that I have encountered. With my textual friends, though I seek this other wisdom yet its crossing is an unchartered terrain and paradoxical.

The texts travel with me onto the edge of the unchartered land, a new place which stands apart from past configurations of wisdom associated with the propositional and is instead nested within a different paradigm of the imaginal.

Herein I am reminded of the story of Gionitus and the astronomers who followed him. Each one looking farther onto the creation than the one before. Though they could never capture all that was present, the limitless expanse of the creation did not deter them from looking onto the uncharted land. Their story offers an exemplar for my own story and the character of inquiry as an endless journey whose mileposts are questions and not answers.

Encounters With Texts as Ontological Acts: A Transit Begins With Artists and Holistic Writers

The educator Robert Yagelski observes how for him writing configures his being, and in this is "an ontological act" (Yagelski, 2011, p. 104)

Yagelski's idea invites extension beyond writing. For the craftsperson, their being is formed in moments of craft making, while for the teacher, it is formed in classroom encounters when the scintilla of learning suddenly emerges from within the student. And for me, within meditative encounters with texts and art.

Within such moments, being is not an ontological singularity in a Platonic sense, that is, some ideal form that stands apart from everyday life. Instead, following in Heraclitus' spirit, being is within a formative domain, that is, within acts of engagement which not only connect us to our authentic selves but in so doing also connect us to our world and others, therein underscoring an understanding of being, not as objectified or disencased, but as connected presence.

In my being such a presence configured by texts, such as the child's workbook, whose critical presence shifted and opened onto new discoveries upon my self, encounters with texts become ontological acts. That is, engaging with them within acts of reflection become my mode of being during the often solitary journey of inquiry.

During that journey texts have joined me in friendship to transit its path.

Amongst these encounters, there was a seminal one with John P. Miller's *Educating for Wisdom and Compassion*.

The question of the relation of wisdom and art initially emerged when reading Miller's *Educating for Wisdom and Compassion* (2006), becoming initially crystallized around his observation of the non-dualistic nature of *timeless learning*. Unlike a *transmission* model of learning, *timeless learning* is not about acquiring knowledge; authentic learning resides not in its temporality, but in the heightened immediacy of the present (Miller, 2006). Miller observes how timeless learning has several characteristics; amongst these his observation on its *nondualistic* character was generative in the initial formation of my inquiry. Sparking my initial intuitions into the relation of art and wisdom was his retelling of Emerson's story of the painter,

> Timeless learning tends to be nondualistic in that the knower and known become one. Emerson wrote. "A painter told me that nobody could draw a tree without in some sort becoming a tree." He adds: "By deeper apprehension . . . the artist attains the power of awakening other souls to a given activity" (p. 134). For Emerson, non-dual knowing can awaken others. Non-dual knowing is also called contemplation.
>
> (Miller, 2006, p. 10)

The way of art can carry us into such moments of awakening when by heightened comprehension we become closer to what Miller observes as "the grand Mystery of being and the cosmos" (Miller, 2006, p. 11).

Reading the story stuck with me. I ponder his retelling of Emerson's story of the painter and wonder if the profound apprehension that Emerson observes in the painter's craft can be named wisdom.

Such deeper knowing suggests a special relationality between the artist and her art—one of intimacy, alignment, or *being one with* wherein as Emerson observes in the story of the painter, the painter becomes the tree. The painter's being is with the being of the tree, in kindred manner that the being of the writer, following Yagelski, is configured by acts of writing or my being in its encounters with texts.

Others have alluded to such relationality. The spark that emerged from my encounter with Miller's retelling offered a lens through which I would meditate upon the reflections of artists upon their art practice and other writers in the field of holistic education.

Photographer Henri Cartier-Bresson observes that "To take a photograph is to align the head, the eye and the heart. It's a way of life" (Cartier-Bresson, n.d.). Landscape photographer Edward Burtynsky speaks of a similar alignment which for him is also meditative, one which is marked by a deep focus wherein the subject guides you onto it (Khachadourian, 2016). Burtynksy's and Cartier-Bresson's sentiments echo my own engagement with photography when the moment of the camera's shutter release is accompanied by a sense of completeness when I *feel* that the composition and the lighting is optimal and nothing more needs to be done to the image. In a similar spirit, Vicki

Kelly, a teacher-artist, likens the artist's act of seeing to "beholding... within our innermost being"—a deep relationality in which "one stretches towards and unites with the object, or the other." "By this act of indwelling" Kelly observes this "leads to an apprehending or deeper understanding... the artist completes the intended wholeness of creation.... Sometimes artists experience profound moments of grace when, with insight, they see into the heart of things" (Kelly, 2006, p. 3). Within such encounters, subject-object boundaries evaporate and, as Bai observes, become moments of "co-emergence" (Bai, 1997, p. 45).

In his essay *Concerning the Spiritual in Art*, the painter Wassily Kandinsky describes such relationality poetically:

> colour is a power which directly influences the soul. Colour is the keyboard, the eyes are the hammers, the soul is the piano with many strings. The artist is the hand which plays, touching one key or another, to cause vibrations in the soul.
> (Kandinsky, 1977, p. 25)

Kandinsky's musical metaphor of such aesthetic intimacy, when colour and the soul are aligned, is echoed by John Coltrane, the American jazz musician, who in the spirit of the American Transcendentalist writers simply observes that

> All a musician can do is to get closer to the sources of nature, and so feel that he is in communion with the natural laws. Then he can feel that he is interpreting them to the best of his ability, and can try to convey that to others.
> (Coltrane as cited in Woideck, 1998, pp. 108–109)

Such closeness to nature, which Coltrane speaks of, is mirrored in painter Jean-Michel Basquiat's observation, "I don't think about art when I'm working. I try to think about life" (Basquiat as cited in Graw, 1999, p. LXVII), and in the words of the indigenous writer, Gregory Cajete: "For, historically Indigenous artists created for *Life's Sake. Be with Life!*" (Cajete, 2019, p. 147).

Regarding the closeness with nature and life which Coltrane, Basquiat and Cajete speak of respectively, Arthur Zajonc writes of the transformative promise of the aesthetical encounter—one which is configured by moments of *reshaping, recentring and realignment* of self. Using the metaphor of the circle such moments are marked by the movement from eccentricity to concentricity. Engaging with art centres and transforms us. On the transformative presence of art, Zajonc in *The Heart of Higher Education* quotes the artist Paul Cezanne and adds

> "There is only nature, and the eye is trained through contact with her. It becomes concentric through looking and working." That is to say, we start eccentric, off-center. Through our constant attention to her

we become concentric; we reshape ourselves with every stroke on the canvas to be in alignment with her. Only in this way does the artist learn to see the as-yet-unseen and so become capable of rendering it visible to others.

(Palmer & Zajonc, 2010, pp. 107–108)

Zajonc's reflection on Cezanne's painting evokes the spirit of the centred self in Fra Angelico's *Mocking of Christ* (1440), an image, which like Miller's retelling of Emerson's painter, resonated deeply in my psyche when I encountered it in Florence and one which I reflect upon in Chapter 1 of this study. For Zajonc, the encounter with the aesthetical is one that reshapes us; it is a transformative event whose transit from the eccentric towards the concentric echoes the centring of self portrayed in Fra Angelico's fresco.

Of the spirit of connection between artist and subject that Zajonc ponders in the aesthetical encounter is one which is not exclusive to the domain of the arts but reflected in other fields of inquiry. Amongst scientists are found echoes of kindred descriptions of their relational encounters with the subjects of their laboratory studies. Amongst these is the story, retold by Tobin Hart of how Barbara McClintock, a Nobel Prize winner, described her relation to the corn plants she researched. The scientist's attentiveness to her plants involved a soft empiricism; "'a feeling for the organism' and an 'openness to let it come to you' (Keller, 1983, p. 198)" (Hart, 2004, pp. 32–33). The language McClintock uses to describe her relation to her plants evokes the intimacy and spirit of Coltrane's intent for the musician, in his work, to get closer to nature, or Burtynsky's strategy of letting the subject guide his photographic composition.

Amongst such artists, musicians and scientist there emerges a shared observation of a special alignment or oneness that is present between the artist and their creation. Such unity evokes the spirit of holism, one from which, as Emerson observes leads to a deeper knowing; or as Kelly observes moments when grace is present (Kelly, 2006).

While problems of epistemology are not a central concern of such writers, they guide us to reflect upon whether such deep knowing is closer to one which is aesthetical, contemplative, intuitive and embodied in nature rather than simply described as rational and demonstrable. The special alignment which Emerson, Cartier-Bresson, Burtynsky, Kelly, Zajonc and Kandinsky observe occurring between the artist and the soul evokes Curnow's observation on Pascal that "intuition and experience are the domain of, or exercises of, the heart, and reason is helpless without them" (Curnow, 1999, p. 131). Without the pauses of rational demonstration, there is instead the suddenness with which direct perceiving happens—a moment of intuitive grasping, a moment of clarity, a leaping into understanding when the encounter with the imaginal touches us. Of the power of intuitive and embodied knowing, Coltrane observes

> When you are playing with someone who really has something to say, even though they may be otherwise quite different in style, there's one thing that remains constant. And that is the tension of the experience,

that electricity, that kind of feeling that is a lift kind of feeling. No matter where it happens, you know when that feeling comes upon you, and it makes you feel happy.

(Coltrane as cited in Hentoff, 2010, p. 212)

Regarding the intimacy of the intuitive touch, others in the field of holistic arts education parallel such sentiments. Michael Grady explores the notion of "art as spiritual inquiry"—a holistic notion about the reintegrating of self through the arts which he examines in the context of the alienation of self in contemporary society (Grady, 2006, p. 84). Alain de Botton parses a similar notion, but through the idea of the art gallery as a space—what he also names the "apothecary for our deeper selves"—which he views as a healing space for the psychic recovery of self (de Botton, 2013, p. 1). The holistic arteducator Seymour Simmons observes how art making is a platform for existential inquiry and the artist serves to make public those ideas which are deeply held and private (Simmons, 2006, p. 48). In the same spirit arts educator Peter London observes how the purpose of art is to engage with the core questions of life: "Who am I? Why am I here? Where am I going? Who are you? Who are we?" (London, 2004, p. 5).

Interestingly, such sentiments amongst holistic writers in the arts and transformative learning are synchronous with Merton's writings upon Zen. Of Zen, Merton observes that it is not about understanding enlightenment as a philosophical system; rather it "seeks an existential and empirical participation in that enlightenment experience" (Merton, 1968, p. 36). Regarding such participation, Merton writes of the essential nature of Zen. In *Zen and the Birds of Appetite* (1968), in a passage which evokes similarities with London's meditations upon the core questions of life or Basquiat's desire not to think but to paint life, Merton observes

> But the chief characteristic of Zen is that it rejects all these systematic elaborations in order to get back, as far as possible, to the pure and unarticulated and unexplained ground of direct experience. The direct experience of what? Life itself. What it means that I exist, that I live: who is this "I" that exists and lives? What is the difference between an authentic and an illusory awareness of the self that exists and lives? What are and are not the basic facts of existence?
>
> (Merton, 1968, p. 36)

While such questions have been the terrain of philosophers since antiquity, the answers they offered have not satisfied us. We continue to ponder them; and we turn to the artist for insights upon such answers. As the writer James Baldwin observes, "The artist cannot and must not take anything for granted, but must drive to the heart of every answer and expose the question the answer hides (Baldwin, 1962, p. 19).

For the artist, the answers to the life questions are not corralled by the domain of the analytical philosopher but instead are configured within a different knowing—an intuitive one informed by the creative and aesthetical. Within the latter terrain, of such questions, Merton's observations on Zen echo those of Peter London on the arts. The questions are similar and nurture the idea that engaging with the arts can guide us towards wisdom—a deep knowing upon the existential questions which both London and Merton pose.

Reflecting upon Merton's words in tandem with texts by artists guides my reflection that the authentic aesthetical encounter constitutes, extending Yagelski's view of writing, "an ontological act" (Yagelski, 2011, p. 104). Of the character of such act, it is formed of the alignment that happens within moments such as those between Emerson's painter and the tree, Cartier-Bresson's alignment with his photographic subjects, Yagelski's writing as an act of being, my own encounters with texts. While such moments are aesthetical in ethos, they are also ones which configure our being and within such formative moments constitute ontological events.

Within such aesthetical-ontological moments our being is formed in alignment with others and the world. "Being" is not simply a singularity qua "being"; rather it is, co-opting Heidegger's suggestion, a "being-in-the-world" (Heidegger, 2001, p. 85). But a being in the world configured within a contemplative and aesthetical ethos, that is, seeded by the aesthetical encounter our being in the world becoming an ethical alignment with it, one wherein the promise of wisdom resides.

My friends who emerged in the encounter with texts guided me towards this view.

Seeking Wisdom From Wisdom Studies

Though my first university studies were in history and philosophy, the topic of wisdom, which the ancient philosophers had viewed in intimate relation to philosophy, had not figured within them. Being curious about this absence I revisit my first philosophy anthology, Edwards and Pap, A Modern Introduction to Philosophy (1973) and observe that there are no index entries for wisdom. Neither are there entries for art. The absences are puzzling: to speak of philosophy without wisdom within a book about philosophy seems counter intuitive; while speaking of philosophy without art feels soulless.

While this text was part of my early studies, I had since transited onto other places and my circle of friends had expanded. Writers in wisdom studies, which had been absent in my earlier schooling, now joined my caravan of texts by artists and holistic writers as we crossed the terrain of inquiry together.

My initial intuitions about the relation of art and wisdom which had first emerged from reflections upon Miller's *Educating for Wisdom and Compassion* and kindred texts by artists and holistic writers led to a general reading on the subject of wisdom beginning with Ferrari's and Potworowski's *Teaching for Wisdom* (2008). Pondering their anthology foregrounded how my undergraduate study of philosophy excluded the ethos of wisdom, and one which many years later seeded my retelling which introduces this section.

My reflection upon my earlier studies, while highlighting a gap within them, also brought into focus an insight into our relation with texts in inquiry and how such relation is not disencased from but intimate with one's narrative. While the old philosophy text foregrounds itself within my narrative about the study of philosophy with which it is entwined it also reveals how the ontological configuration of my being, formed of texts in inquiry, is marked by absences as well as presences.

Reading Ferrari and Potworowski's *Teaching for Wisdom* (2008) stood in opposition to such absence in the philosophical anthology that I had read as a young student. Only years later when I began my inquiry into the relation of art and wisdom in the context of reading *Teaching for Wisdom* did I realize how my experience of analytical philosophy had been marked by the absence of a pedagogy of wisdom.

With the character of my early academic experiences emerging into focus through reading *Teaching for Wisdom*, I ponder how the dearth of wisdom that I had experienced as a philosophy student was later replaced by an abundance of understandings of wisdom. Ferrari and Potworowski's anthology parse such understandings through the lens of pedagogy, histories of eastern and western philosophies and development psychology. Through reading their text I learn that understandings of wisdom are not singular but manifold.

Underscoring their inquiry into wisdom is the question "Can wisdom be taught or at least fostered" (Ferrari & Potworowski, 2008, p. v)? Ferrari and Potworowski's text reveals how responses to this question have diverse answers—ones which range from Curnow's historical overview, Stange's and Kunzman's scientific approach to the understanding of wisdom as captured in the Berlin Paradigm; Sternberg's, Jarvin's and Reznitskaya's "Balance Theory of Wisdom" (Sternberg et al., 2008, p. 38), Reeve, Messina and Scardamalia's understanding of wisdom as a deep knowing nurtured within communities, Rosch's particular interest in Buddhism's notion of "beginner's mind" (Rosch, 2008, p. 135) and general interest in what is common between wisdom traditions, to Bright's (2008) exploration of wisdom within the Christian context. While their foci are diverse, all recognize that understandings of wisdom are much more than knowledge of the world; instead such understandings are an amalgam of how we know and live in the world.

> *While reading* Teaching for Wisdom *filled what had been an absence in my early studies, it also seeded a fundamental question in my thought: How does the aesthetical fit into historical and contemporary discourses of wisdom? The presence of the aesthetical in wisdom studies seems a topic not central to it. Such absence puzzles and the question remains as I seek out new friends.*

Following Ferrari and Potworowski I turned to the work of the development psychologist Paul Baltes, who, like the former, explores multiple understandings of wisdom. In *Wisdom as Orchestration of Mind and Virtue*, Baltes (2004) presents an encyclopaedic overview which, through its inquiry into the history and scholarship on wisdom, ponders whether a psychological theory of wisdom is possible. While Baltes observes that historical understandings of wisdoms share "the core notion that wisdom constitutes deep knowledge about life, its conduct, and its interpretation" (Baltes, 2004, p. 41), he also observes that such understandings are marked by many configurations—to understand wisdom is to engage "a collection of wisdoms rather than a singular wisdom (Assmann, 1991, quoted in Baltes, 2004, p. 8)".

Baltes' view of the multiple configurations of wisdom is shared by others in the field of wisdom studies, notably Trevor Curnow whose writings on wisdom joined with kindred texts in my study. While recognizing that wisdom has no single definition, Curnow, in his text *Wisdom* (2015), overviews the history of wisdom to show how wisdom has been understood in different ways. Amongst these, wisdom understood as being identified with knowledge, or with a healthy soul, or alternatively, in the Christian context, with piety. That wisdom has multitudinous understandings is a theme Curnow explores in his other texts, *Wisdom in the Ancient World* (2010), and *Wisdom, Intuition and Ethics* (1999).

Reading Baltes', Curnow's and Ferrari and Potworowski's writings in wisdom studies brought into focus how such studies have centred on the text as the primary expression of wisdom. Proverbs, maxims, the wisdom literature of the ancients (Buddha, Greek philosophers, early Christians) and writings of Renaissance thinkers such as Nicholas of Cusa (1996), for example, are witness to the form of the text as the primary modality of wisdom. In his overview of the history of wisdom, Curnow observes how its history parallels the evolution of language, writing and literacy and is often associated with the presence of the scribe in ancient historical accounts (Curnow, 2015).

> *Such relationality between texts and historical accounts of wisdom was one I found both intriguing and generative. While wisdom stands in relation to the word and text form as the formal conveyance of wisdom, the subject of wisdom in relation to a different modality of the arts is less apparent.*
>
> *While it is associated with the propositional within these works, I seek to locate wisdom within a different terrain, that is, within an aesthetical understanding that stands apart from the narrow register of the text.*
>
> *My earlier question repeats itself: Can wisdom be associated within the encounter with art?*
>
> *Baltes' work does not suggest such an association. However, neither do interpretations of wisdom share singular understandings. Perhaps within the ethos of multitudinous understandings of the character of wisdom will I discover an aesthetical interpretation.*

Allusions to the Artful and Imaginal in Wisdom Studies

I seek another association of wisdom with the artful and non-propositional. I am impelled towards it by an intuitive sense that such association exists. I return to Baltes and begin to sift faint nuggets.

In my journey through texts the question of the relation of art and wisdom became crystallized while reflecting upon Baltes' work. In his writing there are few references to arts except for allusions to poetry. Of wisdom in poetry Baltes observes how poetry became highly regarded historically because it revealed insights into the nature of humanity (Baltes, 2004).

Reading Baltes' work foregrounded a conundrum within my study of wisdom; though much has been written on wisdom, less has been written on the intersection of the arts with wisdom. Except for poetry the arts in general have little presence in the terrain of wisdom. Yet nuggets of such presence begin to emerge. Though his comments on poetry are cursory, they hint at the possibility of such intersection. In pondering how the art of poetry embodies wisdom Baltes guided my inquiry towards a general meditation upon the relation of wisdom and art.

Such peripheral references to the insights offered by the arts onto the human condition are alluded to by Curnow in his writings on the history of wisdom. In *Wisdom* (2015) he explores, for example, the story of the cave from Plato's *Republic* where the inhabitants of the cave observe shadows: observations set within a philosophical story about the nature of reality and how it can only be understood when the inhabitants leave the cave and emerge into the light (Curnow, 2015). Of the meaning of the cave story for understanding wisdom, Curnow writes,

> Whether we take the connection between wisdom and perception in a metaphorical or a literal sense, it is a theme that is encountered at many different times in many different cultures. The wise are those who can see the bigger picture, whose horizons are broadest, whose vision is clearest, who live in the light.
>
> (Curnow, 2015, p. 10)

Though an aesthetical interpretation of the cave story is not central to its retelling, the cave story is rich in its visuality and perception. The journey from the cave is an evocative visual narrative about seeing; it is a transit into wisdom marked by an imaginal presence and made by those "whose vision is clearest" (Curnow, 2015, p. 10).

Of the possibility of such presence, reading Curnow's text nurtured kindred interpretations in my study. In his overview of Zoroastrianism, for example, Curnow describes how the idea of wisdom is aligned with "creative process" (Curnow, 2015, p. 22) in the creation story of the world. Of the aligning of wisdom with creativity, Curnow observes such affiliation is a common theme found in the ancient mythologies of the Greeks, Norse and Indian sub-continent. Within such affiliation though, the artist is absent from Curnow's account, except for the poet who he observes is often associated with wisdom (Curnow, 2015).

In Curnow's account as it is for Baltes' the aesthetical relation to wisdom is largely absent but the route to understanding such relation is present in their writings. The rich history of wisdom literature and wisdom studies provides a scaffold for beginning to formulate the relation of the aesthetical with wisdom. That is, when Curnow observes, for example, that the proverb, had a "didactic" (Curnow, 2015, p. 179) purpose from which one would learn, such notion of didacticism is one that can also be applied to the work of art; for example, the didactic ethos that is observed in the photographs of Edward Burtynsky and which I explore in Chapter 2 in this study.

Of the aesthetic and imaginal aspect of the proverb, Curnow observes, "A proverb is something that is 'well express'd', there is an aesthetic dimension to it. In literary terms a proverb is like a tiny polished gem . . . the proverb is a triumph of economy and imagery" (Curnow, 2015, p. 180). Of the proverb's imaginal presence, Curnow quotes the medieval Hebrew philosopher Moses ibn Ezra who says "'A proverb has three characteristics: few words, good sense, and a fine image'" (Curnow, 2015, p. 181). Curnow's description of the wisdom of the proverb and its didactic possibilities offers an entry point for kindred understanding of wisdom's relation to the aesthetical.

On such a relation, Curnow, in *Wisdom, Intuition and Ethics* (1999), alludes to the imaginal presence of wisdom in his retelling of the story of Job from the Old Testament. Job encounters God and speaks to him of his dire life. Through his seeing of God, Job achieves enlightenment. Job says "I heard of thee by the hearing of the ear, but now my eyes see thee; therefore I despise myself, and repent in dust and ashes (Job, ch. 42, vv. 5–6)" (Curnow, 1999, p. 15).

Of the visuality of wisdom that is suggested by Job's story, Curnow observes "The vocabulary of wisdom in a variety of cultures talks in terms of illumination and enlightenment, which are both explicitly visual notions. The primary meaning of intuition also links it to the faculty of sight" (Curnow, 1999, p. 15).

While my study of the relation of art and wisdom was guided in part by the thesis of the imaginal in Curnow's interpretations of wisdom; such relation was also enriched by Curnow's reflections upon the relation of the divine to wisdom. Of the divine, Curnow observes how, within the wisdom traditions, it is nested following Heraclitus within one's search for self-knowledge (Curnow, 1999).

Heraclitus emerges as an ongoing presence amongst my textual friends; and reading Curnow on the relation of the divine and wisdom within such presence returns me to Merton. With Merton, such relation is enriched with the imaginal presence of the aesthetical, one which is seen in his visually rich meditations in *The Other Side of the Mountain* (1998a) or the poem *Hagia Sophia* in *A Thomas Merton Reader* (1974) where he seeks his inner *Sophia* within the aesthetical encounter with nature. Reading Curnow aligns with the imaginal character of wisdom in Merton's writings, one whose ethos is also linked to the divine.

While for Curnow and Baltes the aesthetical is not central to the academic study of wisdom their writings help us to begin to scaffold a relation of the arts with wisdom which, by contrast, for Merton is already present. When Merton speaks of Sophia "the highest wisdom principle" (Merton, 1972, p. 141), he does so within a story about nurturing the artist that is present within us; and contemplation which is coloured by acts of artful engaging (Merton, 1972). When we create or contemplate art Merton observes how "the psychological conscience is able to attain some of its highest and most perfect fulfillments." (Merton, 1983, p. 34). For Merton, contemplating the spiritual essence of a poem or painting or music transports us onto an enlightened terrain of being.

Seeking Wisdom From Brother Louis

Reading Merton returns me to another time when as a philosophy student I was inducted into a different paradigm of analytical epistemology in which matters of art and heart were unwelcome. To seek knowledge through the arts was incommensurable with such paradigm. Years later, its incommensurable presence impelling me towards a different modality—one wherein I ponder how artistic inquiry can hold an elevated epistemic standing as wisdom. As I reflect upon Merton, I am reminded of Emerson's poem The Poet (1950) and layer their words onto mine. Of the relation of artistic inquiry to the creation Emerson and Merton speak forcefully. For Emerson, this is "true science" (Emerson, 1950, p. 329), while for Merton this is the "law" (Merton, 1983, p. 36). Such co-opting nurturing an ancillary question of my inquiry, that is, if artful inquiry can lead to wisdom, then does this elevate the arts as a pathway of knowing?

Reading Baltes and Curnow offered primordial texts which hinted at the affiliation of the imaginal with wisdom. Reading Merton confirmed such presence.

While Curnow's and Baltes' writings offer historical interpretations of wisdom, the aesthetical is not fundamental to such interpretations. In Merton's writings, the opposite is observed—the aesthetical is closely intertwined with wisdom and spirituality—an intertwining which in turn became a central pillar of my study.

While Merton is best remembered for his autobiographical text The Seven Storey Mountain (1998b), it was another text by him, first encountered in a graduate seminar on holistic education, Love and Living (1979), that provided a spark to my journey. In that text Merton contemplates how the purpose of education is not to enforce a view of the world but to nurture one's authentic self from within. Of the inner path, Merton speaks of the spark which is vital to the birth of the authentic self. Reading about Merton's spark resonated with my intuitions about the ethos of the authentic self and ignited my inquiry into the relation of wisdom and the imaginal.

Reading *Love and Living* (1979) and Merton's *The Seven Storey Mountain (1998b)* marked entry points in my study of his writings. Of those other writings, though, Merton's oeuvre is immense; and I pondered—which other writings of his should I explore? Merton was a prolific writer; his works spanning poetry, literary criticism, theology, Zen Buddhism, autobiography, correspondences, and mystical writing. An ocean of writing presented itself; how does one navigate such literary vastness?

The unscripted journey, like the pictorial story of the *Navicella of St. Peter the Apostle*, presents a metaphor for inquiry, its open-ended quality suggesting that there are multiple entry points into a body of literature and one marked by the serendipitous interaction between primary and secondary sources. An encounter with Ross Labrie's text *Thomas Merton and the Inclusive Imagination* (2001), while browsing the library shelf, marked such a critical and unanticipated entry point. Though the encounter was serendipitous, it was also fortuitous marking a key turn in my study towards exploring the relation of art and wisdom in light of Merton's aesthetical evolution towards paradisal consciousness. Such turn follows Labrie's exploration of the paradisal within the context of Merton's aesthetics, one which in turn was followed with exploration of Michael Higgins' *Heretic Blood* (1998), a spiritual biography of Thomas Merton wherein the ideas of the paradisal and the aesthetical are also explored; and Robert Inchausti's exploration of Merton's ideas in American thought in *Thomas Merton's American Prophecy* (1998).

Reading Labrie, Higgins and Inchausti was generative to the life of this study nurturing it towards an understanding of spiritual growth in which the paradisal, as an aesthetical notion in general and imaginal one in particular, is central. Such interpretation of the unity of art and spirituality in turn aligned with the spirit of holistic learning in education (Miller, 2008; Schiller, 2014) while drawing on the kindred paradigm of arts based research (Eisner, 1988, 2001, 2002, 2008; Eisner et al., 1996; McNiff, 2008; Diamond & Mullen, 2001) in curriculum studies.

Of the paradisal idea, pondering Labrie and Higgins shifted my inquiry to a rereading of Merton's *Love and Living* (1979) where Merton explores the paradisal within contemplations upon the goal of education. For Merton, the idea of the paradise is not about a knowing which is held by teachers. Rather, it is centred on the student who discovers his inner self (Merton, 1979).

Seeking to understand the *paradisal* in Merton's thought followed my reading of *Love and Living* and led to the exploration of other texts by him; amongst these were his *Conjectures of a Guilty Bystander* (2014) and his poem *Hagia Sophia* in *A Thomas Merton Reader* (1974). *Conjectures* is a collection of poetic and literary meditations wherein Merton expands the meditation upon the paradisal idea from the realm of education, as parsed in *Love and Living*, to life itself. Complaining of the noise and distraction that infests contemporary life, Merton laments that we do not see the paradise which surrounds us (Merton, 2014). In *Hagia Sophia*, Merton writes of the paradisal, but the language he uses departs from that in *Conjectures*. While in *Conjectures* the paradise is contemplated within the clamour of contemporary culture, in *Hagia Sophia*, the paradise is rendered in love and beauty and within an intimacy of one's self with the aesthetical and rhythm of nature.

Regarding such intimacy of the aesthetical with the paradisal, Merton's writings offer other entry points—ones which collectively reveal an evolution of his ideas on such intimacy. In an early essay, *Poetry and the Contemplative Life* in *Figures for an Apocalypse* (1947) Merton ponders the aesthetical within a configuration framed by theological and categorical understandings of contemplation. By the 1960s, the categorical rigidity with which Merton understood such configuration is eroded with his explorations of Zen, one which is observed in his essay *Zen in Japanese Art* (1968) from *Zen and the Birds of Appetite* (1968) wherein he meditates upon the intimacy of spirituality and art and how within the "unifying power of Zen" they are "inseparably fused" (Merton, 1968, p. 90). In *Raids on the Unspeakable* (1966), categorical understandings of art and contemplation are not present. Instead Merton, writing within the spirit of Zen in his essay from *Raids* titled *Signatures, Notes on the Author's Drawings*, moves towards abstraction distilling the drawing to an energetic and transcendent power.

While Merton meditates on the power of art within contemplations upon his own drawings within the interiority of his own spiritual journey, central to such journey and the intimacy of the aesthetical and contemplative is a *being* with nature. In his later journals, *Woods, Shore, Desert A Notebook, May 1968* from *The Other Side of the Mountain* (1998a) Merton poetically records his experiences of being in the American southwest. In writings which are evocative of both Zen and the American Transcendentalist writers, Merton meditates upon wisdom within an artful contemplation upon the landscape.

Collectively, the exploration of such texts marked entry points into understanding the relation of Merton's aesthetical ideas to wisdom and art as were other texts of his such as *Raids on the Unspeakable* (1966), in particular the *Prologue, The Author's Advice to His Book* and chapter *Letters to an Innocent Bystander* where Merton speaks directly to his reader or text, a strategy which I also adopted in my own dialogical discourse with Merton and one which was generative for my inquiry.

The encounter with the dialogical, through Merton's writings, became a seminal presence in my study as it was foundational to several themes, notably, the relation to texts which extends beyond their referential status in inquiry to another, which following Palmer (1993), is about friendship and a second theme about the contemplative ethos which is engendered by such approach when dualisms of subject and object or text and reader in research are eroded. With its contemplative spirit the dialogical is also kindred with the reflective quality of narrative, one which is also central in my study and nurtured by my reading of Merton's *The Seven Storey Mountain* (1998b) where the spiritual journey is nested within the retelling of Merton's narrative.

> *In Raids on the Unspeakable (1966) Merton writes of his texts as children within a spirit of dialogical relation. His way of writing, which is reflective and about connection with self, draws me with its contemplative holism; and seeds my own writing.*
>
> *Merton's presence joins with the caravan of texts that I nod to; and within my reflective writing which emerges in dialogue with it I transit onto the question of wisdom and the artful. Within such dialogical emergence is seeded my being in the world.*

114 *The Friendship of Texts*

Of the Dialogical Character of Transformation: Seeking Wisdom From the Transformative Learning Paradigm

Image 4.3 Rossini, G. (2017). *Transformation*. Sculpture by di Lodovico Buonarroti, Michelangelo. (1512–1530). *Atlas Slave*. [Digital Photograph]. Galleria dell'Accademia, Florence, Italy

Source: G. Rossini

It was early spring and I felt a refreshing chill as I waited to enter the gallery that morning. It was before the oppressive heat that will eventually visit Florence a few weeks later.

I was first in line at the Accademia to visit the sculptures. Once the doors opened I went straight away to visit Michelangelo's David. Seeing it is popular with tourists and I managed to be with it alone and capture his image before the crowds gathered.

The David is located within its own space at the end of a wide gallery which is lined by other sculptures by Michelangelo which are known as the Slaves (1525–1530). These sculptures are not as interesting to some gallery visitors; few linger to pause with them because the sculptures feel unfinished.

I stop to linger with Atlas Slave.

Atlas Slave is raw, and the chisel marks are evident; he stands apart from David's perfection. While he remains unfinished, he is not incomplete; the movement of his narrative is rich and nuanced. He emerges from the stone, or could also seem to be enveloped by it.

Within an entangled ethos of rock and slave Atlas' transit offers a visual metaphor for transformation, one wherein we see Atlas, entwined with the rock, struggling to emerge into his own being.

While my dialogical being in the world is formed of encounters with texts, it is also seeded by kindred ones with art as with the story of *Atlas Slave*. In those moments I am witness to a mysterious metamorphosis when such encounters transmute into an internal dialogue which marks my consciousness. While the emergence of such phenomenon aligns with Bakhtin's view of the "dialogical nature of consciousness" (Bakhtin, 1984, p. 293); it also reveals how the dialogical event is transformational in ethos.

From within my encounter with a text or work of art, an internal discourse emerges within me and which configures my being within that moment and which would not have emerged had I not become entwined with the text or work of art. Such entwining is both dialogical and transformational; and from within it emerges my *dialogical-being-in-the-world*.

Encounters with two bodies of academic literature were generative in seeding the notion of the dialogical nature of transformation. Parallel with reading Merton's writings were texts from researchers in the fields of transformative learning and contemplative studies in education (Miller, 2014; Morgan, 2012; Burrows, 2015; Byrnes, 2012; Dencev & Collister, 2010; Gunnlaugson, 2007; Zajonc, 2006) and recent scholarly work on the development of a spirituality research paradigm (Lin, 2016; Miller, 2016; Ergas, 2016).

Reading the work of these researchers provided a contextual lens through which Merton's aesthetical ideas and their relation to the idea of the *wisdom image* could be bridged to transformative and contemplative studies in education. Reading them also provided a methodological scaffolding for the narrative retellings and dialogical strategies which are adopted in parts of my study.

While such texts enrich a reading of Merton, it is also hoped that the nurturing is reciprocal and that interpretations of Merton's work return to enrich the fields of contemplative and transformative studies.

My study is guided by retellings from childhood and experiences of school and other writings which seek to explore Merton's ideas through the dialogical address to him. While such strategies broadly align in intent with arts-based (Eisner, 2001, 2008; Diamond & Mullen, 2001) and narrative (Clandinin & Connelly, 2000) approaches within curriculum studies, they are also enriched by the paradigm of transformative learning and contemplative studies in education. As with narrative and arts-based approaches, research in transformative learning seeks to expand the tools of inquiry beyond the narrower register of analytical and reductionistic methodologies. Within the transformative learning paradigm, as it is also with those in narrative and arts-based approaches, the way of inquiry takes on an ecumenical formation wherein are engaged intuitive, emotional and artful modes of knowing in addition to the rational and analytic.

It is within such expansive spirit that Gunnlaugson's understanding of transformative learning (TL) is adopted as a lens through which my strategy of dialogical speaking and narrative retellings are, in part, interpreted. It was from reflection upon Gunnlaugson during the early phase of my inquiry that initial intuitions about the relational nature of discourse with the self and art first emerged; and which were followed by explorations into the theory of dialogical discourse through Bakhtin (1984) and the recent scholarship of Hermans and Gieser (2012). Although I depart from the second person notion of "generative dialogue" (Gunnlaugson, 2007, p. 138) in TL, Gunnlaugson's thesis is instructive and formed an initial methodological lens through which I began to reflect upon the strategy of dialogical discourse as a tool for engaging with Merton's writing and with the kindred thesis of discourse as a basis for the formation of self within encounters with the textual and artful.

Of the nature of *transformative shift*, researchers in transformative learning span an array of pedagogical interpretations ranging from Gunnlaugson's socially contextualized "second person contemplative approach" (Gunnlaugson, 2011, p. 3) to Burrows' notion of "interior alchemy" and its focus on learning from within (Burrows, 2015, pp. 127–128). Within such a range of understandings there are kindred ones such as Byrnes' (2012) whose interpretation of transformation in contemplative education straddles the interweaving of our interior lives with the outer world.

Byrnes' observation that contemplative learning is centred upon oneself and Burrows' kindred focus upon the alchemical character of the interior life resonated with my exploration of dialogical discourse with Merton, and the view of its ethos as one, which like Burrows, holds at its core the transformative potential of the inner life. Byrnes' and Burrows' *turn towards* the interior life aligned with the spirit of my dialogical engaging with Merton which I view as a reflective practice and like the spirit of Merton's life and writings *turned towards* the life of contemplation.

Of the contemplative terrain, Hart views it as a way of knowing which supplements the paradigms of the rational and empirical (Hart, 2004). Reading Hart on the ethos of contemplation informed my strategy of dialogical engagement and narrative reflection in my study, one which I view as falling within the range of contemplative practices which Hart, like Byrnes and Burrows, observes nurture reflection.

Within such practices narrative, retellings are like comets' tails, signatures of moments which have past but which remain present within a formative spirit. Pondering such presence draws upon Dencev's and Collister's (2010) view, following Crowell, that transformation is characterized by ceaseless creation (Dencev & Collister, 2010)—a view which evokes the presence of the aesthetical with the transformative—and the story of *Atlas Slave* who resides in two entwined domains: one of the rock from which he struggles to transcend and the other of the emergent form. Within such transformation both domains are unique but also inseparable within a ceaseless movement.

The story of *Atlas'* emergence from the rock offers a second metaphor for the concept of *presence* in transformative studies, one which I draw from the work of Gunnlaugson (2011) and Hart (2008). Gunnlaugson explores presence as a knowing nested within an attentiveness to that which emerges (Gunnlaugson, 2007), as is evoked in the story of *Atlas*, whereas Hart explores an "epistemology of presence" (Hart, 2008, p. 237) within contemplative practices. In my study these notions are co-opted to ponder the question of whether dialogical speaking with Merton is a form of presencing, a strategy by which learning emerges, following Hart, when we allow "opening into our selves . . . and a willingness to really meet and, therefore, be changed by the object of inquiry, whether a new idea or a new person" (Hart, 2008, p. 236). For Hart, such encounters possess a vital nature; they are like "living words" (Hart, 2008, p. 236)—a notion which returns me to the character of dialogical discourse as one which also has a vital essence when, within my discourse with Merton, I too am willing, following Hart, to be changed by it.

Although Hart observes the vital quality of transformation, its promise is not possible without the presence of the child which, in my study, is formed of the synergetic dialogue between reflections upon my childhood drawings and idea of the contemplative child. In this I draw on Montessori's (1970) view of children's spirituality, one which is also synergistic with Hart's suggestion that children are "natural contemplatives" (Hart, 2004, p. 43) and Merton's kindred notion of the "child mind" (Gardner, 2016, p. 3).

With my narrative retellings of childhood as a backdrop these notions are pondered in relation to Morgan's "ground of being experience" (Morgan, 2012, p. 43) as a way of exploring the thesis that the seeds of inquiry are planted early and synonymous with the nascent spirituality of one's childhood. And with this I return to the example of the workbook, which begins this chapter where, within the "vague fragments" of my childhood (Merton, 1998b, p. 12), was seeded a primordial spirituality where the promise of transformation lay.

5 Towards a Methodology of One
The Personal Versus the Socio-Empirical in Inquiry

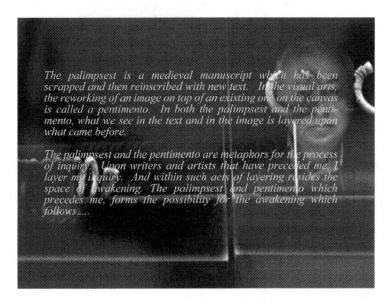

Image 5.1 Di Rezze, G. (2017). *Pentimento*. Image Based on Damien Hirst's *Treasures From the Wreck of the Unbelievable*. [Digitally Edited Photograph by G. Rossini]. Palazzo Grassi. Venice, Italy

Source: G. Di Rezze & G. Rossini

Writing Within and Between Analytical and Aesthetical Texts: Of the Contemplative Ethos Formed of a Methodology of One

Traversing the terrain of the imaginal and narrative domains sculpts the relation I have with texts and the way I engage with them through my writing.

Were I only an analytical philosopher I could dwell in a place where my relation to texts was configured about third-person writing. In this I would simply be a witness to another.

Were I only an artist, I could dwell in another place where encounters with texts and art are captured in first person writing and my art which is witness to my story.

But my "being-in-the-world," co-opting Heidegger's language (Heidegger, 2001, p. 85), is sculpted of both places. I am neither one of these modalities exclusively but formed of both. Instead I meander between them within an ecumenical spirit. The image of the pentimento, a metaphor for such movement, like the markings on the pentimento, first person textual voices sometimes prominent while at other times the third will emerge to inscribe over the first. The encounter with such textual voices is fluid and layered, and herein forming the internal dialogue which is witness to such moments of inscribing, layering and meandering.

Within such movement the texts impress themselves upon other texts within a dialogical discourse within me; and in so doing, forming the palimpsest of my being in the moment.

As I write I am often reminded of the balance I feel that I must maintain within such ecumenism. But the balance I seek is weighted by the texts that I encounter in the moment. Sometimes the balance will tilt towards the analytical and at other times the aesthetical.

I feel that my being is configured within such fluidity of textual voices. My contemplative writing formed within such movement, when I both listen to and am in dialogue with my self within encounters with texts. In such moments I am within my place of "witness consciousness" (Walsh & Bai, 2015, p. 25). A place which is uniquely my own and central to my crossing onto the terrain of inquiry.

The map of this crossing marks my method for research, its configuration sculpting a methodology of my own making: a methodology of one.

But the map of such method is also a paradoxical one as its pathways only emerge into view as I cross the contemplative terrain.

As I traverse this place with my wondrous map, I follow strategies of textual weavings and juxtapositions as ways for moving between my first and third-person voices. A chapter begins with an image or a retelling followed by a third-person reflection on a secondary text and a further retelling. To which side the balance will swing within such weaving with texts is unknown. In its fluidity the weaving is Heraclitean in ethos.

But what feels assured is that within such encounters there will be a formation of voice and being in that moment. Sometimes in the first person, sometimes in the third person. Other times in a synthetic first-third person where I am present within both voices, that is, when I write in the first person and am aware of this writing as I write it and of the presence of the third person which I am also aware of but whose writing is not written but could be. In this, a moment of heightened awareness and of my being formed in "the act of writing" (Yagelski, 2011, p. 104), but which I extend onto how the encounter with texts is also formative of my narrative-palimpsest which is my being in the moment.

Such formative events though feel paradoxical; within such moments there is my awareness of first and third-person voices which are present together in the writing but which also stand apart.

How do I reconcile the paradox with contemplative writing? Or can I simply be with the paradox as Merton is when he speaks of the beauty of the mountain—"it is and is not" (Merton, 1998a, p. 286)?

If I seek reconciliation perhaps it is to be found in a meta-awareness of the third-person presence. That is, I am aware of the third person through my first-person voice as I am in this moment now with you; and in that awareness I write of the third person within my narrative voice which feels artful and authentic. And in this meta-awareness I begin to integrate the analytical of the third person into the aesthetical of the first person.

I pause. I reflect upon Tobin Hart who speaks of "metacognition" which happens when we turn inward "which allows us not only to inquire into the question at hand, but also toward the asker of the question. We can become the object of inquiry as well as the instrument, as we look into self and subject" (Hart, 2019b, p. 340)

Within my meta-cognition the analytical enters into the aesthetical. And within such moments of meta-awareness the texts I encounter and the writing which follows configures my being in this moment.

Naming the Imponderable: Unravelling the Layers of My Palimpsest of Being

> In such perfect poverty, says Eckhart, one may still have ideas and experiences, yet one is free of them.
> (Merton, 1968, p. 10)

> I start in the middle of a sentence and move both directions at once.
> (Coltrane as cited in Webb, 2018)

> If you can speak what you will never hear, if you can write what you will never read, you have done rare things.
> (Thoreau, 1892, pp. 347–348)

In reflections upon the ethos of his art making the street photographer, Saul Leiter observed,

> There are the things that are out in the open, and then there are the things that are hidden, and life has more to do, the real world has more to do with what is hidden, maybe. You think? . . . We like to pretend that what is public is what the real world is all about.
> (Leiter as cited in Cole, 2013)

Towards a Methodology of One   121

While Leiter's observations emerge from his artistic practice, they are also applicable to reflections upon the character of methodology in contemplative studies in general and spirituality studies in education in particular. The paradigm for research in the university is dominated by analytical methods whose core is configured about the bifurcation of the researcher from the object of research. Yet the study of spirituality remains complicated. Central to its core is the inner life; one nested within reflection and meditation and configuring a domain of knowing centred about the personal, and what some may also view as the imponderable. Like Leiter's art practice, Coltrane's musical method or the paradoxical words of Thoreau and medieval mystic Meister Eckhart, spirituality's domain is nurtured by a hidden presence, often mysterious, which we seek to extract.

In my retelling which introduces this chapter I seek to move aside the veil to begin to reveal the hidden world which Leiter speaks of. But to see this world I must turn towards myself. The hidden world I seek is the hidden world that I inhabit and whose witness is my narrative. Its revelation is nested within the imperative of my stories and its emergence from within a dialogical discourse with my self which forms my being-in-narrative.

I am witness to such emergence and must listen attentively to such discourse. From the witnessing of the dialogical I seek to extract the hidden presence, but its extraction must emerge from the compounded layers of stories which constitute the palimpsest of my being.

Each of us is a living palimpsest. Each one of us is a book that has been printed only once yet has also been inscribed many times and can never be reproduced again. And from within this curious book, emerges the "scintilla" (Merton, 1979, pp. 9–10) of the true self.

What compels me to extract the layers of the palimpsest?

I seek to be where my actions align with my beliefs. To achieve such authenticity, I must return to this book; and never forgot to reread and learn from it.

I am reminded of Merton. His words now emerge into pristine clarity. My palimpsest and scintilla constitute my core being, that is, the "Sum, I AM (Merton, 1972, p. 9) Merton writes of in New Seeds of Contemplation.

The Problem of Research Methodology: A Paradoxical Paradigm

The palimpsest is a place for beginning to probe the authentic self. To read it I must turn inwards and extract lessons from the layers of stories which form it. But the contemplative turn towards the palimpsest crosses onto a personal terrain; and the question emerges of the character of the method(s) I use to extract its wisdom.

How do I begin to explore this question in view of the personal ethos of the spiritual journey?

Of this journey Merton speaks of the *"impossible paradox"* (Merton, 1998a, p. 286) while Ergas, in kindred language observes the *"paradoxical creed"* of spirituality (Ergas, 2016, p. 15). The question is nested within a conundrum; and I return to categorical thinking in order to reflect upon the character of the spiritual journey as one which transcends such thinking.

Although analytical study can inform us about the character of spiritual experience, it also remains distant from the spiritual experience. This observation rests upon the fundamental distinction between the analytical-reductive paradigm and spirituality, one which builds upon Ergas' (2016) observations about the character of spirituality and spiritual research in education; and Miller's (2008) and Merton's (1972) kindred criticisms of the spiritually impoverished nature of Cartesian thinking.

The study of spirituality maintains an ambiguous relationship to empirical-analytical research practices, one which is revealed, for example, in the embrace of the mysterious ethos of spiritual phenomenon amongst philosophers of spirituality research in education such as Lin et al. (2016). But while these writers' appeal for the need to construct a new paradigm is a welcome and timely methodological reflection upon the character of spirituality research, their call is incommensurable with a different paradigm for research which dominates the university today. Such dominance is marked by empiricist research methodologies which are configured about rules about data sources, data collection and analyses and ancillary notions of validity and reliability. The power of such paradigm is formidable; and we default to expectations of its role in inquiry.

While empiricism is a powerful research tool and much can be learned about the nature of spiritual phenomenon through its use, foundational to its methodology is a subject-object dualism which strikes at the heart of spirituality. In its boldest configuration empirical research requires that one stand apart from oneself within such binary in order to conduct research. But spiritual phenomenon is complex and to situate its study within such a delimited investigational register does not fully capture its ethos. As Lin et al. observe in their appeal for a new paradigm for spirituality research,

> A spiritual research paradigm requires an ontology that considers all reality to be multidimensional, interconnected, and interdependent. It requires an epistemology that integrates knowing from outer sources as well as inner contemplation, acknowledging our integration of soul and spirit with the body and mind.
>
> (Lin et al., 2016, p. ix)

Against the binary of empiricist methodologies, they invite us to stand, not apart, but with ourselves within inquiry. Their invitation in turn foregrounding the foundational problem of how we perceive research in spirituality studies. While empirically based educational research in general is philosophically distant from such methodological debate, research into spirituality in education is, by contrast, immersed within exploratory arguments upon the nature of its research methods. For some philosophers of education, notably, Lin et al., the methodological problem of doing spirituality research has caused an "urgent need to develop a spiritual research paradigm" (Lin et al, 2016, p. ix) while for others, like Ergas, such urgency is echoed in his call for "de-education" from the Kantian paradigm which had dominated "educational narrative[s]" over the past two centuries (Ergas, 2016, p. 2) and a concomitant call for the "bold reclaiming of subjectivity within academic inquiry" (Ergas, 2016, p. 15). A kindred sentiment is mirrored in Bai, Morgan, Scott and Cohen who appeal for the *re-validation* of the subjective in spirituality research. In their call for a "*Prolegomena to a Spiritual Research Paradigm*" (Bai et al., 2016, p. 77) they echo the urgency of philosophers of educational research, like Lin et al., who have also advocated for a foundational rethinking of how such research is conducted in spirituality studies. Collectively, these researchers invite us to move away from a methodology nested within a socio-empiricist ethos towards another paradigm which is instead centred about the individual and personal.

While the methodological character of such paradigm is paradoxical, what is clear is that it is configured within a personal domain. As Ergas observes "A spiritual research paradigm turns to our very motivations and nests all our endeavors in a deeper quest for meaning, one that is different for each and every one of us (Frankl, 1959, p. 98)" (Ergas, 2016, p. 15). In this the analytical-reductive paradigm, wherein the personal is severed from inquiry, will not suffice as a vehicle to carry us onto spirituality. Instead, the spiritual journey becomes aligned with a paradigm of our own making; that is of a *methodology of one*, primordial in configuration but unique to oneself; never in stasis but fluid within a creative formation nested within the personal and subjective. But also, a methodology which, in its paradoxical configuration, perhaps also heralding, co-opting Hart's words, "the cusp of a new episteme." That is, one which finds "a way to bring together the bits and the bytes in the living of an integrated life in a world of global technical interconnection but human disconnect" (Hart, 2019b, p. 338).

Beginning to Engage the Paradox: A Witnessing of Self Through Writing and Encounters With the Aesthetical

It is within a conundrum that I seek to write of that which cannot be written, but perhaps can be alluded to. To grapple it, I use the tools I have at hand—meditations and meanderings, creativities and heresies, the opposites of the artful and analytical. I open myself onto these tools to explore a paradox which cannot be captured within the bifurcating character of empiricist and rationalist research. Instead my tools seek a contemplative ethos wherein, following Merton, I consent to the paradox and stand with it and not apart from it.

My tools have a complex genesis though; they do not stand apart from the palimpsest of my being. They are not imposed from

> *without as might be a telescope or microscope. Instead, my tools for inquiry emerge from within me. They have grown with me and accrued in tandem with my narrative. My tools form part of the palimpsest of my narrative being. In this, while my being is one in palimpsest, it is also one in inquiry.*
>
> *Upon my palimpsest of being, I begin to create my own palimpsest of inquiry. With this act of creating, all that I am assured of is that the path onto the conundrum is mine. I must travel it on my own, and I am witness to its journey through my writing and art within a dialogic relation with myself. Regarding the personal ethos of this journey I am reminded of Merton's characterization of it as one which one must travel within their own solitude. (Merton, 1972)*
>
> *My crossing of this place is configured about acts of writing and moments within such acts when a reflection emerges onto its meaning. The French writer Jean Malaquais observed, "The only time I know that something is true is the moment I discover it in the act of writing" (Malaquais, n.d., as cited in Mailer, 1967, p. 278). To this I add, my truth emerges, not only in acts of writing, but also in encounters with texts and art.*

My journey of inquiry is nested within the primacy of my narrative to whose presence I am witness in part through acts of writing, a thesis which is sympathetic to that of Malaquais on the entwined character of writing and truth and kindred notion of writing as a form of witnessing. In the activity of writing, consciousness is "activate[d] and magnif[ied]" (Walsh & Bai, 2015, p. 25). But while for Walsh and Bai "writing witness consciousness" is a collaborative engaging—a "'being with,'" another (Walsh & Bai, 2015, p. 26)—my journey follows a different focus where *being with* is a being with *my-self*. My act of writing within collaborations with texts, such as those by Walsh and Bai in this moment, when I also become a witness onto my *being* in this moment.

While I depart from their collaborative ethos their language is familiar and I co-opt it. They write of being witness to their witnessing, a witnessing nested within a cascade of mirrors wherein

> our
> own witnessing words would be like setting
> up more mirrors to the previous
> mirrors universe of mirrors everywhere we turn
> a mirror that mirrors other mirrors.
> (Walsh & Bai, 2015, p. 25)

Their mirrors become a witnessing in reflectivity—an imaginal "echo chamber" (Walsh & Bai, 2015, p. 25) embodying an ethos of witnessing which is fluid, layered, complex and reflective. I am reminded of my palimpsest—a witnessing which like theirs is layered and informed by the presence of narrative and my own echo chamber formed of memories which emerge, submerge and re-emerge. Their method of witnessing, like my palimpsest, is configured within a consciousness in emergence within the act of writing. Of their method Walsh and Bai write,

> our methodology will also have to be one with
> what we are doing which means not
> imposing it from without from the outset but
> letting it arise out of what's
> happening with our writing a methodology
> of recursive emergence witnessing reflecting
> writing with warmth with care a few
> fragments something will emerge.
> (Walsh & Bai, 2015, pp. 24–25)

Their method resonates with mine. The character of "witness consciousness," as one marked by "constant making, unmaking, and remaking of the content of consciousness," (Walsh & Bai, 2015, pp. 25) echoes my wondrous map whose retelling introduces this chapter. Like witness consciousness the pathways of my map, are not pre-existing but, only come into view within my encounters with texts and art and wherein its method of inquiry emerges organically from my narrative. Such encounters are dialogical in spirit when, following Bakhtin, "To live means to participate in dialogue: to ask questions, to heed, to respond, to agree, and so forth" (Bakhtin, 1984, p. 293). Within such dialogical acts of asking, heeding and responding within encounters with texts, such as with Walsh and Bai in this moment, my consciousness emerges.

Such emergence is "recursive" for Walsh and Bai; and I am reminded of how my journey is nested within a recycling of memory within my narrative. Such emergence is also organic, that is, within a methodology which, for Walsh and Bai "means not imposing it from without" (Walsh & Bai, 2015, p. 24); and I am reminded of Merton's question to his readers that the journey onto the self must follow its own path and not be imposed (Merton, 1972). Nested within the personal, "writing witness consciousness" is a generative force which nurtures the "scintilla," the inner spark of the authentic self (Merton, 1979, p. 9).

My thoughts cascade onto an imaginal palimpsest which had gradually emerged when I had initially read and a few weeks later returned to Walsh's and Bai's text; my encounters with their writing are demarcated by my glyphs and notations upon it. Their gradual appearance onto the page denoting a visual witnessing of my emergence into a *consciousness in the moment* within encounters with their text.

The Dialogical as My Witness Consciousness

The palimpsest that slowly emerges in my encounter with Walsh and Bai's text becomes an imaginal exemplar of my witness consciousness.

> *That is, my emergence onto an interpretation of their text is configured within an internal dialogue between me and its words and one whose outcome is manifested in the image of a palimpsest wherein I inscribe my words onto theirs.*
>
> *As my glyphs and notations gradually appear upon their writing, the presence of their text emerges within my dialogical relation to it wherein the being of the text, in the moments of its interpretation within my consciousness, forming part of my dialogical self, that is, when my self emerges in dialogue with their text. In such moments the encounter with the text and the imaginal expression of such encounter within the palimpsest becoming a witnessing of my consciousness.*

While the theory of the relation of self and dialogue has sociological roots (Hermans & Gieser, 2012); the metaphor of the palimpsest as a manifestation of witness consciousness imagines a dialogical self residing closer to the internal domain along the spectrum of the "internal-external axis" which Hermans and Gieser use to describe dialogical self theory (Hermans & Gieser, 2012, p. 2). The fundamental question of the relation to self and others underscores such spectrum; what for Martin Buber is configured about the *I-Thou* (Buber, 1970, p. 14) relationship or for William James as the *I* and *Me* (James, 1891, p. 371) but which for others like the physicist philosopher David Bohm could also be about a different kind of relation and one centred on the relationship with one's self. As Bohm observes "A dialogue can be among any number of people, not just two. Even one person can have a sense of dialogue within himself, if the spirit of the dialogue is present" (Bohm, 1996, p. 6).

Dialogical self theory is scaffolded within a sociological paradigm, but Bohm's observation, though firmly situated within such paradigm, invites extension of the dialogical idea into the contemplative terrain. When Arthur Zajonc, for example, advocates the "silenc[ing of] the social self" (Zajonc, 2009, p. 31) as a way of quieting the clamour that both inhabits our daily lives and inhibits our spiritual lives what remains of the dialogical self if not a silent and reflective discourse with *one's self*?

To pose such question is not to diminish the relation the contemplative has with the world. Following Hermans and Gieser, our dialogical relation to it is within an "extended self, the other belongs to the self and is not simply 'outside the skin'" (Hermans & Gieser, 2012, p. 3), a notion which accords well with the ethos of holistic connection in spirituality studies. But within the theoretical spectrum of the dialogical self, such notion has an internal interpretation wherein the dialogical discourse with *one's self* is central, one which is also enriched by a contemplative ethos. As such, while the notion of the dialogical self is broadly informed by a sociological paradigm, it stands beyond it or at its very least is on its periphery in this study.

While standing apart from a sociological register, the thesis of the dialogical discourse with *one's self* as a form of witnessing is closer to Bakhtin's (1984) view of the dialogical self wherein its focus is internal in spirit and centred about problems of consciousness. The basis for Bakhtin's understanding is his study of literature, in particular Dostoevsky's writings wherein the dialogical emerges between the imagined characters of the story (Hermans & Gieser, 2012). The characters are situated within a dialogical relation between themselves and the author, one wherein the characters partner with and co-create with the writer (Żurawska-Żyła, Chmielnicka-Kuter, & Oleś, 2012). Herein the dialogical self emerges within an intimate relation between the artist and an imagined other within an internal landscape of consciousness. At its core such understanding is anchored by an artful presence nested within the autonomy of the artist and in this stands apart from sociological understandings of the dialogical self as associated with Hermans and Gieser, Buber and Bohm.

The ethos of the dialogical self as one informed by an aesthetical ethos guides extension of this notion from the literary onto the contemplative. But while the literary and contemplative paradigms share the aesthetical, the dialogical self within the former remains within a relational domain of imaginings and in this within a language which also falls short of the ethos of the contemplative paradigm.

The idea of the dialogical self within the latter paradigm requires a different language which extends beyond the literary. Where Parker Palmer, for example, encourages us to be in dialogue with texts within a spirit of friendship (Palmer, 1993), Tobin Hart writes about the power of texts as "living words" (Hart, 2008, p. 236), Merton refers to his texts as children (Merton, 1966) and I am in dialogue with my primary school workbooks, a different vocabulary is sought. It is one which extends beyond that of the literary onto another of the contemplative domain where the understanding of the dialogical self as a sphere of consciousness is captured, not within Bakhtin's configured interpretations of imaginings but within different notions of, for example, *presence, connection and witnessing*.

Within the contemplative paradigm such vocabulary expands the understanding of the dialogical self away from its broadly nested sociological interpretation towards another configuration wherein its interpretation is also located within the domain of the personal. In the second chapter of this study, an exemplar of such configuration is offered by Thomas Merton wherein, following Palmer and Hart, I seek to engage his writing, not simply as a literary artefact, but within a different ethos of connection and contemplative presence. Within the sections which follow I return to reflect upon such ethos but within an exploration of its relation to the dialogical self.

Acknowledging Merton's Call: Dialogue with Brother Louis as a Strategy for Inquiry

> It is not as an author that I would speak to you, not as a story-teller, not as a philosopher, not as a friend only: I seek to speak to you, in one way, as your own self. Who can tell what this may mean? I myself do not know. But if you listen, things will be said that are perhaps not

written in this book. And this will be due not to me, but to One who lives and speaks in both.

(Merton as cited in Giroux, 1998, xvii–xviii)

Brother Louis, do you mean that when you speak to me through your words such moment is not within a binary? That is, there are no authors, storytellers, philosophers or readers? There is no binary of you and me. Instead binaries dissolve within the mystery of the "One who lives and speaks in both." Is my encounter with your words simply a discourse wherein I am witness to myself?

Of the intimacy of the personal with the subject of research Parker Palmer in *To Know as We are Known* (1993) offers an example, one which is told through his retelling of his experiences teaching contemplation through Merton's writings. His approach is a personal one—instead of standing apart from his subject, he encourages his students to be in dialogue (Palmer, 1993) with them. To encourage such strategy Palmer shares with his students images, biographical information and audio tapes of Merton speaking. Palmer's intent is to introduce Merton as if he were a friend; by nurturing his students in communion with Merton's reality they may discover their own. As Palmer observes

when we interview the subject instead of just viewing it, then we find the subject speaking back to us in ways surprisingly independent of our own preconceptions.

(Palmer, 1993, p. 99)

The intimacy with which Palmer engages his subject within a spirit of dialogue mirrors the intimacy with which Merton also speaks to both his *readers* and *texts* in his writings, for example, *A Thomas Merton Reader* (1974) and *Raids on the Unspeakable* (1966). When Merton says he "seek[s] to speak to you, in one way, as your own self" (Merton as cited in Giroux, 1998, pp. xvii–xviii) the dialogical discourse of self is shifted onto a personal terrain. At its core the dialogue has an internal and contemplative ethos, that is, a witnessing onto self which is framed about a personal and not sociological configuration. The personal intimacy with which Palmer and Merton engage with texts underpins the spirit of dialogical discourse that infuses this study, one whose character I seek to align with explorations of the nature of discourse in contemplative and transformative learning studies (Gunnlaugson, 2007; Burrows, 2015; Byrnes, 2012).

The catalyst for dialogical engaging with Merton in this study was sparked when I encountered Merton's *Raids on the Unspeakable* (1966) wherein he begins the text with a prologue which is addressed, not to the reader, but to the text. *The Prologue*, subtitled *The Author's Advice to His Book*, begins with a caution to his text.

Well, Raids, you're grown up now. It is time for you to go out and meet people as the other books have done. They have usually managed pretty well on their own. They were, for the most part, good mannered. Some of them were even fairly devout. As for you, you may need special advice. It's your poetic temperament.

(Merton, 1966, p. 1)

Merton cautions his text about how it speaks about God with advice which echoes the dialogue of a father speaking to a child.

Will you be careful, please, not to overemphasize the titans, the creativity, and the microcosmic subject? And don't make Atlas look like a "world soul" or cosmic Adam. I have been called so many names lately that I don't want to be called a Gnostic anarchist on top of everything else. Please think of your old man, won't you?

(Merton, 1966, p. 2)

But then Merton tempers his caution though with his love for his child for it has a message that he especially likes. For this reason, though he loves all his texts, he adds "But in some ways, *Raids*, I think I love you more than the rest" (Merton, 1966, p. 2).

In his writings, Merton spanned the domains of spiritual writing, poetry and literary commentary. Whereas in *Raids on the Unspeakable* (1966), Merton explores subjects ranging from poetry to the nature of solitude to reflections on images, in his *Prologue* he integrates the element of the personal into his writing. Instead of the text being disencased from the personal and emotion, Merton speaks to it as a vital presence—one whose vitality is integrated into his discourse. In *Letters to an Innocent Bystander*, a chapter in *Raids on the Unspeakable* wherein Merton meditates upon how we are witness to truth, he repeats this strategy except he speaks directly to the reader. He begins by posing the question "If I dare, in these words, to ask you some direct and personal questions, it is because I address them as much to myself as to you" (Merton, 1966, p. 53). Merton invites us into his reality; and herein returns us to Palmer's invitation to his students to be with their subject within a spirit of communion.

Of the presence of internal dialogue in Merton's writings, Labrie observes how Merton's dialogical writing opened onto the reader and was prevalent in his writings (Labrie, 2001). In a similar spirit Inchausti (1998) observes how in his texts Merton seeks to connect with his readers by revealing his own contemplative reality—a revelation which is ultimately about one's self. One whose focus is a contemplative turn inwards wherein the binaries of writer and reader are dissolved and whose spirit is captured in Merton's words which introduce this section.

From pondering Merton's dialogical writings in tandem with Palmer's, Labrie's and Inchausti's observations upon them, their began to emerge a methodological configuration for my own writing, wherein, following Merton, I sought writing whose core was configured, not by the bifurcated research practices of analytical-empirical inquiry, but by another which was instead enriched by the contemplative ethos of dialogical engagement with the subject of research.

Within such an engagement the presence of the aesthetical is central, as is its expression through the imaginal and artful quality of the dialogical voice. My voice finding reassurance in Merton's writings, in particular *Raids on the Unspeakable*, whose example of the artful and dialogical voice, resonated with my intuitions about sculpting a study whose intent, is not only to explore questions with an academic voice, but to do so within an artful presence. Merton's writing offered an exemplar of such presence, one whose spirit I found synergistic support within kindred modes of inquiry represented by arts-based, contemplative and transformative learning in curriculum studies.

Speaking with Brother Louis:
The Seeds of an Organic Methodology

> This book is dedicated to All My Friends
> To the Old Ones and the New Ones
> To Those Who Are Near and Those Who Are Far Away
> To Those on Earth and Those in Heaven
> To Those I know and Those I have Never Met
> To Those Who Agree and Those Who Disagree
> To Those I have Never Heard of
> In the Hope That We May All Meet in the One Light
> (Merton, 1974, n.p.)

Brother Louis, we have never met in this world, but I heed your call within the light we share within a spirit formed, not of imaginings, but of connection, friendship and presence.

When Merton entered the Abbey of Gethsemani he took the name Brother Louis. In this study, the dialogue with Brother Louis becomes a generative entry point for my writing where primordial questions and intuitions about the relation of wisdom and art begin to emerge not from within an empirical strategy where I stood apart from him in inquiry, but from a different contemplative terrain where I sought to understand his ideas by being with him within, following Palmer (1993), in a relational domain of friendship. To be in such a space was generative evoking interpretations of his writings and reflections upon the relation of wisdom and art which would not have emerged had I not engaged Brother Louis in this way. It nurtured insights which an analytical-empirical approach could not. And the character of my relation to his writings, which was nested within an ethos of friendship and dialogical engagement with him, was not a strategy for inquiry that was imposed from without; but instead one which emerged organically from within me. It marked a methodology for inquiry of one's own making. This was my method.

Within dialogical encounters with Merton, I engage him, not simply as a historical memory apart from us, but in a different mode, that is, as a vital and active presence in my study as one with us. A presence nested within an engagement which is integrative, artful and holistic in spirit and wherein "we listen obediently to the voice of the other" (Palmer, 1993, p. 101).

While to sculpt an inquiry in such manner departs from empirical-analytical research practices, such an approach finds precedent, methodologically, following in the spirit of writers in the fields of holistic and arts-based inquiry in curriculum studies. Notably, holistic writers such as Schiller who reflects upon how we need to rethink writing by situating it in the writer's emotional and spiritual world in order for it to be meaningful (Schiller, 2014), a view echoing Palmer's holism about the intimate relation of the knower and known within a spirit of community and one born of love and compassion (Palmer, 1993). For Palmer, to know is to love; by such activity we engage with others within their reality and in so doing, knowing becomes a relational act about community and one which is nurtured, not simply by a rationalist ethos, but in addition by other capabilities of the self, such as emotion, intuition and empathy. Together such capacities nurture, what Palmer in kindred spirit with Merton observes, seeing the world as whole within the unity of the heart and mind.

Though writing from a different perspective of arts-based learning, Elliot Eisner, in kindred spirit to Palmer, departs from binary knowing by the embrace of non-propositional strategies for inquiry, as are associated with the arts (Eisner, 1991). Eisner's openness to alternate strategies extends to the ways we write in inquiry in general and the form of the novel in particular (Eisner et al., 1996), herein aligning well with Schiller's ideas about nurturing ways of writing which may depart from common academic practices.

In his poem *Hagia Sophia*, Merton writes of the wholeness which is nameless and hidden but wherein wisdom resides (Merton, 1974). It is within such spirit, that is, of engaging the creation in its fullness within a spirit of connection that Schiller (2014), Miller (2006, 2008), Palmer (1993) and others in the field of holistic education share that my study is situated. Within such vision inquiry is viewed, not as reductive in the Cartesian sense and restricted in the tools it uses in research but, as one which instead embraces the learner in their aesthetic, intellectual, social, emotional and spiritual complexity—a vision of inquiry which both sees with "wholesight" (Palmer, 1993, p. xxiii) and is nurturing of the "whole person." (Schiller, 2014, p. 1)

It is within such a spirit of seeing with whole eyes that my study seeks to be an *artful contemplative inquiry*, that is, one which is sculpted, not in dualistic relation to an object of research, but instead within a method of inquiry formed of encounters with art, meditations upon wisdom and dialogical engagement with Brother Louis' writing, together sculpting a methodology for inquiry which emerges organically from within *I* the inquirer.

My reflections in this section are introduced with the dedication from his book *A Thomas Merton Reader*. While they may not be yet known or near, in his dedication Brother Louis reaches out to friends who are spiritually present in the "One Light" (Merton, 1974, n.p.). His dedication is both expansive in spirit and artful in its desire to engage in discourse with those who transcend the temporal and spatial confines to which we are accustomed. Following in the spirit of Merton's dedication, this inquiry endeavours to reciprocate his call and *re-turn* towards him in spiritual discourse within dialogical engagement with Brother Louis. By speaking directly to him my inquiry seeks to sculpt a discourse which is holistic and aesthetical and which, following Schiller (2014), also is meaningful to the life of this writer.

From "Generative Dialogue" to Dialogical Speaking: The Inner Alchemy of the "Silent Self"

Although the idea of dialogical engagement as an internal dialogue with self is explored within interpretations of Merton (1966), Miller (2008), Palmer (1993), Schiller (2014), Walsh and Bai (2015) and dialogical self theory, it is also informed by kindred observations about the nature of discourse from writers within the field of transformative learning (TL) studies such as Gunnlaugson (2007), Burrows (2015), Byrnes (2012).

Of the character of TL Gunnlaugson observes how "generative dialogue" is central to the possibility of transformative learning. With TL, also known as "spoken discourse" or what Mezirow describes as "'communicative learning'" with generative dialogue "... "learners can reflect on their actions and uncover insights from the meaning, experiences, and opinions expressed by others" (Gunnlaugson, 2007, p. 138). Such a process is also viewed as a contemplative strategy configured within a second-person strategy. As with the first person, the second-person approach departs from focus on learning in the third person which dominates education (Gunnlaugson, 2011).

Instead, within a second-person approach learning is social; within a community of discourse learners can examine their assumptions and engage with the emotional and intuitive in addition to rational ways of knowing. With generative dialogue learners become attentive to those beliefs which form their views of the world; as Gunnlaugson observes, it allows learners to become witness to their own thoughts (Gunnlaugson, 2007).

The notion of generative dialogue as a second-person approach to learning departs from the strategy of dialogical engagement with Merton. Like dialogical self theory (DST), generative discourse is configured about social exchange, whereas the notion of dialogical engagement in this study is centred about a different exchange which is centred about one's self and internal. But as with the reimagining of DST in this study, can the idea of transformative learning be extended to accommodate the notion of the personal ethos of dialogical engagement? That is, can transformative learning be nested within a discourse which is centred about an *interior generative discourse* in addition to the social context, one which follows Palmer's suggestion to be in a dialogue with the subject which is personal (Palmer, 1993)? In other words, can the social interpretation of generative dialogue in TL be extended onto a different and personal notion of generative dialogue with self? Can the vocabulary of TL enrich the latter notion?

Arthur Zajonc (2009) and Leigh Burrows (2015) offer guidance on this other possibility. While observing that the clamour of life, which he identifies with our external world, needs to be balanced with a commitment to doing our inner work, Zajonc adds that meditation, which is key to such balance, is a solitary endeavour. The "silent self" which Zajonc identifies with doing the solitary work requires a turning inward located beyond the psyche space of ego (Zajonc, 2009, p. 31). Departing from Gunnlaugson's notion of the communicative and social aspects of transformation which is nurtured within the presence of others, Zajonc references Merton's early writings wherein transformation is instead centred about the self extracted from the outer clamour that surrounds it. For Merton, self, creativity and silence are enmeshed with one another. Referencing Merton, Zajonc observes the importance for Merton of silence when one withdraws from the din and instead seeks the self of quietude where creativity lives.

In contrast to Gunnlaugson's view of the role of communicative relationships in transformation, the communal self with which such notion may be allied, is in Zajonc's and Merton's writings diminished and instead stands as a quieting of the self—a self which retreats from the clamour of society and what he names as the "not-I" (Zajonc, 2009, p. 31). It is within the space of the silent self, a space which Zajonc also describes as one of solitude and where creativity is present in silence that the dialogical discourse with Merton is situated. Following Zajonc it is within my interior space of a silent and creative solitude that I speak with Merton.

In a similar spirit to Zajonc, Burrows' (2015) notion of "inner alchemy" explores the centrality of interiority in transformation, one which departs from Gunnlaugson's understanding of the community of dialogue in TL while inviting us to ponder alternative forms of interior dialogue, such as dialogical speaking, as is explored in this inquiry. The aspect of interior discourse which describes dialogical speaking stands apart from Gunnlaugson's understanding of TL by focusing instead upon transformation nurtured by one's interior life. For Burrows the inward turn is a self reflective wherein we arrive at self awareness "through a process of 'learning from the inside out' (Osterhold et al., 2007)" (Burrows, 2015, p. 128). Herein are engaged paths to knowing which are holistic in spirit and informed by intuition and feeling. Of the importance of interiority in Burrow's work is seen in the retelling of her own dreams with which she begins her meditation upon the transformative alchemy of one's interior life (Burrows, 2015).

While it may be viewed as an artful literary strategy, dialogical speaking is also one which, following Burrows, is about learning from within the transformative presence of reflection or, as Zajonc observes, is focused on doing the interior work. In my journey dialogical speaking nurtures my inward reflective turn guiding me towards the promise of wisdom which Burrows observes is innate to our being. Within the crucible of my "inner alchemy" (Burrows, 2015, p. 127) its promise nurtured within the dialogical discourse with Brother Louis, one which both nurtured my journey of inquiry while feeling authentic to the life of this inquirer.

The idea of the alchemical character of transformation offers an artful and expansive metaphor for the nature of inquiry which departs from the narrow registers of rationalism and empiricism. While Burrows speaks of the ethos of the interior alchemy within meditations upon the inner life Gunnlaugson, though focused upon a social understanding of TL, also speaks of the "alchemical vessel" (Gunnlaugson, 2007, p. 141) in which the community of discourse unfolds. Within its alchemical ethos, he also acknowledges a place for creativity within TL, an alignment which is echoed by Merton in his observations upon the artist's place in society. In his essay *Answers on Art and Freedom* (1981), Merton stands the artist with the alchemist. Merton says,

> For today, the artist has, whether he likes it or not, inherited the combined functions of hermit, pilgrim, prophet, priest, shaman, sorcerer, soothsayer, alchemist, and bonze.
>
> (Merton, 1981, p. 379)

For Merton, the artist's role is not singular but is instead immersed within the complexity of creation, one which evokes the messiness of inquiry which Gunnlaugson (2007) ponders and in my own reimaging of such complexity in my photograph of the Venetian street in Chapter 1. Within such messiness the aesthetical is bound with the alchemical; inquiry is informed by ways of knowing which transcend the parameters of rationalist methodology, and transformation is nurtured within a different contemplative terrain. It is within such complexity, one wherein the artist stirs the alchemical, that the dialogical discourse with Merton is also configured.

Dialogical Speaking, Narrative and Contemplative Knowing: A Transformative Journey of Shadows and Paradoxes

> *Though I studied philosophical writing I was never comfortable with the way analytical philosophers wrote. I could not write like them. It was stern and depending upon the topic often unintelligible. Something was missing.*
>
> *I then tried historical writing but could not write as a historian. Historical writing is premised on chronicle and though I could not name it at the time something was missing.*
>
> *I tried writing as a cultural theorist. The way the theorists wrote broke with the shackles of philosophical and historical writing and for a while felt liberating. But while the writing opened up, I still felt unsettled. Something was missing.*

> *I tried such diverse forms of writing and eventually transited onto an awareness that the "something" that was missing was my presence in the writing: my being-in-narrative.*
>
> *After a long journey I had finally reached Merton's question:*
>
> *"How do you expect to arrive at the end of your own journey if you take the road to another man's city?"*
>
> (Merton, 1972, p. 100)

Of the character of contemplative inquiry its introspective ethos in this study is nested within an internal dialogical discourse to whom I am its witness, one whose presence is manifested through the discourse with Merton and in reflective and imaginal retellings of transformative moments in my narrative. While this understanding of inquiry departs from the reductive analytical philosophical tradition in which I was trained, it opens onto another expansive terrain of knowing, one which is knitted of threads drawn from narrative theory (Bruner, 1991, 1986), DST (Hermans & Gieser, 2012) and arts-based inquiry (Eisner, 1993a, 1993b, 1995, 1997). Together, such threads reimagined within a quilt which aspires to Palmer's (1993) and Merton's (1974) appeal to seeing the world, not in parts, but within an ethos of its wholeness.

The language of reductionism tussles with such ethos, and thus the inquirer seeks other words, such as the *alchemical*—to interpret that which cannot be described by the former but which, in the same instance, is a generative vocabulary for those who cross onto the terrain of contemplative and transformative studies in education.

Within this other landscape, the discourse of the alchemical to explore the character of dialogical discourse offers a rich metaphor. In this study, its exploration is guided, in part, by the intersection of Gunnlaugson's social notion of generative discourse with Burrows' idea of our "interior alchemy" (Burrows, 2015, p. 127) and Byrnes' view, which is intermediate between these, in seeing contemplative teaching as embodying a relation of both the internal and external worlds. Following Palmer's (2004) observations on the metaphor of the Mobius strip, Byrnes observes how they are intimately related. While the integrity of a teacher, for example, is nested within interiority, it is also influenced by the world beyond (Byrnes, 2012, p. 23).

While Byrnes' understanding of holism straddles the internal and external worlds, neither Gunnlaugson's externalist notion of generative discourse nor Burrows' internal understanding of the "inner alchemy" exclude the other domain. While TL in Gunnlaugson's account, for example, is set within a social context he also observes that it is "not exclusively group mediated" (Gunnlaugson, 2007, p. 138). Similarly, Burrows while observing that learning happens from the inside, does not discount the importance of one's relation to the external world. Following Krishnamurti, Burrows observes that the transformation of self and society depends upon the non-dualism of the observer and observed (Burrows, 2015).

As such the differences between Burrows' and Gunnlaugson's interpretations of transformative learning suggests one of emphasis, rather than of opposing differences. Meditating upon the strategy of dialogical speaking with Merton falls within the range of such emphases. That is, while constituting a discourse; dialogical speaking departs from Gunnlaugson's understanding of generative discourse by being one which is instead situated within the domain of inner reflection instead of a community of discourse. With this understanding, the idea of dialogical discourse also aligns with Burrows' focus on the central role of reflection in transformative learning.

Of contemplative education Byrnes observes how it is a relational journey enmeshed with the self, "a journey that moves both outward into the world and inward into one's own mind, body and heart. It is a journey of knowledge and self-knowledge towards transformation" (Byrnes, 2012, pp. 36–37). Regarding that journey, an exemplar is offered by my opening reflection about my experience with different forms of writing, one wherein contemplation upon stories of philosophical or historical writing about the world beyond myself gradually transits onto another terrain where my writing becomes a contemplation upon *myself*.

Being witness to the thoughts which inhabit our consciousness both travels the journey and offers a contemplative opening onto the world wherein, as Hart observes, there emerges

> a distinct nonlinear consciousness that invites an inner opening of awareness. This opening within us in turn enables a corresponding opening toward the world before us. Through a fresh lens, our worldview, sense of self, and relationships may be powerfully transformed.
> (Hart, 2004, p. 29)

Following Hart, my story of writing becomes a pathway onto awareness. By meditating upon my relationship with forms of writing my retelling brought into focus aspects of *myself* which had not been nurtured but which are central to the richness of my life. By looking inward, as Byrnes' observes onto the relationship with one's self, I am able to begin the journey of transformation (Byrnes, 2012).

Such story as mine about writing is one which traverses a terrain of lingering feelings, and recycled memories—ones which were ever present but never voiced as such stories did not meet the epistemological expectations of the analytical epistemological paradigm in which I was schooled. In contrast to such knowing, Hart observes "Contemplation involves a softer focus and a lighter touch. The voice of the contemplative lives in these shadowy symbols, feelings, and images as well as in paradoxes and passions" (Hart, 2004, p. 37).

My story of writing dwells within such land of shadows, paradoxes, feelings and images, as do my other stories. Only by journeying into this open terrain and away from the rationalist encampment from which such shadows and paradoxes had been isolated could I begin the journey of transformation. Only by entering this new territory and stirring them, following Burrows, within the crucible of one's interior alchemy could the richness of human experience of which they are its ingredients be brought into meaning within the fullness of the creation.

Of the nature of transformation, Dencev and Collister (2010) observe how it is marked by shifts in consciousness and configured within change and acts of creativity. My retelling of moving onto and beyond ways of writing an exemplar of such shifts wherein transformation transcends stasis. A transformation set within a narrative-dialogical engagement with writing which signalled a gradual departure from ways of knowing and modes of writing in which I had been schooled. A transit whose ethos captured in the observation "that transformation does not happen instantly and it is never finished. Transformation is iterative and continuous" (Dencev & Collister, 2010, p. 180). Its journey, following Miller (2016), is continually unfolding and unending.

The Epistemology of Presence:
Transformation as "Living Words"

> To free the knower from his "knowing"—not just from his error. For the "Known"—to know is not to know but to be.
> (Merton, 1998a, p. 175)

> The reader's mind becomes the screen, the place, the era. To a large extent, readers create the world from words, they invent the reality they read. Reading, therefore, is a co-production between writer and reader. The simplicity of this tool is astounding. So little, yet out of it whole worlds, eras, characters, continents, people never encountered before, people you wouldn't care to sit next to in a train, planets that don't exist, places you've never visited, enigmatic fates, all come to life in the mind, painted into existence by the reader's creative powers. In this way the creativity of the writers calls up the creativity of the reader. Reading is never passive.
> (Okri, 1997, p. 41)

Although the strategy of narrative writing and dialogical discourse is interpreted, in part, through the writings of Dencev and Collister, Gunnlaugson, Hart and Burrows on the ethos of transformative learning, it is also enriched by other notions from these writers, in particular Gunnlaugson's idea of *presence* and Hart's kindred notions of the centrality of *presencing* and *interiority* in education.

Gunnlaugson describes presencing as "the practice, condition, or state of abiding in embodied present-moment-centered awareness—is the quality of attention that we embody in each moment" (Gunnlaugson, 2011, p. 6). Regarding this domain, Merton's writings are rich in evocations of presencing, amongst which are his reflections upon the southwest desert landscape in his journal *The Other Side of the Mountain* (1998a) where he contemplates the character of knowing, not as analytical, but as an embodied state of being—what he has elsewhere described, in contraposition to Descartes, as the "*SUM*, I Am" (Merton, 1972, pp. 8–9) or in his Zen-like words which introduce this section.

While Merton's retellings of his encounters with nature evoke *presencing* can his other writings, in particular his dialogical writings wherein he speaks to his reader and in my own dialogical exchange with him also embody such notion. Can we ponder dialogical speaking as a form of *presencing*?

The strategy of dialogical speaking with Merton in this study was inspired by Merton's writing, in particular, passages from *A Thomas Merton Reader* (1974) and *Raids on the Unspeakable* (1966) where he speaks directly to his readers and text. While being artful Merton's strategy is also holistic as it connects with his readers in a manner which is intimate and dialogical. Merton asks us to listen; and I heed his call by returning to him within a discourse which is configured within a first-person voice in addition to the third person. Adopting such strategy seeds my reflections upon and learning from Merton's ideas, one wherein his ideas are engaged not as a disencased historical presence, but instead within a different and more complex relation configured by a notion of a vital *presencing* and kindred in spirit to Parker Palmer's advice to engage with texts in an ethos of connection. Following such a strategy is generative to my writing. The dialogical discourse with Merton emerges from within, its method is organic in spirit; and reflections arise which would not have if I had remained in the third person.

The notion of *presencing* is adopted from Gunnlaugson's examination of generative dialogue and its definition where he observes "presencing involves learning from attention to what is emerging—knowledge that is sensed but not yet embodied in our experience" (Gunnlaugson, 2007, p. 141). While Gunnlaugson explores the notion of presencing within the social configuration of dialogue and a second person perspective (Gunnlaugson, 2011), his notion is extended onto the idea of dialogical speaking or the life of interior discourse. When Gunnlaugson speaks of *presencing* as a moment of emergent knowing which is sensed, such notion can inform understandings of interior discourse where, in kindred manner, I become present to what is emerging in the dialogue with Merton.

Of the configuration of knowing that emerges within such moments, Tobin Hart writes of the "*epistemology of presence*"—one "that moves past conditioned habits of mind to stay awake in the here and now" (Hart, 2008, p. 237). Such notion is nested within interiority and the idea of contemplation as a way of knowing which both departs from while supplementing rational and sensorial ways of knowing. To know with presence involves both a looking at the world beyond while "opening into our selves" (Hart, 2008, p. 236). By listening to that which emerges within the dialogical discourse with Merton, I become present to a knowing which seeds from within.

To speak of knowing within dialogical discourse as one configured by notions of *presence*, *emergence* and *openings* underscores how such knowing is a vital knowing. That is, of a knowing, following Hart, in the *here and now*—an epistemology of presence which is vital in spirit. With such knowing, words are not dead; instead following Hart, who evokes the tradition of wisdom literature, within the epistemology of presence is nested the idea of *wisdom* as words which are alive (Hart, 2008).

When Merton addresses his readers or I address Merton, the writing departs from modes of academic writing which are bounded by a third-person configuration; and instead is sculpted within a relation of intimacy in which such boundaries are eroded. The objective distancing which marks third-person inquiry is transcended by another relation that is vital and personal; words are exchanged within a relation that transcends the subject-object binary and are instead configured within an intimate discourse where Merton's words touch me and I, within my reflections, reach out to him, not as a text, but as a friend. Of the vital character of such words, Hart observes

> They are in some mysterious way described as alive on the page. This is why in all of the traditions there is invitation to reconsider the words again and again to see what light might be revealed this time around. It is as if the words are encrypted and compressed. To gain access to the mysteries and to reveal the meaning we have to break the code.
> (Hart, 2008, p. 236)

Knowing is not impersonal and disencased from the subject; rather for Hart it becomes living and interconnected. It is knowing in presence. Together with Gunnlaugson's understanding of presence, Hart's interpretation of the epistemology of presence is co-opted to interpret the strategy of dialogical discourse with Merton. His words are engaged not as historical artefacts separate from my life as the inquirer. Instead, I seek to engage with Merton, following Hart, within a relationship which transcends category, and is configured within a domain of presence where I open onto consciousness within the transformative encounter with his words (Hart, 2008). Such transformative space becoming, following Walsh and Bai, my space of "writing, witness, consciousness" (Walsh & Bai, 2015, p. 24); or as the writer Ben Okri observes, in the words which introduce this section, the screen of my "reader's mind" where I co-create my reality in the encounter with the writer's words (Okri, 1997, p. 41).

Inquiry as the Epistemological Touch of Flow

The examples of narrative writing which inform this inquiry emerged from my experiences of schooling, growing up within a working class immigrant family in southern Ontario in the 1960s, and encounters with art. Together with the discourse with Merton to write my stories became my "living words" (Hart, 2008, p. 236) and points of departure for my study. My inquiry, which in its initial iterations had struggled with a third-person approach, was reinvigorated when I rebooted it with the retelling of my stories and conversations with Merton. To inquire within the first person was generative and in the same instance intensely gratifying. To tell the stories and speak to Merton felt natural. The struggles I had experienced when I started my research were replaced with a happy abandon, the writing becoming less arduous and sometimes effortless. I was often not aware of time as I wrote them. Reflecting on them I am in wonder of their emergence from my being. I reread them and ponder rhetorically—*this writing came from me?*

Of such feelings one experiences when absorbed Csikszentmihalyi (1990) describes as a state of flow; one characterized by wonder, focus and suspension of the sense of time. The sense of self is temporarily suspended as one's awareness is immersed within the activity they are engaged with. In Hart's exploration of the epistemology of presence the notion of flow has a kindred relation—one wherein he examines Csikszentmihalyi's notion and ponders how such notion is related to an epistemology of flow. When Hart describes presencing as "stay[ing] awake in the here and now" (Hart, 2008, p. 237) or as Gunnlaugson observes as "embodied present-moment-centered awareness" (Gunnlaugson, 2011, p. 6) such notions evoke Csikszentmihalyi's notion of flow wherein, as Hart observes, awareness and action become fused.

To know in presence is to know in flow. And to know in flow is to be, following Hart, in communion with words as vital presences within a relation that transcends the bifurcation of researcher and research subject and is instead configured within a different relation where one touches the other. Within the epistemology of flow where stories emerge and interior dialogue hears its voice, that is, within the touch that transforms, I seek to be present to what is emerging and from such emergence distil its wisdom.

Voice of the Paradise Child: Emerging from "Vague Fragments" Onto Inquiry

I look at the drawings of the planets that I had drawn in my Grade 4 workbook and reflect upon the words I use to describe them. In the margins I had written "Look back for size etc" and ponder the metaphorical prescience of those words. Many years later within the context of doing a doctoral dissertation I "looked back" onto my narrative in order to arc forward onto inquiry.

My reflections upon the ethos of TL were synchronous with explorations into the idea of interior dialogue as a contemplative strategy inspired by Merton's writings. To engage with Merton through TL provided a scaffold for retelling transformative moments in my life—ones which, following Gunnlaugson, marked shifts, revelatory moments, moments when memories came into clarity and others which brought into focus, as he also observes, the unstudied presumptions that I held (Gunnlaugson, 2007). Such moments marked the seeds of my inquiry.

One such seed is configured within the following story of a medical examination. Retelling it brought to the surface a childhood memory which I had carried for years but only later coming into meaning within a doctoral inquiry, one whose retelling foregrounded the notion of the contemplative child in inquiry.

I had consulted with a medical specialist to help with a disruptive sleep condition. The diagnosis involved a study where I was monitored overnight in a clinic. A harness of electrical wires and probes were attached to my brain and other parts of my body. With the probes, data was collected on heart rate, flow of air, brain activity, REM and non-REM sleep. The study uncovered that my dream sleep was higher than the population average. I dream vividly—the dream images are powerful and memorable—and the observations by the study reconfirmed this.

Later, in the context of doing a doctoral inquiry, this observation, which had remained latent but ever present in my psyche, grew into meaning. As an only child until the birth of my sister eight years later, my life was a solitary one. Except for my caregivers I had very little interaction with playmates until the first grade. In lieu of preschool, day care or kindergarten, I lived within a world of my own making—the Lego buildings I built, a metaphor for that world. Within it the memory of being myself alone in silence on the couch—with my small hands grappling for the dust particles that floated in front of the sunny window. Within such moments the inner alchemy of one's core is fermented and though, as a child I could not name it, my inner life began to form. Within its solitudinous presence were seeded the beginnings of my inquiry.

In beginning to know our core selves it feels that we need to allow those memories—ones that are ever present but unspoken—to ferment and then come into calm. It is within such alchemy that the dialogical speaking with Merton is blended. To speak to Merton returned me to a place I had known as a child. Such speaking aligned with my inner life whose presence was manifested in the richness of its dream world. A presence which I do not discount but one which I am now open to learning from. Within such presence is nested the dialogue with Merton. And within such presence is the promise of my own "innate wisdom" (Burrows, 2015, p. 129) which I seek to tap.

Seeking the core self though feels like a quest without end. The discourse with Merton nurtures more questions; doubts set in as they did with Descartes when he pondered his dreams. Is the discourse a fantastical one which merits no place within inquiry? The analytical philosophers who taught me would assent to this question, but my intuition says no. To dismiss my story would be to grant Descartes' desire to dismiss the epistemic power of ways of knowing and forms of inquiry— ones sculpted by dreams and stories; and intuitions and feelings—which complete the fullness of the creation, are meaningful to the life of my inquiry and cannot be dismissed as Descartes would have it.

I seek to protect my dreams as Merton protects his literary children as he does in Raids on the Unspeakable (1966). Thus, what seems fantastical is reimagined within a holistic understanding about the

> *interconnectedness between others past and present as Merton himself alludes to in his writings. And so, with this, in my discourses with Merton, I seek to engage him, not as a historical artefact, but rather as a vital presence in my inquiry.*

The relation of the contemplative child and wisdom is one that has been explored by researchers in both Merton studies and the field of transformative learning in education. In his advocacy of contemplative practices in the classroom, Hart reflects upon the contemplative nature of children. They have a spiritual self which is rich in interior awareness and wisdom, what Hart also names "the wise child" (Hart, 2009, pp. 129–130).

> Children—young children especially—are natural contemplatives. They ponder big questions, they daydream, they fall in wonder with nature, they reflect on their own existence and find silence in their "special spot," perhaps under the arms of an old tree.
> (Hart, 2004, p. 43)

Similarly, Merton scholar Fiona Gardner explores the theme of the "child mind" in Merton's writings. Gardner observes how for Merton spiritual enlightenment was nurtured within "the adult mind uncovering, discovering, recognizing, and then integrating the eternal child—the Christ child—who is present and within the psyche of everyone" (Gardner, 2016, p. 3). In his poem *Grace's House*, Merton (1977) reveals such sentiment in the idea of the paradisal. By coming into consciousness, we travel away from the false self towards the core self, that is, of the configuration of the paradisal self, which for Merton, is also identified with the child mind. On the relation of the paradisal and the child Merton reflects,

> O Paradise, O child's world!
> Where all grass lives
> And all the animals are aware!
> (Merton, 1977, p. 331)

Regarding the child mind in Merton's writings, other writers have explored kindred themes—in particular Del Prete's exploration of the innocence of the "child's voice" (Del Prete, 1990, p. 85); or Labrie's study of the relation of "child's vision" to paradisal consciousness (Labrie, 2001, p. 142). Another parallel with Merton offered in Montessori's (1970) notion of the spiritual child; a notion which echoes Hart's observation of children as contemplatives and Gardner's interpretation of the paradisal child in Merton's thought. For Montessori the ethos of the spiritual child as one that is present within us and seeks to grow. The wonder that children have for the great questions evoking Montessori's kindred notion of cosmic education (Miller, 2010) as one which nurtures the child's interest in the big picture and understanding of their purpose within it.

Reading Hart's idea on children as contemplatives together with kindred notions by Gardner, Del Prete, Labrie and Montessori brought clarity to my childhood memory which was ever present and persistent but whose meaning was never captured. I found silence under a window—a moment which became a vivid and recurring memory but which only much later in adulthood came into meaning in the context of writing a doctoral dissertation, one whose contemplative spirit had been seeded many years earlier in a solitary childhood of silence, dreams and imaginations and which collectively seeded my "spiritual embryo" (Montessori, 1970, p. 18).

Returning to this memory is also a return to my childhood when, I now reflect, this inquiry began. The seeds of inquiry synonymous with the nascent spirituality of my childhood mirrored, for example, within a page from the child's workbook which is used to introduce Chapter 4 of this study. Of such generative moments in one's early growth, Thomas Merton, recalls how reading stories of the Greek heroes were formative to his later life. Of the bearing of those childhood experiences on his later life and work Merton writes in *The Seven Storey Mountain*:

> I unconsciously built up the vague fragments of a religion and of a philosophy, which remained hidden and implicit in my acts, and which, in due time, were to assert themselves in a deep and all-embracing attachment to my own judgement and my own will.
> (Merton, 1998b, p. 12)

Like Merton's story, seemingly innocuous events in childhood were both prescient and formative to my later growth and the beginnings of my inquiry. Spirituality and narrative intertwined; one mirrored in Merton's memories of his early childhood and Clandinin and Connelly's kindred observation of narrative inquiry that it "is a form of living, a way of life" (Clandinin & Connelly, 2000, p. 78).

In my story those "vague fragments" that Merton speaks of foreshadowed my later interests in philosophy and art, fascination with connections and having a global perspective. Seeking the big picture began with my colourful drawings of the planets in my grade school workbook; subsequent study of philosophy and history of ideas and my later transit through the territories of architecture and post-structuralist theory. As I journeyed away from those places the "vague fragments," which were ever present and silently seeding, eventually came into bloom when I transited onto a new terrain of holistic education. During my transit the fragments were fleeting and elusive as when one looks through the window of the speeding train. But once I had journeyed onto and disembarked at this new land, those fragments, which had remained blurred, now came into focus and were embraced within a spirit of welcome.

In *New Seeds of Contemplation*, Merton observes how every moment of one's life is a moment of potentiality. Of such moments he speaks of them as "germs of spiritual vitality" (Merton, 1972, p. 14) which often die if they are not nurtured with freedom and love. In this new place of holistic knowing that I had journeyed onto later in life; those intuitions, predispositions and feelings about connection and creation, that had their earliest manifestations in my childhood found fertile ground. They had seeded within Merton's "good soil of freedom, spontaneity and love" (Merton, 1972, p. 14).

In my childhood, such intuitions were present but unnamed; later as a young university student, the same intuitions were present but unnurtured. Without a map I journeyed, often stumbling and sometimes failing, but in the same moment sustained by curiosity, moments of discovery and an intuitive feeling that the authentic path to reflecting upon connection and self could not but follow such a journey.

The physicist Fritjof Capra observes how we cannot talk about our world without talking about ourselves (Capra, 1991). To Capra's observation I add that if we must talk about ourselves, then one aspect of such discourse is to embrace the presence of the child within us. Within such embrace—one which is nested within the configuration of the spiritual child (Montessori, 1970) or Merton's paradisal child—to know about the world is to honour such presence in our spiritual journey, one which in this inquiry gradually emerged from its vague fragments into meaning. The embrace of the child also revealing an insight into the character of inquiry, that is, how the child's story is originary with the cradle of narrative from which emerges the primordial configuration of one's being and the beginnings of a methodology for inquiry of one's own making.

Transiting From the Ground of Being to Transcendence of Being: A Journey of the Spiritual Embryo

The thesis of the contemplative child guided my reflection upon how the contemplative presence, seeded within childhood, is core to the terrain of self. I co-opt Morgan's notion of a "ground of being experience" to interpret such core. That is, one which is foundational to self: "a benign, foundational ground that is conceived of here as a transconceptual, elemental substrate that founds reality" (Morgan, 2012, p. 43). In her research into students' contemplative experiences Morgan observes how her study participants described it as a core psychic place which felt grounded and peaceful.

As a space of anchorage and transcendence, the ground of being is core to the interior life; and aligns with the notion of the contemplative child. To return to the spiritual seed of childhood feels both a passage towards and one away from the ground of being. That is, one which in my story of a medical examination transited through childhood memories, reflections on Merton and others on Cartesian rationalism. A connecting of stories, workbook images and philosophical reflections which were ever present but had remained unspoken. Like an elevator ride the journey transits down through them towards the ground of being; and having reached it transiting away again towards another domain of transcendent understanding. For Morgan, such movement towards the ground of being is described as a passage through "layers of space" (Morgan, 2012,

p. 49)—one where there is a sense that the journey penetrates through deeper layers of one's interior landscapes. Having transited through them, one arrives within a domain which is marked by what Morgan, following Clark and Wilson (1991) describes as 'perspective transformation' (Morgan, 2012, p. 44).

The perspective shift that is associated with the ground of being evokes kindred sentiments amongst writers in transformative learning such as Burrows' (2015) exploration of the alchemical configuration of interiority or Hart's (2004) observations on how the epistemology of presencing nurtures awareness. Similarly, Gunnlaugson's (2007) exploration of meta-awareness, which he develops in relation to generative discourse, suggests how consciousness is nurtured when the ground of being is touched.

Of meta-awareness, Gunnlaugson describes it as a tumbling through of thoughts and emotions when we become attentive to them within our consciousness. Such movement through psychological states evokes the observation of how the journey towards the ground of being is one of passage—where assumptions which are unconsciously present transmute into awareness (Gunnlaugson, 2007). In my retellings of my early childhood, such passage witnessed within stories which were triggered by lingering memories and reflections upon images within my workbooks. To reflect upon them was to tumble through them, but one wherein such movement also hopefully opened onto a transcendent terrain of awakening.

The Map of the "Contemplative Turn"

> *In philosophy graduate school, the students were required to study a predetermined set of questions in preparation for the comprehensive examination. I recall studying the question on the subject of Kant's Third Antimony on the nature of causality. Although the question was an exemplar of a transmissional pedagogy, it was not sustained by a pedagogy which was transformational in ethos. Cultivating knowledge as wisdom, that is, as ethical, about self-reflection and my being in the world was absent.*
>
> *Later I had cycled onto another terrain, its orbit mapped by a contemplative ethos where I looked inward towards the spark of the authentic self which lit the journey. And as I travelled this new trajectory, its route necessarily visited narrative, its journey onto story mapped by acts of writing and encounters with texts and art which were self-reflective in spirit. Within this new trajectory I began to ponder my ethical relation to the world, and within its contemplative ethos lay the promise of wisdom.*

Standing apart from the analytical methodology in which I had been schooled, my research journey traverses a different methodological terrain, one which is instead mapped by a turn towards the contemplative. Of that turn, the map is marked by the interweaving of ideas—*presencing*, of the *spiritual embryo* that configures our core selves, notions of *transcendence of being*, *alchemical* metaphors for transformation, reflections upon inquiry as *palimpsest*, the aspect of the *silent self*, the presence of feelings as tools which enrich inquiry and notions about how knowing is crafted within movement and *flow* instead of stasis. Together, such ideas configure a paradigm for research which departs from the binary and reductionist ways of analytical thinking by instead following a research path which is holistic, artful and contemplative and which embraces the creation within the fullness of its complexity. Collectively forming a contemplative ethos nested within the personal from which emerges a path onto inquiry of one's own making.

In the introduction to Merton's text *The Inner Experience* (2004), William Shannon, observes how for Merton contemplation did not stand apart from one's life but *is* life (Merton, 2004). Following Merton, the contemplative spirit which my inquiry seeks is entwined with the necessity of my narrative wherein the "summonses to awareness" (Merton, 1966, p. 182) finds its earliest roots within a childhood narrative. The beginnings of inquiry are seeded within the nascent spirituality of childhood.

Reading Palmer (1993), Zajonc (2009) and Miller (2010) in tandem with Merton's autobiographical and contemplative writings nurtured the latter reflection. Of the relation of contemplation to inquiry, I ponder how the relation of the contemplative life to inquiry is not simply to *inquiry* abstracted from the life of the inquirer, but rather to the *life of inquiry* in the same way that Merton speaks of the life of contemplation. That is, it is a life of inquiry which is not separate from how one engages life but is instead continuous with it holistically, in the same way, that for Merton, contemplation is life. Following Merton, I reflect upon how the *life of inquiry* is the *life of contemplation*.

The intimacy with which contemplative inquiry is embedded in life follows in the spirit of Bai et al. (2013) who advocate for pedagogies of higher education which move beyond "objectified learning" to another which encourages "self-cultivation" (Bai et al., 2013, p. 9). That philosophy, for example, should not simply be learned but lived evokes the colloquialism about *walking the talk*; an observation which both touches on how self-cultivation is about integrating learning with life; and how far higher learning today has become removed from such ethos. In addition, touching upon the ethical demand that is placed upon teachers in contemplative studies, perhaps more so than in other departments of a university, to walk the talk, that is, to live the learning we teach.

Engaging with narrative and art nurtures the character of learning integrated with life which is central to the contemplative journey. To engage story through acts of writing nurtures reflection upon self and our relation to others and the creation; while to engage with art, as for example in Burtynsky's landscape photographs, offers an imaginal manifestation of the ethical themes that are embodied in our stories. Art and story turn us towards reflection upon *ourselves*, a turning which seeds the contemplative spirit.

The notion of the *turn* towards the contemplative terrain follows Ergas who, like Bai et al., or Palmer and Zajonc (2010) advocates for a revival of higher education in what he observes as an emerging "contemplative turn" (Ergas,

2016, p. 2, 2019, p. 251) in academic research practices. For Ergas, such practices are broad and expand beyond the narrow rationalist register of Kantian knowing and evoke Merton's kindred observation that spirituality emerges from "the heart of a spiritual person" even when "things are not patently spiritual" (Merton, 1993, p. 90).

For Ergas, Palmer and Merton the contemplative turn is an expansive one whose register of knowledge extends upon Kantianism in, for example, Ergas' critique or the critique of Descartes by Merton. With Palmer they stand apart from binary paradigms configured within sensorial or rationalist methodologies; instead offering *another path*, the contemplative turn, which crosses a different epistemic terrain. That is, one in which the idea of inquiry is reversed (Ergas, 2016) and moves from a position of disencased observation to another where to engage in inquiry is also transformative to the life of the inquirer. Of the transit onto this new orbit, my story of thinking about Kant in philosophy school, which begins my reflection, is offered. I cycled away from the analytic paradigm. Instead, following Palmer, I walked onto my own path to knowledge.

Of the character of that path, Ergas invites us onto a different paradigm which departs from dualism by instead embracing holism and the presence of spirit in inquiry.

> A spiritual research paradigm is not about knowing spirit from without, as an object—that, as stated, or the potential to further advance such knowing, which is already present within current research paradigms. A spiritual research paradigm is rather about looking at the world from the vantage point of spirit itself. It implies accepting a knower who is not confined to reason and senses, but is rather an impregnated being who is also (or fundamentally) spiritual.
> (Ergas, 2016, p. 6)

Ergas' metaphor of the pregnant being speaks to the fullness of the spiritual life; and one which resonates with Merton's observation on how for the contemplative *life is contemplation* (Merton, 2004). The contemplative terrain is a pregnant place where life is embraced within an ethos of holism instead of one of bifurcation and exclusion; and where the ethos of knowledge, as Hadot (2002) observes, extends beyond knowledge of the world, onto a different knowing as a way of being in the world. Herein, contemplative knowing as ethical living where the promise of wisdom lives.

But while the contemplative turn which Ergas offers is a turn towards a pregnant domain, it is also a *re-turn* to such ethos of ancient philosophy which Hadot explores and which is represented, for example, by Socrates *daimon* or the Hindu *Atman*; and later writers such as Rousseau and American Transcendentalists (Miller, 2019) who believed that the promise of enlightenment emerged from the inward turn towards the soul.

It is within such turn and *re-turn* towards a contemplative land that my study is nested. Its transit seeded by a "spiritual embryo" (Montessori, 1970, p. 18) captured within the vision of a child's drawings upon the cosmos, its scintilla for the contemplative journey which followed.

I return to the necessary letter which introduces this study. In it I outline a bricolage formed of childhood memories, encounters with schooling and others with art which sculpt my narrative. The bricolage guided my inquiry. I now look back on the crossing, and the map of my contemplative methodology emerges into view . . .

A methodology of one's own . . .

Formed of a rare map

It turns inward towards the self

The scale of the map determined by the Imperative of my narrative and Presence of the Artful

Its narrative seeded by Montessori's "spiritual embryo"

With my stories the embryo formed into The palimpsest of my being

From the palimpsest I emerge into Consciousness within the dialogical encounter with Acts of writing, texts and art

A discourse with self which stands Apart from the Binary

Towards presence and Transcendence

Towards transformation and the Silent self

A map which emerges within questions and Not final answers

But which seeks

To live in ethical relation to my world

Where wisdom resides

and
Merton's "Sum, I Am"

On the Method of One: The Heart of the Map of Wisdom

The blueprint lays out the plan of the building before it is constructed. It does not emerge as the building is raised.

Unlike the building plan, my map for inquiry was not present when I started, yet the way of inquiry has a paradoxical ethos. Without a map I began the journey on the basis of intuitions, conjectures and predispositions and whose witness was my bricolage. Within this diverse domain, such witnessing was organic as it emerged from within the imperative of my narrative. Its necessity a critical presence as I felt that I could not engage inquiry unless I was witness to the necessity of my story.

As I allowed such necessity to reveal its presence through writing and visual retellings of encounters with art, there slowly but gradually emerged my method. That is, I came onto the view that the stories I retell with words and image; and the tools I use to express are core to my being and method. Within my narrative there is the seed of my method—a methodology of one's own. And from within the unity of narrative and method there emerges my making of meaning in my world.

This study into the relation of wisdom and contemplative inquiry, while being informed by understandings of curriculum as arts-based (Pinar, Reynolds, Slattery, & Taubman, 1995; Barone, 2001; Diamond & Mullen, 2001; Diamond & van Halen-Faber, 2008; Eisner, 2008; Knowles & Cole, 2008; Leavy, 2018) and "autobiographical/biographical text" (Pinar et al., 1995), is also informed by notions of curriculum as contemplative text—one which is nurtured by Merton's writing while also drawing upon the fields of contemplative and transformative studies in education (Zajonc, 2009; Palmer, 1993, 2004; Gunnlaugson, 2007; Dencev & Collister, 2010; Miller, 2014; Hart, 2004; Burrows, 2015; Gunnlaugson, Sarath, Scott, & Bai, 2014; Walsh & Bai, 2015). In this, my study is nested within an methodology which seeks to be embracing and holistic in spirit—one which draws on rich understandings of inquiry as aesthetic, narrative and contemplative exploration while also aligning such understandings with the project by Lin et al. (2016) to sculpt a formal paradigm for spirituality research; with contributions to that project by such researchers as Ergas (2016, 2019) and Miller (2016).

These writers to which I have found my self *returning* in my inquiry sustain the intent of my study to be both artful and contemplative in spirit. Amongst them meditating upon Merton's autobiography *The Seven Story Mountain* (1998b) and his other texts, such as *Raids on the Unspeakable* (1966) where he uses the strategy of dialogical speaking nurtured the intent of crafting an inquiry which drew on narrative while also being contemplative and artful in configuration. By using research tools informed by narrative and dialogical writing, inquiry departs from modes of academic research which are confined by analytical reductionist methodologies set within the third person, and are instead enriched by an expansive strategy which is configured within a first person approach in addition to the third person.

While such strategy departs from the narrow register of a third-person approach, it also foregrounds the question of methodology within a contemplative study, which is broadly put as follow:

> *While a methodology can be viewed as one shared by a community of researchers, can it also be understood as unique to one's self? That is, can the methodology of my inquiry be viewed as intertwined with my life experiences; and if it is, then how do we describe such intertwining? Is the character of method in contemplative studies in curriculum one marked, not by a singular path, but by multiple ones? Each individual follows their own path. And each individual is guided by their own method—one which emerges organically from within—along such path.*

The questions are guided by the reflection that a contemplative method does not stand apart from the life of the researcher; but is present in holistic relation to their lived experience. Instead of being understood as something borrowed from curriculum studies, a contemplative method is viewed as one which emerges organically from within the researcher. That is, one which follows in the spirit of Hart's focus on "on contact over categorization" (Hart, 2008, p. 236) in knowing; or Parker Palmer's advocacy of listening to the "voice of the subject" (Palmer, 1993, p. 98) in inquiry. Departing from the idea of methodology as a tool, which is intimate with inquiry but viewed as separate from the life of the researcher, the idea of methodology in this study follows in the spirit of Hart's and Palmer's holistic observations on a non-binary relation of the researcher to their subject of research.

While such method is holistic in spirit, its discourse opens onto a paradox. To speak of a method of one's own configured in narrative is to speak of a way of doing inquiry which stands apart from understandings of methodology which are configured about scientific method. Herein is foregrounded the paradoxical discourse of methodology, one which Ergas, in the kindred field of spirituality studies in education, describes as a "nonparadigm" (Ergas, 2016, p. 15). Insofar as method is nested within the core of the individual and not within an analytical undersanding of method, its discourse which is shared by spirituality and contemplative studies in education presents a paradox. Its conundrum is explored in greater detail in the section *The Problem of Research Methodology: A Paradoxical Paradigm*.

While the paradox is present, it is not insurmountable and can perhaps be viewed as a necessary component of contemplative inquiry. Centred about the interior life, introspection is at its core; its ethos nurtured by tools for inquiry formed of narrative and the presence of the artful which emerge organically from within. In my inquiry, their presence witnessed by my bricolage, a sundry assemblage of intuitions, feelings and conjectures, which both seeded the journey and transformed into its method.

In his reflections upon the tools used in arts-based research Eisner observes:

> our capacity to wonder is stimulated by the possibilities that new forms of representation suggest. As we learn to think within the medium we choose to use, we also become more able to raise questions that the media themselves suggest; tools, among other things, are also heuristics.
>
> (Eisner, 1997, p. 8)

While Eisner writes from a different paradigm of arts-based research in curriculum studies, his observations are extended onto the terrain of arts-based contemplative inquiry wherein introspection upon self and our ethical relation to others and the creation is seeded by the presence, at its core, of the aesthetical. The spirit of Eisner's observations on the character of the tools we use in inquiry echoed in Parker Palmer's observations on the nature of truth and method in spirituality studies.

> Authentic spirituality wants to open us to truth—whatever truth may be, wherever truth may take us. Such spirituality does not dictate where we must go, but trusts that any path walked with integrity will take us to a place of knowledge.
>
> (Palmer, 1993, p. xi)

Palmer invites us to reflect how getting to the truth is not so much dependent on following prescribed methods of research as it is upon the character of those methods. In this, sharing with Eisner, the personal nature of inquiry as one wherein the choice of tools expand beyond the prescriptive register of empirical methods. Herein, an ethos of research in which its methods are not imposed from without but instead nested within a different terrain sculpted of the personal and transformational, spiritual and contemplative. One wherein the map of wisdom emerges from within its own method; a place where as Kathryn Byrnes, commenting upon the character of contemplative education, observes "begins with the most intimate relationship possible—relationship with oneself" (Byrnes, 2012, p. 36).

Towards the Artist as Atman: The Way of Arts-Based Contemplative Inquiry

With Eisner, the spirit of inquiry is configured about *wonder* and *possibilities*; from which is seeded an ethos of creativity and discovery. In my study, such spirit motivated by my bricolage; from which emerged the view that what is core to the character of inquiry is, extending Eisner, the personal quality of method and how we make it our own. That a methodology can be particular to one's inquiry also resonating with Ergas' (2016), notion of the personal character of paradigms in the making of meaning.

The centrality of narrative in the forging of reality follows Bruner (1991, 1997); and one which is extended in this study onto the metaphor of the palimpsest of being as a unique expression of both one's self and one's method. The self as palimpsest sculpted of my *being-in-narrative*, that is, of the stories we carry and the artful tools with which I choose to study them, following Eisner, and whose meaning, in this study, emerges through retellings both textual and imaginal within the dialogical discourse with one's self.

While at its heart the palimpsest idea is about an understanding of self and how wisdom as ethical knowing emerges from within it; the bricolage I use to explore the palimpsest also speaks to a way of doing inquiry in curriculum studies. At the core of such method is the presence of the personal; it drives the inquiry through imaginal encounters and narrative retellings within a terrain of contemplative introspection. The discourse with self within such moments is central to such reflective witnessing, as is also the dialogical discourse with Merton.

But to speak of wisdom within the terrain of the personal is to offer an interpretation of its character which is one amongst many. Much has been written on the subject of wisdom; to inquire upon wisdom is to engage a rich landscape of scholarship manifold in approach and ranging from discourses scaffolded by, for example, historical research, psychological investigation, literary theory and wisdom studies. But while such discourses inform the study of wisdom, the present study also departs from them. To inquire upon the character of wisdom through the lens of the personal and aesthetical is to engage with a method, introspective in ethos where I place myself within its study. In this, departing from the bifurcation of researcher from the subject of research which characterizes other discourses of wisdom.

Instead my study of wisdom returns to older philosophical exemplars, that is, to archetypes more so than traditions of wisdom and represented for example, by notions of the Hindu *Atman* or Socrates' *daimon*. When Socrates, for example, spoke about the *daimon* or in the Hindu tradition the *Atman* is evoked, such notions configure the "divine spark" that resides within the individual (Miller, 2019, p. 6); and ones which in turn resonated with my reading of Merton's *scintilla* in *Love and Living* whose kindle he viewed as key to the "fruit of education" (Merton, 1979, pp. 9–10) and authentic self.

Merton's scintilla returns to the *daimon* and the *Atman*; in so doing his text offers a bridge which spans such ancient understandings of the *divine spark* with more recent ones reimagined within the intersection of holism, spirituality and contemplation in curriculum studies. The presence of the personal is core to these domains; and the question emerges: *what method(s) captures the ethos of the daimon or Atman today*?

I depart from textual configurations of the Atman within Hindu understandings; and am drawn towards another wherein the spark of the Atman also evokes the figure of the artist. Like the Atman, the artist seeks the inner most self, a place of self knowledge. For the contemplative Merton, this place was the "inmost center . . . a freedom beyond freedom . . . a self beyond all ego" (Merton, 1979, p. 9) while for the artist Fra Angelico, in kindred spirit with Merton, expressed in the imaginal depiction of the centred Christ who is immune to the mocking by his captors. The image of Fra Angelico's fresco is reproduced in Chapter 1 of this study.

That the spirit of the Atman is interpreted as one with that of the artist is reimagined through teachers whose writings are sympathetic to one another; in particular holistic educators like Miller (2019) and Schiller (2014) and those in contemplative studies in education, for example Bai (1997) and Hart (2004) whose welcome to the role of the arts within learning echo that of arts based educators like Eisner (2001, 2002, 2008), McNiff (2008) and Diamond and Mullen (2001) who view artistic process as integral to the understanding of human experience.

These writers, some of whose words are reproduced upon the following image, have been a germinal presence in my inquiry. I keep returning to them, and like my encounter with writing on witness consciousness by Walsh and Bai (2015), they inscribe themselves upon my writing. Except this time I layer their words onto my art: what seems an image of sails, or shells or perhaps an abstract sculpture but whose inspiration emerges from a photograph of the curved walls of a building. Their inscription upon my art becoming my imaginal metaphor for the palimpsest like nature of both inquiry and the character of self as one nested within an ethos of ceaseless accrual and layering. A process wherein the act of extracting meaning from such accrual is also a ceaseless *forming* and *reforming* of my being in that moment and ones which follows. Such moments are generative. Their words inscribe my reflections; the encounter between their words and my art seeding a dialogical conversation with self whose witness is my art and writing in this moment. And from within this discourse the idea of the Atman emerges and is reimagined within the terrain of arts-based contemplative inquiry.

Departing from the narrow epistemological register of scientific method, William Pinar observes, "Reality is a matter of revelation. Subjectivity, not the laboratory, is its site. The artist's studio houses both" (Pinar, 2015, p. xv). Pinar's words return me to my interpretative photograph; and I am reminded how the artist's *revelation* opens onto pathways where scientific method cannot journey. She nurtures Merton's scintilla and transits onto the terrain of the authentic self where the Atman rests. In this, the path of the artist is kindred with that of the Atman. Both paths are personal and emerge from within.

I am present to their journey but must seek my own wherein, following Walsh, Bickel and Leggo, my journey is rooted within the "possibilities and potentialities" offered by research strategies configured by the artful and contemplative (Walsh et al., 2015, p. 1). In my path such possibilities, sculpted by an engaging with the arts, opened onto an expansive epistemological domain which looked beyond the horizon of scientism in which I was trained as a young philosopher many years ago. It could go where science could not; its end point, the seeking of the divine self of the Atman, Fra Angelico's centred Christ, or Merton's *Sum I am*.

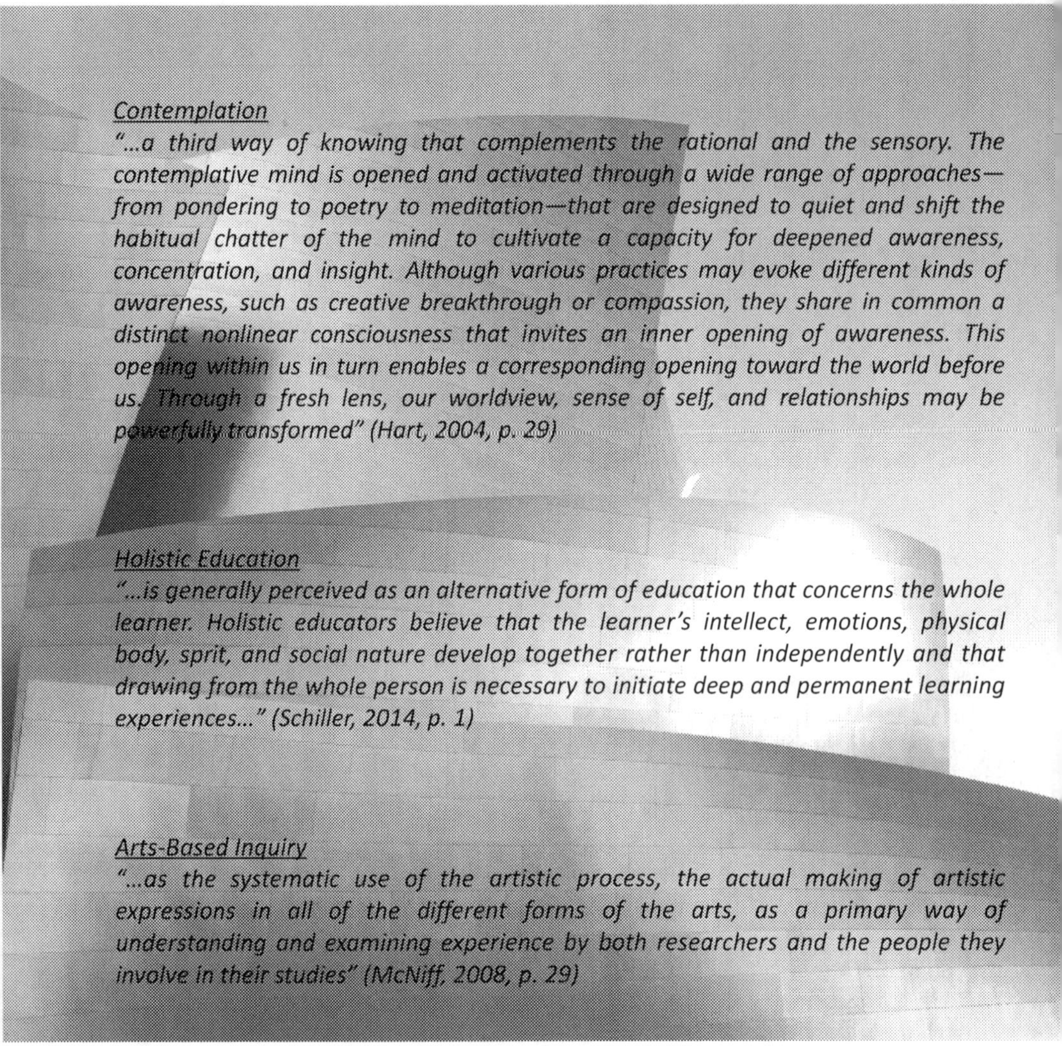

Contemplation
"...a third way of knowing that complements the rational and the sensory. The contemplative mind is opened and activated through a wide range of approaches—from pondering to poetry to meditation—that are designed to quiet and shift the habitual chatter of the mind to cultivate a capacity for deepened awareness, concentration, and insight. Although various practices may evoke different kinds of awareness, such as creative breakthrough or compassion, they share in common a distinct nonlinear consciousness that invites an inner opening of awareness. This opening within us in turn enables a corresponding opening toward the world before us. Through a fresh lens, our worldview, sense of self, and relationships may be powerfully transformed" (Hart, 2004, p. 29)

Holistic Education
"...is generally perceived as an alternative form of education that concerns the whole learner. Holistic educators believe that the learner's intellect, emotions, physical body, sprit, and social nature develop together rather than independently and that drawing from the whole person is necessary to initiate deep and permanent learning experiences..." (Schiller, 2014, p. 1)

Arts-Based Inquiry
"...as the systematic use of the artistic process, the actual making of artistic expressions in all of the different forms of the arts, as a primary way of understanding and examining experience by both researchers and the people they involve in their studies" (McNiff, 2008, p. 29)

Image 5.2 Rossini, G. (2018). *A Formation of My Being-in-the-Moment*. Image Based on Frank Gehry's *Walt Disney Concert Hall*. [Digital Photograph Superimposed With Text]. Los Angeles, California

Source: G. Rossini

The journey of inquiry felt far and complicated when I started it. In the beginning I sought a map for an end point before I started but soon learned that the ethos of the journey remains in questions and less so in answers. As I travelled, its map only began to emerge when I was already in the midst of my crossing. The discovery of a child's notebook along the way revealing that its map was closer than I had thought. It was right in front of me all the time, the possibilities of the journey emerging from within the necessity of my narrative.

I am comforted in this discovery by Merton's words, what I also now name a mantra, which sustained me in my crossing.

If one reaches the point where understanding fails, this is not a tragedy: it is simply a reminder to stop thinking and start looking. Perhaps there is nothing to figure out after all: perhaps we only need to wake up.
(Merton, 1968, p. 53)

Rooted in the necessity of narrative, its *possibilities* for my passage through arts-based contemplative inquiry began to emerge within the intersection of such necessity with research strategies which were ecumenical in spirit. While guided by narrative I also meandered along a spectrum of first- and third-person voices, sometimes inclined towards the third person while at other times within the first person in the dialogical discourse with Merton, and within an ethos which follows Tobin Hart's view of contemplation as a "a third way of knowing that complements the rational and the sensory" (Hart, 2004, p. 29). In this, the third person included within a meta-awareness that I have of its presence in this moment as I reflect upon it within my first person voice. And within this *awareness of my awareness* I begin to integrate the analytical of the third voice within the aesthetical of the first voice within writing that is guided by the personal and introspective spirit of contemplation.

The imperative of narrative is driven by the imperative of such voices and within the meta-awareness I have of them I seek to construct meaning from what emerges from their necessity. A necessity formed of many moments, amongst them: the child's story found in an old workbook, a story about a philosophy student's difficult encounters within the academy, the encounter with Fra Angelico's fresco of *Mocking of Christ* (1440). A bricolage of encounters which seeded my narrative but whose meaning and transformative promise only emerged when I left the shackles of scientism behind and journeyed onto the freedom of the aesthetical.

With this freedom the first- and third-person voices emerge within a sometimes ambiguous presence. While I seek to integrate and draw meaning from them they are imaginally represented by the italics of the first person and the upright font of the third person. And sometimes neither as in this moment when I speak of the third person within the first person voice. Herein, the seeming ambiguity where I imaginally distinguish them; but in the same moment, I also reflect upon and seek to integrate their relation to the other within a contemplative and holistic spirit.

The artful and ecumenical character of contemplative inquiry allows for such ambiguity. Its ethos of openness to human experience and the tools we use to decipher it encourages meaning making in a way which would not be possible had I remained within a reductionist paradigm. It allows the philosopher, who had been once chastised for not following the canon of analytical philosophy, to reclaim his being as philosopher. A reclaiming, which in addition became an act of pedagogical resistance wherein, as Gianna Di Rezze observes "to resist is to speak in our own voice about our lived experience" (Di Rezze, 2000, p. 76).

Through art making, which in my story involves doing photography, I construct meaning of human experience in part through the imaginal presence, but the philosopher who forms part of my narrative also seeks to understand the character of and motivation for its construction; a discovery of a child's workbook, for example, a primordial place for beginning such search. And hence the philosopher's voice, expressed in the third person or a synthetic voice when combined with the first as I am with you in this moment. But whose *witness consciousness*, co-opting Walsh's and Bai's (2015) language, is also centred about a dialogical discourse with self. That is, from within an inner place, a layered narrative from which is sculpted my being-in-palimpsest; and not from a canon imposed from without.

Of the character of contemplation, Hart writes of how it nurtures "awareness, concentration and insight" and observes how the turn onto self is also an opening onto the world beyond (Hart, 2004, p. 29). Following Hart, *I turned* inwards in order to *return* to the world. As I ventured upon the contemplative terrain, the turns I took within it were my own, its method seeded deep in the necessity of my narrative and whose witnessing emerged through dialogical writing and aesthetical encounters.

In the spirit of the Atman, the way of the artist turns us inwards onto Merton's *scintilla* wherein the authentic self resides. The aesthetical and dialogical discourse with self guides us towards this place, towards the promise of wisdom as ethical knowing. And in this, the spirit of the Atman is reimaged with that of the artist.

6 The Imaginal as a Pathway Onto Wisdom

A Prolegomenon for a Classroom Practice

Image 6.1 Burtynsky, Edward. (2000). *Manufacturing No. 18. Cankun Factory, Zhangzhou Fujian Province, 2005*. [Chromogenic Print]

Source: © Edward Burtynsky, Courtesy of Nicholas Metivier Gallery, Toronto

> *From an encounter with Burtynsky's images in a graduate seminar on educational research methodologies, there emerged the primordial thesis that the imaginal presence has the potential to nurture wisdom—a view which builds uponHadot's (2002) view of wisdom, not simply as knowledge of the world, but as a mode of being within it.*
>
> *Hadot's view is reimagined in the following questions: How can the encounter with the arts nurture reflection upon our ethical relation to the world? That is, how can wisdom, as ethical knowledge, be taught through the arts? How can art nurture our mode of being in the world?*

158   *The Imaginal as a Pathway Onto Wisdom*

> *Meditation upon artists' work, such as Burtynsky's photograph of a factory complex in China shown in Image 6.1 or his image Navajo Reservation/Suburb: Phoenix Arizona, USA (2011) guided my initial reflections upon this question, as did exemplars by other artists; in particular Fra Angelo's fresco, The Mocking of Christ (Convent of San Marco, Florence, 1440); and the performance piece by Marina Abramovic, The Artist is Present (Chermayeff & Dupre, 2012).*
>
> *Also guiding me onto this question were researchers in wisdom studies; in particular those who explore the narrative character of wisdom as do Ferrari, Weststrate, and Petro (2013). They retell a story of the Buddha; and I am reminded of how the imaginal, like the text, can also convey a wisdom story. Burtynksy's image of a bifurcated urban and rural landscape in his Arizona photograph evoke ethical and cultural reflection upon our relation to self, others and the environment. The narrative spirit of the artist's image is kindred with that of the text. It resonates with Ferrari et al.'s observation upon the retelling of the Buddha "a story like this invites the reader to transport him or herself into the storyworld, simulating the experience firsthand and provoking insight about fundamental personal matters, and so helps develop personal wisdom" (Ferrari et al., 2013, p. 138).*

The field of wisdom studies is informed by diverse academic disciplines—in part by historical study (Hadot, 2002; Curnow, 2015) and secondly by its emergence as a subject of psychological investigation (Baltes, 2004; Sternberg & Jordan, 2005; Ferrari et al., 2013; Bruya & Ardelt, 2018). The recently published anthology *The Cambridge Handbook of Wisdom* (Sternberg & Glück, 2019) is a recent testament to such emergence, one which engages the study of wisdom from philosophical, sociological and neurobiological perspectives in addition to its psychological study.

Within such registers, though, the exploring of the relation of wisdom to the artful is largely absent. While a central question of the psychological study of wisdom is whether wisdom can be taught, the presence of the imaginal seems not germane to such question.

To ponder, therefore, the question of whether wisdom can be taught through the arts is to engage a problem which departs from the historical and psychological registers which at present scaffold the academic study of wisdom. In view of its absence from such discourses, the question of art's relation to wisdom enters onto an unchartered terrain. My suggestions for its crossing are therefore offered as a prolegomenon which I hope will stimulate exploration amongst researchers in wisdom studies, curriculum studies in education and the arts.

While the question stands on the periphery of wisdom studies, it is not removed from it entirely. The topic of wisdom's relation to art turns upon the fundamental question that is posed by Ferrari and Potworowski in their anthology *Teaching for Wisdom*. To ask *"Can wisdom be taught, or at least fostered?"* (Ferrari & Potworowski, 2008, *p. v)* is central to my own study. To ask *"Can wisdom be taught, or at least fostered" through the imaginal*? extends the foundational question that was originally posed by them.

The strategy towards the question of wisdom's relation to art is in turn extended onto the methodological problem for teaching wisdom through the arts. That is, in like manner that the question emerges from wisdom studies, so are also the methodological possibilities for a classroom practice. Such possibilities are expressed through the following question: what can we extract from the methods and findings of wisdom studies which would begin to inform a classroom practice whose focus is wisdom's association with the arts?

The exploration of this question is ecumenical in spirit. That is, while it draws upon wisdom studies, in particular the work of Ferrari and Potworowski (2008), Weststrate (2019) and Sternberg and Glück (2019), it also reimagines their ideas, in particular the notion of *"personal wisdom"* (Ferrari et al., 2013, p. 137) and the centrality of *"self-reflection"* (Weststrate, 2019, p. 500) from the perspective of contemplative studies in education.

The methodological paradigm for wisdom studies, following Ferrari and Weststrate is a scientific one; while the ethos of method in the contemplative field is not guided by scientific reductionism and is instead, following Hart (2004) expansive with regard to the tools we use in inquiry and holistic in vision. But while differences of method are evident, there are also synergetic moments between them; ones which are reimagined within the terrain of "trading zones" (Ferrari & Weststrate, 2013, p. 334), that is, a descriptor of method, originating with the philosopher of science Peter Galison, to describe the exchange of information amongst researchers when there is not common agreement. While the descriptor is used to characterize such exchange within a research discipline, it is broadly reinterpreted in this study to apply to exchanges *between* disciplines as I am in this moment with you as I seek to draw linkages between contemplative studies in education and the psychological study of wisdom.

Wisdom Emergent from the Self Reflective Mirror of Narrative

A striking exemplar of such interdisciplinary bridge is seen in the metaphor of the mirror used by the psychologist of wisdom Nic Weststrate to explore the self-reflective ethos of wisdom (Weststrate, 2019), and Walsh and Bai, in contemplative studies in education, who write poetically of the mirror in *Writing Witness Consciousness* (2015) as a self-reflective trope for witnessing onto self.

To engage with narrative is to engage an organic path to self-reflection. It is a mirror which illumes a reflective emergence from the personal. For Weststrate, such emergence is illustrated through a Renaissance pictorial depicting the allegory of fortune and wisdom; and wherein wisdom is represented by a female figure that holds the "mirror of wisdom" (Weststrate, 2019, p. 500). While the figure of fortune is blind, *Lady Wisdom* sees her image reflected in the mirror and framed by cosmological references to planets and stars. Herein, the promise of wisdom is nested within the self-reflective turn. For Walsh and Bai the mirror, like *Lady Wisdom's* mirror, is a turning onto self, a self-reflective domain "a mirror that mirrors other mirrors" (Walsh & Bai, 2015, p. 25) which is witness to consciousness through writing; and which I also view and extend as a witnessing onto the promise of wisdom.

The story of the mirror, one found within a psychological study of wisdom while a second in writing upon the character of contemplative reflection, accords well with the ethos of wisdom as one whose core is configured about self-reflection and the kindred presences of the personal and narrative. Within the psychological research paradigm Weststrate views self-reflection "as the intentional and effortful processing of autobiographical experience" (Webster, 2019, p. 502); an understanding which is core to psychological theories of wisdom. In the Berlin Model, for example, such centrality reimagined through the notion of "life review"—a thesis which is synergistic with other theoretical descriptors, in particular Webster's wisdom model wherein "' reminiscence and reflectiveness'" is key; or Staudinger's thesis of "'life reflection'" (Weststrate, 2019, pp. 504–505). A kindred thesis is the *MORE* wisdom model proposed by Glück and Bluck and consisting of four markers: "*m*astery, *o*penness, *r*eflectivity and *e*motion regulation and empathy" (Glück & Bluck, 2013, p. 75). As with the preceding theories the aspect of reflection is central to the *MORE* model of wisdom.

Characterizations of the reflective process in these models is generative for beginning to scaffold a pedagogical theory of wisdom's relation to the arts. Weststrate's theory of "self-reflective processing modes" (Weststrate, 2019, p. 507), and in particular, the relation of narrative to the notion of "*contextual coherence,*" is instructive in this regard. Weststrate observes

> *Contextual coherence* concerns the setting of the narrative, such as time and place, and information concerning the story's characters. Contextually coherent narratives are richly detailed and vivid, sometimes evoking a mental image so complete that the reader feels transported directly into the story.
>
> (Weststrate, 2019, p. 508)

Narrative is formidable, the construction of "a mental image" an expression of its power; and one which in turn invites extension onto the relation of narrative with the imaginal. In this study such relation is developed in part through the notion of "explorative processing" which is co-opted from Weststrate's study of wisdom and described as "a relatively prolonged and effortful process of examining the deeper meaning of an event" (Weststrate, 2019, p. 509). It involves a critical self-reflectiveness about the events which configures one's life from which emerge, observes Weststrate, "paradigmatic or conceptual shifts in thinking about the self, others, or the world" (Weststrate, 2019, p. 509).

While such notion is developed within a domain scaffolded by narrative and autobiographical writing, its ethos is synergistic with the imaginal encounter. Self-reflective writing which emerges from narrative through a process of *exploratory processing*, following Weststrate; or *witness writing consciousness*, following Walsh and Bai, is a mirror onto self. But if story is also formed within acts of seeing within encounters with art, or moments of *contextual coherence* when the imaginal is stoked from within, then how does the imaginal also participate within the mirror of self?

The story which begins this chapter about a seminar encounter with images, such as those by Burtynsky of urbanistically complicated or distressed landscapes, is illustrative in interpreting this question. The encounter with such images sustained moments of *exploratory processing* wherein reflection upon our ethical relation with the environment and others, through dialogue and pictorial responses from seminar participants, was also generative of reflections upon self. A detailed retelling of the imaginal encounter with Burtynsky's images is explored in the sections which follow.

The encounter with the imaginal seeds our narrative and together with autobiographical writing, nurtures a reflective ethos which guides us onto and mirrors the self. Herein, the imaginal standing with the autobiographical in the power it has to foster reflection upon ethical relation with others and the creation while, in the same moment, turning us inwards towards reflection upon our own self. Of such power, Thomas Moore, in his advocacy of holistic learning writes of how the arts offer a "depth and layered presentation of experience" (Moore, 2019, p. 54). The experience of the artful guiding us onto the depth which Moore speaks of from which emerges the "mirror of wisdom" (Weststrate, 2019, p. 500).

Wisdom as Narrative-Imaginal Stimulus

The mirror of wisdom is a reflective metaphor; its ethos for an understanding of wisdom evoking an imaginal presence but one whose core is also nested within a narrative domain. Herein suggesting a view of wisdom which is expansive in character, that is, one in which a narrative configuration of wisdom is also informed by an imaginal terrain. While such association is not central to the questions of wisdom studies, the developing of such linkage in this study builds upon Ferrari et al. (2013) characterization of personal wisdom.

Of the character of wisdom, they observe "personal wisdom involves narrative at its core" (Ferrari et al., 2013, p. 138); an understanding which stands apart from a second view of wisdom which they also observe, following Bruner, as paradigmatic or theoretical wisdom. Such distinction foregrounds that what is key to the character of personal wisdom is an inward turn where wisdom emerges organically from within reflection upon one's narrative.

For Ferrari et al. the nature of such turn is configured about two markers. The first, "narrative simulations individuals create of (a) hypothetical situations that may come to pass and (b) situations lived by others" while the second involves reflection upon stories which emerge from one's life experiences and which they describe as "autobiographical reasoning" (Ferrari et al., 2013, p 138). While such characterizations of personal wisdom are explored through written retellings of stories in their account, it is also accords well with a reimagining of personal wisdom as one which is also informed by the presence of the imaginal.

The notion of "narrative simulations" is co-opted here in part to explore such reimagining. Ferrari et al.'s understanding of the character of such narratives is instructive. They observe:

> According to Oatley (1999; Mar & Oatley, 2008), literary narratives are simulations of the real world: "Narrative fiction models life, comments on life, helps us to understand life in terms of how human intentions bear on it" (Mar & Oatley, p. 173). By projecting ourselves mentally into such simulations, we can extract general and personal wisdom from them. In understanding a story, readers or listeners participate in a meaning-making process whereby they "read between the lines" of the story, interpreting and analyzing their lived experiences to achieve a deeper meaning in the text, and through this process, extract lessons to live by.
>
> (Ferrari et al., 2013, p. 147)

Their understanding of the literary narrative is extended onto the notion of the *imaginal narrative*. As with the literary narrative, the imaginal whose exemplar in this study is the photography of Edward Burtynsky, opens onto experiences which following Ferrari et al. are not readily accessible (Ferrari et al., 2013). Like the literary, the pictorial exemplar offers a narrative about a life moment which allows the viewer to *project* themselves into the depiction. And from within such acts of immersion a "meaning-making process" is engaged which allows for "'reading between the lines' of the story" (Ferrari et al., 2013, p 147). From the encounter with the pictorial, an inward turn is fostered wherein the witness to the image also encourages a witnessing onto one's own narrative experiences. A witnessing wherein, following Ferrari et al., life lessons begin to emerge.

A theme which is shared by wisdom researchers is how such life lessons are associated with difficult or stressful narratives (Webster, 2019; Ferrari & Kim, 2019; Weststrate, Bluck, & Glück, 2019). In their investigation of the relation between wisdom and life experience Weststrate et al., for example, observe "emotionally negative and culturally non-normative event memories contained the highest levels of meaning-making (i.e. lessons, insights), suggesting that these types of events may provide an important facilitative context for wisdom development (Weststrate et al., 2018)" (Weststrate et al., 2019, p. 109).

Such observation accords well with the thesis of the relation of wisdom to the imaginal narrative, in particular, pictorial depictions of distressed landscapes such as those by the photographer Edward Burtynsky. A seminar encounter with his images evoked students' responses which spanned global narratives about ecological, social and political distress to others wherein such universal themes were also accompanied by personal responses of anxiety. Personal narratives were touched by the stories evoked in the encounter with the difficult pictorial; and within such moments narrative enters into relation with the pictorial and life reflection is fostered in the encounter with the latter. Like the encounter with narrative, the imaginal presence, becoming an opening onto self-reflection.

While the notion of the *imaginal simulation* extends Ferrari et al.'s notion of narrative simulation, it is not proposed in this study as part of a scientific strategy whose intent is to predict or measure. In this regard, a distinction is to be made between the notions of *imaginal simulation* and an *imaginal stimulus*. In theory a marker of imaginal simulation can form part of an empirical model for assessing wisdom. As this descriptor evokes a methodology which is not mine in this study I choose to follow the less restrictive and more phenomenologically expansive notion of the *imaginal stimulus* to describe how the encounter with the artful nurtures self-reflection. It is hoped that the term is closer to a holistic and contemplative ethos of connection, that is, one which recognizes that images, such as Burtynsky's, are not pictorial simulations, but instead harsh depictions of what humanity has done to an environment with which we are in intimate relation.

In the story which introduces this chapter, encounters with his images encouraged discourse amongst students. Within the bleak reality of broken landscapes that are depicted in Burtynsky's images, there emerged reflective conversations, both oral and visual, that both touched and carried us onto ethical reflection upon our relation to environment and others. The encounter with the image returned us onto our own stories; the intensity of the mirror an imaginal "witness consciousness" (Walsh & Bai, 2015, p. 24) to our hopes and fears.

"Think[ing]–Aloud" With the Imaginal

While the notion of the *imaginal stimulus*, as an element in the fostering of wisdom, extends Ferrari et al.'s research, it also draws upon the kindred strategy of *vignettes* in the Berlin Wisdom Paradigm. In the Berlin model, vignettes are used to measure wisdom, wherein a life problem is presented and test participants are asked to think through the problem out loud. Participant responses are in turn scored in accordance to a wisdom scale from 1 to 7. While the "think-aloud technique" (Stange & Kunzman, 2008, p. 27) forms part of a method of measuring wisdom within the Berlin model, it is also an apt descriptor to apply to scenarios where participants think aloud about life questions; but within a different context wherein their observations emerge from either *vignette-images* which are presented to them, images which they themselves craft, or a combination of these. Interestingly, the possibilities for the use of such strategy in wisdom research is starting to emerge, in particular in the work of Kunzmann, who has proposed using film clips, instead of vignettes which are text-based, to study people coping with life problems (Kunzmann, 2019). While the thinking aloud method within the Berlin model is intended as a measure rather than a characterization of how wisdom develops; the retelling that introduces this chapter is offered as an extension of this strategy but from within a developmental understanding of wisdom (Weststrate, 2019) and the contemplative perspective of this study, as opposed to one focused about its measurement.

In the retelling which introduces this section graduate students are presented images of distressed or urbanistically complex landscapes by the photographer Edward Burtynsky and are asked to capture their responses to them pictorially on 11" × 17" sheets of paper which were then pinned to the classroom wall for shared viewing. With the artist's images and student observations acting as starting points a conversation ensued—a *thinking aloud*—amongst students and instructor which traversed a broad range of social, political and cultural themes.

The students' responses to Burtynsky's images invite reflection upon how encounters with art within the classroom nurture us to towards contemplations upon the core questions of life (London, 2004); or upon our way of being in the world where wisdom resides (Hadot, 2002). In transiting onto such contemplative moments, the imaginal helps us. Images, such as Burtynsky's, are clear and colourful and easily accessible. Their narratives are seemingly straightforward and engage us easily but become complicated and nuanced in a gentle way once we begin to ponder them. They draw us in easily, in the image of the factory which begins this chapter, the line of the pavement which transects the image softly guiding us into its narrative. Following Merton, the imaginal draws us onto awareness (Merton, 1966).

Seminar students responded to Burtynsky's landscape images with observations about globalization, environment, culture, creativity and the power of art. Their encounter with them evoked observations which were global and relational in spirit and graphical in addition to being textual. Within some of their responses, the figure of the earth is central with observations which radiated about it, depictions revealing a holistic recognition of connection. Other comments upon the images evoked feelings amongst the seminar participants with some finding the images too strong. The power of the image was formidable; their feelings were accompanied with observations about the power of the artist and soft complaints that I could have "found hopeful images on globalization" (Student Observations, 2011).

Researchers in the fields of contemplative and environmental education have recognized the pedagogical possibilities of such images for student engagement and reflection in the classroom. Environmental educators, such as Gary Babiuk have recognized in Burtynsky's images a powerful pedagogical presence guiding students in their reflections upon humanity's relationship to the environment (Babiuk, 2014), one which has been complicated by issues of environmental damage, climate change and social unrest. Such issues underscore for Babiuk an urgency which threatens our survival; and one which he addresses through his advocacy of an "education for sustainability" (Babiuk, 2014, p. 27). In his appeal for such pedagogy, Babiuk recommends programs offered by UNESCO, in particular, *Education for Sustainable Development* and *Teaching and Learning for a Sustainable Future* (UNESCO, n.d.). Informed by Miller's notions of connection, inclusion and balance (Babiuk, 2014) education for sustainability is understood holistically and enriched by notions of interdisciplinarity; critical engagement and participation in decision making; and a multitude of pedagogical tools including drama, art, and play (Babiuk, 2014).

Interestingly, a kindred view is shared amongst some researchers in wisdom studies such as Ferrari and Kim (2019) who view education for sustainability as one, amongst several strategies for fostering wisdom in the classroom. Like Babiuk, they look to the UNESCO programs as models for encouraging children to reflect upon contemporary issues of sustainability, environment and citizenship (Ferrari & Kim, 2019). Their wisdom project is also holistic in ethos as they draw upon, as does Babiuk, Miller's *The Holistic Curriculum* (2008); and its theory of connection as one configured by the domains of intuition, mind-body, soul, community, earth and subject. For Ferrari and Kim, Miller's model is interpreted as foundational to the several definitions that have been advanced by researchers in wisdom studies and the basis for teaching of what they view the "Six Wisdom Connections" (Ferrari & Kim, 2019, p. 357).

The encounter with the imaginal and in particular landscape pictorials, such as those by Burtynsky, guide us onto the connections which Babiuk, Miller, Ferrari and Kim contemplate. In the image that begins this chapter we see rows of regimented workers, a depiction which nurtures reflection upon the character of soul connection and community connection. Other student observations about connection, as seen through the encounter with Burtynsky's images, are summarized in the table which follows.

Burtynsky's photographs are powerful imaginal meditations upon humanity's relation to environment in particular, which nurture a kindred meditation about our relation to self and others in general. They seed ethical reflection upon our conduct and by nurturing a discourse about life questions guide us onto the terrain of wisdom. A terrain whose contemplative map emerges from the encounter with the pictorial—one which extends the strategy of *thinking aloud* from the Berlin model wherein the engaging with the pictorial, in like manner to the textual narrative, stimulates ethical reflection upon life questions.

The strategy of *thinking aloud*, which is reimagined from the Berlin wisdom model, accords well with an imaginal strategy for fostering ethical reflection in the classroom. Encounters with pictorial narratives of distressed landscapes, such as those depicted in Burtynsky's photographs, encouraged discursive engagement upon life questions. The engaging with the pictorial, through discussion and graphical responses from students, in turn fostering moments of learning which became ethical in ethos.

While the strategy of *thinking aloud* is co-opted from the Berlin model, it is one amongst kindred strategies for nurturing wisdom through the imaginal

> *"Global Village"*
> *Marshall McLuhan*
> *Education tied to economic agenda*
> *More Injustice. How much have we really progressed?*
> *Loss of individual thought/creativity*
>
> ---
>
> *How long will this last?*
> *Where is the sun?*
> *Is this going as planned?*
>
> ---
>
> *Implications of technology*
> *Language of corporations*
>
> ---
>
> *Globalization making world smaller*
> *Who is in control, 1 percent*
> *Environmentalism*
> *Corporatization of cultural, political, economical*
> *Destruction of villages*
>
> ---
>
> *Stark Images*
> *Hope?*
> *Power in the art of the photographer*
> *Need art*
> *Question: Could John have found hopeful images on globalization?*

which can be extracted from the domain of wisdom studies. Amongst these, for example, is the notion of "lifespan contextualism"—a criteria for wisdom also extracted from the Berlin model and underscored by the view that life events are enmeshed in contexts, such as the cultural, familial and biographical (Stange & Kunzmann, 2008, p. 26; Staudinger, 2019, p. 184). Such expansive understanding of wisdom in turn inviting the question—how can the criteria of lifespan *contextualism* within the Berlin model be informed by the arts?

A kindred question can be posed with Staudinger's thesis of "life reflection"—a model for wisdom wherein reflection is nurtured within the recall of life events followed by their analysis (Staudinger, 2013, p. 6; Weststrate, 2019, p. 505). An element of "life reflection" is Staudinger's notion of "comparison processes" where reflection is fostered through, for example, comparison of one's life path with others; and one wherein such comparative exercise is facilitated when done with another (Staudinger, 2013, p. 7). While such aspect of life reflection is fostered through comparative questions and

The Imaginal as a Pathway Onto Wisdom 167

Image 6.2 Unknown. (2011). *Student Group Reflections on Paper of a Burtynsky Photograph.* [Digital photograph by G. Rossini]

Source: G. Rossini

168 *The Imaginal as a Pathway Onto Wisdom*

within dialogue with another, can the imaginal form part of that comparative ethos? Can the encounter with the imaginal within a comparative process akin to the one proposed by Staudinger and one which is also modelled by way of example in the students' encounter with Burtynsky's images of distressed landscapes, stimulate life reflection?

The spirit of such questions is extended onto other proposals within wisdom studies; in particular, Sternberg's "Balance Theory of Wisdom" (Sternberg et al., 2008, p. 38) which is centred about a set school curriculum wherein structured lessons involving classroom units in history are adapted as a way of encouraging students to reflect upon how to live the ethical life; and less structured approach by Reeve et al. (2008) in which the teaching of wisdom is centred about a different ethos of student collaboration. As with the earlier proposals the question is posed—how can such approaches be adapted to include the presence of the arts in fostering reflection upon the ethical life?

The question is focused when applied onto the proposal by Reeve et al. (2008) and viewed through the thesis of the personal character of method in inquiry which is explored elsewhere in this study and named the *method of one*. For Reeve et al. wisdom is fostered not necessarily from exercises which are assigned to children but instead from a different process which is centred upon the child and which emerges organically from within. Wisdom emerges within an open process marked by what they observe as, for example, "epistemic agency" wherein children identify their own goals; the exploration of "improvable ideas;" and the fostering of inquiry which is not delimited but about "idea diversity" (Reeve et al., 2008, pp. 80–81). While such process is configured within collaborative interactions within the classroom, its character resonates with the contemplative view of inquiry in this study as one which emerges organically from within a terrain where the individual uncovers their own path for its crossing.

Towards an Imaginal Re-Imagining of Wisdom

Of the character of wisdom's relation to self-reflection Weststrate observes how little it is understood (Weststrate, 2019). To this conundrum we may add the kindred problem of sculpting a pedagogy of wisdom informed by the relation of self-reflection to the imaginal. Methodological exemplars, such as *contextual coherence, exploratory processing, thinking aloud, life-span contextualism*, and *narrative simulation* are co-opted along with others from the study of the psychology of wisdom; and together with my own reimagining of the latter notion as *narrative-imaginal stimulus* are offered for beginning to think about a pedagogy of wisdom enriched by the presence of the arts. From the "'trading zones'" (Ferrari & Weststrate, 2013, p. 334) of the psychological study of wisdom I assemble such methodological bricolage; and offer it as a prolegomenon for beginning to reflect upon how the "mirror of wisdom" (Weststrate, 2019, p. 500) is one whose reflexivity, while nested in narrative, is also enriched by the presence of the imaginal.

7 The Journey of *Gionitus* and *"Newton's Child"*

Concluding Reflections on the Imperative of the Personal and Aesthetical in Arts-Based Contemplative Inquiry

The Story of the Watchmaker and Artist

Of the watchmaker's story...

During the early modern period of science, theologians and philosophers seeking to account for the existence of God looked to the creation and reasoned that its complexity was proof of a divine presence. The creation was viewed as a finely tuned watch and God its watchmaker (McMahan, 2008, p. 79; Paley, 2009, pp. 1–4, 2009).

While the watchmaker argument persists today as a strand of theological thinking, the argument from intelligent design upon which it is based evokes imaginal depictions of the creation from the Middles Ages. Then, the creation of the Bible story was a closed and bounded vessel; its determinate cosmology witnessed by Ptolemaic astronomy—one wherein the known celestial bodies circled the earth within fixed circular orbits. Its imaginal presence similar to wheels of the clock. Like the clock mechanism, the creation was a fixed instrument which was bounded and known.

Since then our microscopes and telescopes have revealed a different creation story. Bilocality in quantum theory; counterintuitive notions of the existence of universes other than our own; the folded space of relativity science; and immense measures for the size of the universe reveal a much more complex creation—one which defies the watchmaker's skill.

Instead of being framed by limits, the creation seems unbounded. Instead of remaining within the known, it remains within the unknown. Instead of a closed cosmology, we remain within a modality of wonder and questioning. Instead of stasis and order, there is discovery, surprise, contradiction and beauty. Far from being a space of stasis, the creation is rich in becoming.

What standing does the watchmaker have to such creating?

The watch has a beginning and end defined by the hours on its face. How can the timepiece be configured if that which is to be timed cannot be timed?

I wonder if the watchmaker has been falsely privileged in the creation. If God is a watchmaker, then to equate her as such would be to diminish her standing in relation to the creation.

Opposite the watchmaker stands the artist's story . . .
The creation is rich and boundless, timeless and unknown, transient and unsettled—a space of unceasing wonder and beauty. What presence could have crafted such a place? If the watchmaker cannot capture such ethos, then do we open ourselves onto other possibilities? If God is not a watchmaker, is she instead an artist?

Of the wonder and beauty of nature Merton observes,

> *Nay, I see that God is in all creatures,*
> *Man and Beast, Fish and Fowle,*
> *And every green thing from the highest cedar to the*
> *Ivey on the wall;*
> *And that God is the life and being of them all . . .*
>   (Merton, 1969, p. 66)

While the cosmologists estimate that the creation, that Merton meditates upon, is 13.6 billion years old they also speculate that it emerged from a primordial scintilla. Every moment of being proceeding from the initial spark—what they also call the "big bang" when the light of creation first flickered. From that primal moment, galaxies have been sculpted, stars lit and planets formed.

Collectively, with the stars and earth, we have come into being within continuous moments of light. We have transited into creation together within an aesthetical trajectory of becoming.

Every moment of being feels within such cosmological lineage and every moment within such lineage is a point of creation within the creation journey.

As I write I look through my window surveying the city and tree canopies which frame it and ponder how the present moment is nested within such lineage—one which connects us collectively to the creation and primal spark of 13.6 billion years ago.

I meditate upon such lineage and reflect that what is fundamental to such presence are continuous moments of becoming formed of light and nested within an aesthetical presence. The spirit of the artist is manifest; and we are witness to the original scintilla within such presence.

The Healing of the Splinter

Tobin Hart observes how humanity has been "splintered from the divine" (Hart, 2019a, p. 26); an observation which mirrors the story of the artist and watchmaker which introduces my concluding reflections. Science and art are fragmented, a division which Hart views as artificial, as humanity is innately drawn to beauty. When beauty is divorced so are we from the divine. But when beauty is embraced Hart, referencing Plotinus, observes how "our soul carries its imprint and in beauty we get a glimpse of that divinity, our true home base. Whenever we get a sense of the perfection of that other world, our soul strives to reunite with it" (Hart, 2019a, p. 26).

Hart's observations upon Plotinus are evocative and guide reflection upon the ethos of knowledge. To speak of "our true home base" as one configured of beauty and divinity foregrounds the interpretation of such domain as a fundamental epistemological presence, that is, as an account of the character of knowledge which is radically configured about the aesthetical, yet one which also remains within an epistemological tussle with empiricism. Following Kuhn's (1975) characterization of paradigms, the analytical-empiricist lens constitutes the dominant paradigm for knowledge today. We default to its dominance yet are unaware, extending Hart's observations, of its reductive outcomes. Art is excised from science, as is also beauty from the divine. Disintegration rather than connection configures such terrain, its presence as the dominant epistemological paradigm foregrounded, for example, in Palmer's and Zajonc's criticisms of higher education as an "epistemology of separation" (Zajonc, 2006, p. 1744) and in my own encounters with the academy which I reflect upon in Chapter 1.

The call for a reintegrated epistemological paradigm which Palmer, Zajonc and Hart share departs from the reductionist lens by being instead nestled within a different epistemological register enriched by the presence of the aesthetical. While the analytical-empiricist lens remains formidable as a method of knowing, its standing with regard to this alternative epistemological register is not insurmountable. In his text *On Knowing: Essays for the Left Hand* the psychologist Jerome Bruner (1997), for example, ponders the character of mathematical beauty by way of the work of the theoretical physicist and philosopher Henri Poincaré. Bruner contemplates the character of such beauty within a discourse shared with reflections upon Dostoevsky and Picasso. In kindred manner Hart also looks to Poincaré who sees the spirit of science within an aesthetical discourse (Hart, 2019a). Poincaré observes:

> The scientist does not study nature because it is useful to do so. He studies it because he takes pleasure in it, and he takes pleasure in it because it is beautiful. If nature were not beautiful it would not be worth knowing, and life would not be worth living.
> (Poincaré, 1914, p. 22)

It is knowledge as beauty, but also as shape shifting and fluid, its ethos captured within a domain of incessant formation, reshaping and becoming, one alluded to in the creation story which opens this chapter and in the story of the first astronomer, Gionitus and those that followed him—"perpetual seeker[s]" (Miller, 2016, p. 138) in the expansive and ceaseless journey of knowledge.

It is a story which tussles with expectations of the indubitable presence of empirical knowledge and whose character is instead captured, for example, in Bruner's observation upon the analytical philosopher W. O. Quine who believed that "physics is 99 percent speculation and 1 percent observation" (Bruner, 1986, p. 14) or in the writer Ben Okri who, in kindred spirit, appeals for an expansive and unbounded ethos of knowing. In language which is familiar with Parker Palmer's observation about those who lead "one-eyed lives" (Palmer, 1993, p. xxiii) Okri, in his essay *Newton's Child*, observes:

> We were not born with one eye, with only one thought in our heads, and with only one direction to travel. When we look out on the world with all its multiplicity of astonishing phenomena, do we see that only one philosophy can contain, explain, and absorb everything? I think not. The universe will always be greater than us. Our mind therefore should be like Keats' thoroughfare, through which all thoughts can wander. It should also be a great cunning net that can catch the fishes of possibility.
>
> (Okri, 1997, p. 19)

Okri's observations along with those of Poincare and Quine test assumptions about the edifice of analytical-empirical knowing. While Quine, for example, views physics as speculative Poincaré offers a stronger observation that reimages scientific inquiry within an aesthetical understanding. If the scientist is drawn by the presence of beauty in scientific inquiry, as is Poincaré, then this in turn invites expansion of the empiricist methodological register to include the presence of the aesthetical.

But the character of such expansion involves more than an epistemological turn as it also entails ethical and spiritual outcomes. As Hart observes beauty and divinity are enmeshed. If we are "splintered from the divine" (Hart, 2019a, p. 26), then we are also, extending Hart's notion, splintered from self; and our ethical relation to the world is misaligned. But if we embrace beauty, we begin to heal the splinter when we are carried onto the divine from which emerges the self beyond alienation and which for Merton is "nobody but the man, or the artist, that God intended you to be (Merton, 1972, p. 100).

The encounter with the aesthetic begins to heal the splinter. And if the aesthetic conveys us onto reflection upon our relation with self, others and the creation, then the aesthetic becomes an ethic. Herein, following Bai's (1997) observation upon the unity of the ethical and aesthetical wherein to live aesthetically is to live ethically; and her concomitant advocacy for a pedagogy of art education as moral education.

If physicists like Poincaré also see the presence of beauty within scientific inquiry than the union of ethics and aesthetics, which Bai observes, crosses onto a different epistemological terrain. That is, an epistemological terrain where the ethos of epistemological investigation is not corralled by the bifurcating walls of empiricism and ethics is no longer splintered from ontology (Bai, 2013). Instead it is one configured by another where the walls are broken and the ethos of thinking about problems of knowledge is nested within a holistic and inclusive terrain where questions of ethics and ontology, and aesthetic and scientific inquiry, are together and not apart. And within such unity, the question of the metaphysical nature of our being in the world is no longer separate from its ethics or our way of being in the world. As Zajonc observes, "Our epistemology, our way of knowing, rests on our ethics" (Zajonc, 2013, p. 93). Knowing and ethics come together, their reunion seeded by the presence of the aesthetical where is nurtured the promise of wisdom.

To seek such knowing crosses a holistic terrain which embraces rather than excludes the complexity and fluidity of experience, and in so doing stands apart from the narrow and bifurcated map of the analytical. The artist guides us onto the crossing where she leads the watchmaker, the divine travels with beauty and the splinter, which, following Hart, divides the former, is healed.

The Return to Wonder: A Return to Seeking the Divine

> There are many mysteries, continents, and planets in writing that we haven't yet discovered. There are many oceans of literary possibilities that we don't suspect exist. We are still like Newton's child, playing on the shore, turning over pebbles, while great possibilities of wonder stretch out ahead of us into eternity. This is the beauty of it all. The full potential of human creativity has not yet been tapped. Along with the ever-renewing miracle of love, this fact is one of the brightest hopes for the human race.
>
> (Okri, 1997, p. 28)

In *New Seeds of Contemplation*, Thomas Merton reflects upon the character of the authentic self and asks us poetically how we can expect to arrive at our destination if we travel another person's path (Merton, 1972). While Merton's question meditates upon the character of the integrated self, one whose ethos is shared in kindred reflections by Zajonc (2009), Palmer (1993), Miller (2008) and Bai (2013), it is also a reflection upon the ethos of inquiry.

In my meditations upon the relation of art and wisdom, Merton's question both introduces my journey and informs its concluding reflections. Between these places of departure and destination the arc of my study was seeded by a sometimes serendipitous but alchemical bricolage of narrative retellings, childhood memories, conversations with Merton and encounters with art which collectively summoned me onto inquiry.

While forming an arc for my study, its transit was also epicyclical in character, one which, following the metaphor of Tycho Brahe's astronomy, was perpetually *recycling* between the guideposts of such experiences. Such recycling in turn painting an allegory for the seeking of the authentic self which Merton asks of us.

Of such seeking, encounters with art were generative bringing into focus the presence of the aesthetical within understandings of the authentic self. Reflecting upon Merton's writings upon the aesthetic experience was central in this regard as were also my own encounters. Amongst the latter a surprise encounter with Fra Angelico's fresco *Mocking of Christ* (Convent of San Marco, Florence, 1440) offered a visual metaphor for the centring of self beyond the clamour that sometimes envelopes us—a vision of the interior life which writers in the holistic paradigm, such as Merton (2014), Miller (2008), Palmer (1993) and Zajonc (2009), also share. Accompanying such encounters were others, in particular, encounters with Edward Burtynsky's images of distressed landscapes. Reflecting upon them expanded the discourse of self onto its relation with others and the environment we collectively share. With Fra Angelico's painting, meditations upon Burtynsky's images in turn reinforced the intuition with which I began my inquiry, that the aesthetical encounter offers us the gift of wisdom.

Art awakens us, and within such moments when we reflect upon our being in the world, is seeded its transformative promise. For Merton, such promise resides in the artist within us (Merton, 1972) and one whose transformative potential, as the indigenous educator Gregory Cajete observes, lives in all of us (Cajete, 2019). For Cajete the divine which resides within is made manifest through the encounter with art, in kindred manner with Merton who speaks of the inner artist (Merton, 1972). Or, in Burtynsky's depictions of landscapes which he describes as a seeking of the divine, but also ones where we, as witnesses, begin to reflect upon our being in the world.

Of such promise the aesthetical experience not only returns us to reflecting upon the character of self, but also in so doing summons us to contemplate the great questions of life of which writers such as London (2004) and Hart (2004) in the holistic paradigm speak. Carrying us towards wisdom the encounter with art is also a pedagogical one, nurturing within the classroom dialogue upon such questions. My experience with classroom explorations of Burtynsky's images, for example, was reaffirming of such possibility, its wisdom lessons sparked by the vision of the artist. It is an encounter from which emerged my primordial suggestions upon what can be extracted from the field of wisdom studies in education for beginning to craft a pedagogy of wisdom and art.

My crossing onto inquiry was also one of epicyclical returns to narrative reflections and the *imaginal presence* which formed my initial bricolage for its journey—and from which the thesis was seeded that its map was not imposed from without but emerged from within. The seeds of bricolage flowered into a method for inquiry which originated from the unity of the necessity of one's narrative with the aesthetical, together underscoring the spirit of an arts-based contemplative inquiry whose turn to reflection upon self was guided by the embrace of artistic practices, such as dialogical discourse and encounters with the imaginal. Collectively, these sculpted a method for inquiry of one's own making.

Along my path the journey sought wisdom, but in its crossing it also sought to honour the ethos of wonder. As Abraham Heschel observes:

> A return to reverence is the first prerequisite for a revival of wisdom. . . . Wisdom comes from awe rather than from shrewdness. It is evoked not in moments of calculation but in moments of being in rapport with the mystery of reality. The greatest insights happen to us in moments of awe.
>
> (Heschel, 1976, p. 78)

For Heschel, wisdom resides within the presence of mystery and reverence. It is an observation which returns to Merton who extends Heschel's observation by enriching such a presence with that of the aesthetical encounter. Art transports us into the space of awe where wisdom seeds. Of the power of art to awaken us, Inchausti makes a kindred observation when he observes how Biblical scripture requires "a way of reading that changes the person in the act of interpreting the text" (Inchausti, 2014, p. 39). His observation about the transformative presence of reading in turn aligns with the metaphor of the palimpsest as a layering of such presences within our narratives. In my inquiry, these were manifested within narrative retellings and encounters with art which collectively seeded both the living palimpsest that forms my self and constructs my reality, one whose transformative presence emerged from the imperative of the personal in inquiry.

In my study, within the alchemical union of narrative and aesthetical, the palimpsest was also layered by the presence of the child, who gradually foregrounded itself into inquiry within reflections upon my school workbooks. Its "spiritual embryo" (Montessori, 1970, p. 18) informed the arc of my project and its presence within it reaffirmed Merton's observation that contemplation does not stand apart from life, but *is* life (Merton, 2004). Its presence also sustaining the dialogical discourse with Merton, its first person strategy for inquiry nurturing reflection while returning me to a place I had known as a child and echoing Gardner's observation on Merton's spirituality about the recovery and integrating of the "Christ child" that is present within us (Gardner, 2016, p. 3).

In my story, such recovery witnessed within a child's workbooks; finding them in turn fostered the view that the contemplative terrain is centred about the relationship with one's self (Byrnes, 2012) and that within the "vague fragments" (Merton, 1998b, p. 12) of my childhood narrative lay the seeds of the beginnings of my inquiry. This is a revelation which would not have emerged had not the child many years before protected and cared for his workbooks. Their discovery enriched my methodology wherein inquiry, following Palmer, moves beyond a dualistic relationship to the subject of research to another configured within a spirit of connection and dialogue (Palmer, 1993). My story was fostered by the child's workbooks whose figural representations of the planets formed part of an arc of a project whose trajectory many years later was manifested within the adult who continues the cosmological reflections of the child. Within such a trajectory, the dissolution of the binary within a research methodology extends onto the dialogical discourse when Merton calls us within his writings and reflection is nurtured within the dialogical return of his call.

A serendipitous but seminal conversation with colleagues at OISE about the relationship we have with texts during the research process highlighted the holistic character of such methodological dissolution. With Brother Louis, the dialogical discourse became a way of penetrating the text, wherein the binary of researcher-subject of research is replaced by another in which, following Hart (2008), words are viewed as possessing a vital presence. Of the vitality of words, Merton, in *Raids on the Unspeakable* (Merton, 1966), spoke of them as his children and, I, in my inquiry, as friends.

To speak of the friendship of texts signalled a departure from the analytical and rationalist philosophy in which I had been schooled, one whose bifurcating ethos of knowing, as Zajonc observes, dominates higher education today (Zajonc, 2006, 2014) and is echoed in Merton's critique of Cartesian thinking and in my own encounters with the university. To speak of the friendship of texts indicates a different way: a knowing nested within a contemplative presence in inquiry and one which draws support from new directions in spirituality and contemplative studies in education (Lin et al., 2016). To speak of the friendship of texts is a turn toward the contemplative embrace of aesthetical approaches to inquiry within a spirit of inclusion and welcome.

In the *Geography of Lograire*, Merton writes:

> A poet spends his life in repeated projects, over and over again attempting to build or to dream the world in which he lives. But more and more he realizes that this world is at once his and everybody's. . . . In this wide-angle mosaic of poems and dreams I have without scruple mixed what is my own experience with what is almost everybody else's.
>
> (Merton, 1969, p. 1)

Merton's words are familiar. It is within such spirit that my inquiry seeks its core, wherein the turn to narrative is a turn toward retellings, dialogical conversations and personal encounters with art which collectively sculpted my way of contemplation. Its map is configured by the palimpsest of my self—its "*SUM*, I Am" (Merton, 1972, p. 9)—and the source of its "scintilla" (Merton, 1979, p. 9). Of the touch of art to awaken and guide us towards wisdom, meditations upon Merton's writings in tandem with the arc of narrative illuminated the road for my journey. Its map, sculpted of the unity of narrative and the aesthetical, served as my "summonses to awareness" (Merton, 1966, p. 182) from whose call emerges the promise of *Sophia*.

Bibliography

Alsubaie, M. (2015). Hidden curriculum as one current issue of curriculum. *Journal of Education and Practice*, *6*(33), 125–128.
Arya, R. (2011). Contemplations of the spiritual in visual art. *Journal for the Study of Spirituality*, *1*(1), 76–93. doi:10.1558/jss.v1i1.76
Babiuk, G. (2014). Sustaining life: Education for sustainability. In S. Schiller (Ed.), *Sustaining the writing spirit* (pp. 27–44). Lanham, MD: Rowman & Littlefield Education.
Bai, H. (1997). Ethics and aesthetics are one: The case of Zen aesthetics. *Canadian Review of Art Education*, *24*(2), 37–52.
Bai, H. (2005). What is inquiry? In W. Hare & J. Portelli (Eds.), *Key questions for educators* (pp. 45–47). Halifax: EdPhil Books.
Bai, H. (2013). Peace with the earth: Animism and contemplative ways. *Cultural Studies of Science Education*, *10*, 135–147.
Bai, H. (2014). Life lessons. In A. Cohen, H. Bai, C. Leggo, M. Porath, K. Meyer, & A. Clarke (Eds.), *Speaking of learning . . . . recollections, revelations, and realizations* (pp. 29–42). Rotterdam: Sense Publishers.
Bai, H., Cohen, A., & Scott, C. (2013). Re-visioning higher education: The three-fold relationality framework. In J. Lin, R. Oxford, & E. Brantmeier (Eds.), *Re-envisioning higher education: Embodied paths to wisdom and social transformation* (pp. 3–22). Charlotte, NC: Information Age Publishing.
Bai, H., Elza, D., Kovacs, P., & Romanycia, S. (2010). Re-seaching and re-storying the complex and complicated relationship of biophilia and bibliophilia. *Environmental Education Research*, *16*(3), 351–365.
Bai, H., Morgan, P., Scott, C., & Cohen, A. (2016). Prolegomena to a spiritual research paradigm. In J. Lin, L. Oxford, & T. Culham (Eds.), *Towards a spiritual research paradigm* (pp. 77–96). Charlotte, NC: Information Age Publishing, Inc.
Bakhtin, M. (1984). *The problem of Dostoevsky's poetics* (C. Emerson, Trans.). Minneapolis, MN: University of Minnesota Press.
Baldwin, J. (1962). The creative process. In J. F. Kennedy, D. D. Eisenhower, H. S. Truman et. al. (Eds.), *Creative America* (pp. 17–19). New York, NY: Ridge Press.
Baltes, P. B. (2004). *Wisdom as orchestration of mind and virtue*. Unpublished manuscript, Max Planck Institute for Human Development. Berlin. Retrieved from http://library.mpib-berlin.mpg.de/ft/pb/PB_Wisdom_2004.pdf
Barone, T. (2001). Science, art and the predispositions of educational researchers. *Educational Researcher*, *30*(7), 24–28.
Barthes, R. (1981). *Camera lucida* (R. Howard, Trans.). New York, NY: Hill and Wang.

Bibliography

Basquiat, J. (1999). Interview: By I. Graw. In *Basquiat* (p. LXVII). Milan: Edizioni Charta.
Beattie, M. (2019). Conducting narrative inquiry research from a holistic perspective: Honouring story and soul. In J. P. Miller, K. Nigh, M. J. Binder, B. Novak, & S. Crowell (Eds.), *International handbook of holistic education* (pp. 252–259). New York, NY: Routledge.
Bohm, D. (1996). *On dialogue*. London: Routledge.
Bright, P. (2008). Ascending to wisdom: A Christian pedagogy. In M. Ferrari & G. Potworowski (Eds.), *Teaching for wisdom* (pp. 163–178). Ann Arbor, MI: Springer.
Bruner, J. (1986). *Actual minds, possible worlds*. Cambridge, MA: Harvard University Press.
Bruner, J. (1991). The narrative construction of reality. *Critical Inquiry*, *18*(1), 1–21.
Bruner, J. (1997). *On knowing: Essays for the left hand*. Cambridge, MA: The Belknap Press of Harvard University Press.
Bruner, J. (2004). Life as narrative. *Social Research*, *71*(3), 691–710.
Bruya, B., & Ardelt, M. (2018). Wisdom can be taught: A proof-of-concept study for fostering wisdom in the classroom. *Learning and Instruction*, *58*, 106–114.
Buber, M. (1970). *I and thou* (W. Kaufmann, Trans.). New York, NY: Charles Scribner's Sons.
Burrows, L. (2015). Inner alchemy: Transforming dilemmas in education and mindfulness. *Journal of Transformative Education*, *13*(2), 127–139. doi:10.1177/1541344615569535
Burtynsky, E., Davis, W., & Lord, R. (2013). *Burtynsky water*. Gottingen: Steidl; New Orleans, LA: New Orleans Museum of Art.
Burtynsky, E., & Ewing, W. (2016, October 1). *Salt pans/essential elements*. Talk presented at Nicholas Metivier Gallery, Toronto.
Byrnes, K. (2012). A portrait of contemplative teaching: Embracing wholeness. *Journal of Transformative Education*, *10*(1), 22–41. doi:10.1177/1541344612456431
Cajete, G. (2019). Transformation through art and vision: An Indigenous perspective. In J. P. Miller, K. Nigh, M. J. Binder, B. Novak, & S. Crowell (Eds.), *International handbook of holistic education* (pp. 139–147). New York, NY: Routledge.
Capra, F. (1991). *The tao of physics*. Boston, MA: Shambhala.
Cartier-Bresson, H. (n.d.). *Magnum photos*. Retrieved from https://pro.magnumphotos.com/C.aspx?VP3=CMS3&VF=MAGO31_9_VForm&ERID=24KL53ZMYN
Chermayeff, M. (Producer), & Dupre, J. (Producer). (2012). *Marina Abramovic: The artist is present* [DVD]. Chicago, IL: Music Box Films.
Chitwood, A. (2004). *Death by philosophy: The biographical tradition in the life and death of the Archaic philosophers Empedocles, Heraclitus, and Democritus*. Ann Arbor, MI: The University of Michigan Press.
Clandinin, D., & Connelly, F. (2000). *Narrative inquiry*. San Francisco, CA: Jossey-Bass.
Clark, C., & Wilson, A. (1991). Context and rationality in Mezirow's theory of transformational learning. *Adult Education Quarterly*, *41*, 75–91.
Cole, T. (2013, November). Postscript: Saul Leiter (1923–2013). *The New Yorker*, n.p.
Cronin, J. (2016). The poetics of history: Thomas Merton's use of the past to imagine possible futures. *The Merton Journal*, *23*(2), 46–52.
Csikszentmihalyi, M. (1990). *Flow: The psychology of optimal experience*. New York, NY: Harper and Row.
Curnow, T. (1999). *Wisdom, intuition and ethics*. Aldershot, UK: Ashgate Publishing Company.
Curnow, T. (2000). Wisdom and philosophy. *Practical Philosophy*, *3*(1), 10–13. Retrieved from www.society-for-philosophy-in-practice.org/journal/pdf/3-1%2010%20Curnow%20-%20Wisdom%20and%20Philosophy.pdf

Curnow, T. (2008). Sophia's world: Episodes form the history of wisdom. In M. Ferrari & G. Potworowski (Eds.), *Teaching for wisdom* (pp. 1–22). Ann Arbor, MI: Springer.
Curnow, T. (2010). *Wisdom in the ancient world*. London, UK: Duckworth.
Curnow, T. (2015). *Wisdom: A history*. London, UK: Reaktion Books Ltd.
Davis, W. (2013). *Water notes*. In E. Burtynsky, W. Davis, & R. Lord (Eds.), *Burtynsky water* (pp. 20–25). Gottingen: Steidl and New Orleans, LA: New Orleans Museum of Art.
de Botton, A. (2013, October). Art galleries should be apothecaries for our deeper selves. *The Guardian*. Retrieved from www.theguardian.com/uk
Del Prete, T. (1990). *Thomas Merton and the education of the whole person*. Birmingham, AL: Religious Education Press.
Dencev, H., & Collister, R. (2010). Authentic ways of knowing, authentic ways of being: Nurturing a professional community of learning and praxis. *Journal of Transformative Education*, 8(3), 178–196. doi:10.1177/1541344611407202
de Pencier, N., Burtynsky, E., & Baichwal, J. (n.d.). *The anthropocene project*. Retrieved from https://theanthropocene.org/
de Pencier, N. (Producer), Burtynsky, E., & Baichwal, J. (Directors). (2014). *Watemark*. Canada: Mongrel Media.
Descartes, R. (1960). *Discourse on method and meditations* (L. Lafleur, Trans.). Indianapolis, IN: The Bobbs-Merrill Company Inc.
Diamond, C. (2009). Taking the inner and outer journeys: Successfully completing your thesis. In B. Garrick, S. Poed, & J. Skinner (Eds.), *Educational planet shapers: Researching, hypothesising, dreaming the future* (pp. 19–32). RHD Conference. Brisbane: Post Pressed.
Diamond, C., & Mullen, C. (2001). Attractions on the midway: Carnivalesque inquiry. *Journal of Curriculum Theorizing*, 17(1), 3–12.
Diamond, C., & van Halen-Faber, C. (2008). A history of the arts in research: A postmodern guide for readers-flaneurs. In J. G. Knowles & A. L. Cole (Eds.), *Handbook of the arts in qualitative research: Perspectives, methodologies, examples and issues* (pp. 569–590). London, UK: Sage Publishing.
Di Buonaguida, P. (1310–1315). *L'albero della vita* [tempura su tavola]. Galleria Dell'Accademia di Firenze, Florence, Italy. Retrieved from http://galleriaaccademiafirenze.beniculturali.it/collezioni/?form_search_key=&form_id_autori=7&form_id_collezioni=&search=1
Di Rezze, G. (2000). *Becoming and being a teacher: Arts-based narratives of relational knowing, response-ability and resistance* (Unpublished doctoral dissertation). University of Toronto, Toronto, Canada.
Dutton, T. (1991). The hidden curriculum and the design studio: Toward a critical studio pedagogy. In T. Dutton (Ed.), *Voices in architectural education: Cultural politics and pedagogy* (pp. 165–194). New York, NY: Bergin & Garvey.
Education for Sustainable Development. (n.d.). Retrieved from http://en.unesco.org/themes/education-sustainable-development
Edwards, P., & Pap, A. (Eds.). (1973). *A modern introduction to philosophy*. New York, NY: The Free Press.
Eisner, E. (1988). On the differences between scientific and artistic approaches to qualitative research. *Educational Researcher*, 10(4), 5–9.
Eisner, E. (1991). What the arts taught me about education. *Art Education*, 44(5), 10–19.
Eisner, E. (1993a). Forms of understanding and the future of educational research. *Educational Researcher*, 22(7), 5–11.

Bibliography

Eisner, E. (1993b). The emergence of new paradigms for educational research. *Art and Technology*, *46*(6), 50–55.

Eisner, E. (1995). What artistically crafted research can help us understand about schools. *Educational Theory*, *45*(1), 1–6.

Eisner, E. (1997). The promise and perils of alternative forms of data representation. *Educational Researcher*, *26*(6), 4–10.

Eisner, E. (2001). Concerns and aspirations for qualitative research in the new millennium. *Qualitative Research*, *1*(2), 135–145.

Eisner, E. (2002). *The arts and the creation of mind*. New Haven, CT: Yale University Press.

Eisner, E. (2008). Art and knowledge. In J. G. Knowles & A. L. Cole (Eds.), *Handbook of the arts in qualitative research: Perspectives, methodologies, examples and issues* (pp. 3–12). London: Sage Publishing.

Eisner, E., Donmoyer, R., Gardner, H., Cizek, G. J., Gough, N., Tillman, L., Stotsky, S., & Wasley, P. (1996). Should novels count as dissertations in education? In A. Saks (Ed.), *Research in the Teaching of English*, *30*(4), 403–427.

Emerson, R. (1950). *The complete essays and other writings of Ralph Waldo Emerson* (B. Atkinson, Ed.). New York, NY: The Modern Library.

Ergas, O. (2016). Knowing the unknown: Transcending the educational narrative of the Kantian paradigm through contemplative inquiry. In J. Lin, L. Oxford, & T. Culham (Eds.), *Towards a spiritual research paradigm: Exploring new ways of knowing, researching and being* (pp. 1–23). Charlotte, NC: Information Age Publishing, Inc.

Ergas, O. (2019). A contemplative turn in education: Charting a curricular-pedagogical countermovement. *Pedagogy, Culture and Society*, *27*(2), 251–270. doi:10.1080/14681366.2018.1465111

Ewing, W. (2016). *Edward Burtynsky: Essential elements*. London, UK: Thomas & Hudson Ltd.

Ferrari, M., & Kim, J. (2019). Educating for wisdom. In R. Sternberg & J. Glück (Eds.), *The Cambridge handbook of wisdom* (pp. 347–371). Cambridge, UK: Cambridge University Press.

Ferrari, M., & Potworowski, G. (Eds.). (2008). *Teaching for wisdom*. Ann Arbor, MI: Springer.

Ferrari, M., & Weststrate, N. (2013). The scientific study of personal wisdom. In M. Ferrari & N. Weststrate (Eds.), *The scientific study of personal wisdom* (pp. 325–341). Dordrecht: Springer.

Ferrari, M., Weststrate, N., & Petro, P. (2013). Stories of wisdom to live by: Developing wisdom in a narrative mode. In M. Ferrari & N. Weststrate (Eds.), *The scientific study of personal wisdom* (pp. 137–164). Dordrecht: Springer.

Francis. (2015). *Address to joint meeting of Congress*. Retrieved from www.washingtonpost.com/local/social-issues/transcript-pope-franciss-speech-to-congress/2015/09/24/6d7d7ac8-62bf-11e5-8e9e-dce8a2a2a679_story.html

Frodeman, R., & Briggle, A. (2016, January). When philosophy lost its way. *The New York Times*. Retrieved from https://opinionator.blogs.nytimes.com/2016/01/11/when-philosophy-lost-its-way/

Galilei, G. (1989). *Sidereus nuncius, or the sidereal messenger* (A. van Helden, Trans.). Chicago, IL: The University of Chicago Press.

Gardner, F. (2016). *The only mind worth having: Thomas Merton and the child mind*. Cambridge, UK: The Lutterworth Press.

Giroux, R. (1998). Introduction. In T. Merton (Ed.), *The seven storey mountain* (pp. xi–xviii). Orlando, FL: A Harvest Book - Harcourt, Inc.

Giroux, H., & Penna, A. (1979). Social education in the classroom: The dynamics of the hidden curriculum. *Theory and Research in Social Education, 7*(1), 21–42.

Giroux, R. (1998). Introduction. In T. Merton (Ed.), *The seven storey mountain* (pp. xi–xviii). Orlando, FL: A Harvest Book-Harcourt, Inc.

Glück, J., & Bluck, S. (2013). The MORE life experience model: A theory of the development of personal wisdom. In M. Ferrari & N. Weststrate (Eds.), *The scientific study of personal wisdom* (pp. 75–97). Dordrecht: Springer.

Grady, M. (2006). Art and consciousness: The pedagogy of art and transformation. *Visual Arts Research, 32*(1), 83–91.

Green, S., Pohlad, B., Pitt, B., Gardner, D., & Hill, G. (Producers), & Malick, T. (Director). (2011). *The tree of life* [Motion picture]. Los Angeles, CA: Fox Searchlight Pictures.

Gunnlaugson, O. (2007). Shedding light on the underlying forms of transformative learning theory: Introducing three distinct categories of consciousness. *Journal of Transformative Education, 5*(2), 134–151. doi:10.1177/1541344607303526

Gunnlaugson, O. (2011). Advancing a second-person contemplative approach for collective wisdom and leadership development. *Journal of Transformative Education, 9*(1), 3–20. doi:10.1177/1541344610397034

Gunnlaugson, O., Sarath, E., Scott, C., & Bai, H. (Eds.). (2014). *Contemplative learning and inquiry across disciplines*. Albany, NY: State University of New York Press.

Hadot, P. (2002). *What is ancient philosophy?* (M. Chase, Trans.). Cambridge, MA: Belknap Press of Harvard University Press.

Hart, T. (2004). Opening the contemplative mind in the classroom. *Journal of Transformative Education, 2*(1), 28–46. doi:10.1177/1541344603259311

Hart, T. (2008). Interiority and Education: Exploring the neurophenomenology of contemplation and its potential role in learning. *Journal of Transformative Education, 6*(4), 235–237. doi:10.1177/1541344608329393

Hart, T. (2009). *From Information to transformation: Education for the evolution of consciousness*. New York, NY: Peter Lang.

Hart, T. (2014). *The integrative mind: Transformative education for a world on fire*. Lanham, MD: Rowman & Littlefield.

Hart, T. (2019a). Beauty and learning. In J. P. Miller, K. Nigh, M. J. Binder, B. Novak, & S. Crowell (Eds.), *International handbook of holistic education* (pp. 25–31). New York, NY: Routledge.

Hart, T. (2019b). Toward an integrative mind. In J. P. Miller, K. Nigh, M. J. Binder, B. Novak, & S. Crowell (Eds.), *International handbook of holistic education* (pp. 336–343). New York, NY: Routledge.

Heidegger, M. (2001). *Being and time* (J. Macquarrie & E. Robinson, Trans.). Oxford, UK: Blackwell Publishers.

Hentoff, N. (2010). *At the jazz ball: Sixty years on the jazz scene*. Berkeley, CA: University of California Press.

Hermans, H., & Gieser, T. (2012). Introductory chapter: History, main tenets and core concepts in dialogical self theory. In H. Herman & T. Gieser (Eds.), *Handbook of dialogical self theory* (pp. 1–22). Cambridge, UK: Cambridge University Press.

Heschel, A. (1976). *God in search of man: A philosophy of Judaism*. New York, NY: Farrar, Straus and Giroux.

Higgins, M. (1998). *Heretic Blood: The spiritual geography of Thomas Merton*. Toronto: Stoddart.

Inchausti, R. (1998). *Thomas Merton's American prophecy*. Albany, NY: State University of New York Press.

Inchausti, R. (2014). *Thinking through Thomas Merton*. Albany, NY: State University of New York Press.
James, W. (1891). *The principles of psychology* (Vol. 2). London, UK: Macmillan and Co., Ltd.
Jenkins, A., Villard, R., & Kelly, P. (2018, April). *Hubble uncovers the farthest star ever seen*. Retrieved from www.nasa.gov/feature/goddard/2018/hubble-uncovers-the-farthest-star-ever-seen
Jung, C. (1955). *Synchronicity: An acausal connecting principle* (R. F. C. Hull, Trans.). New York, NY: Pantheon.
Jung, C. (1989). *Memories, dreams, reflections* (A. Jaffé, Ed.). New York, NY: Vintage Books.
Kabat-Zinn, J. (2005). *Coming to our senses: Healing ourselves and the world through mindfulness*. New York, NY: Hyperion.
Kandinsky, W. (1977). *Concerning the spiritual in art* (M. Sadler, Trans.). New York, NY: Dover Publications Inc.
Kelly, V. L. (2006). *The arts as catalyst, catharsis, and crucible: Towards a personal philosophy of art* (Unpublished doctoral dissertation). University of Toronto, Toronto, Canada.
Khachadourian, R. (2016, December). The long view: Photographing environmental destruction. *The New Yorker*, 80–95.
Knowles, J., & Cole, A. (Eds.). (2008). *Handbook of the arts in qualitative Research: Perspectives, methodologies, examples and issues*. Los Angeles, CA: Sage Publications.
Kuhn, T. (1975). *The structure of scientific revolutions*. Chicago, IL: The University of Chicago Press.
Kunzman, U. (2019). Performance-based measures of wisdom: State of the art and future directions. In R. Sternberg & J. Glück (Eds.), *The Cambridge handbook of wisdom* (pp. 277–296). Cambridge, UK: Cambridge University Press.
Labrie, R. (2001). *Thomas Merton and the inclusive imagination*. Columbia, MO: University of Missouri Press.
Labrie, R. (2014). Merton on art as truth. *The Merton Annual, 27*, 140–164.
Leavy, P. (Ed.). (2018). *Handbook of arts-based research*. New York, NY: The Guilford Press.
Levi, C. (1947). *Christ stopped at Eboli* (F. Frenaye, Trans.). New York, NY: Farrar, Straus and Company.
Lin, J., Oxford, L., & Culham, T. (2016). Introduction: The urgent need to develop a spiritual research paradigm. In J. Lin, L. Oxford, & T. Culham (Eds.), *Towards a spiritual research paradigm* (pp. ix–xix). Charlotte, NC: Information Age Publishing, Inc.
London, P. (2006). Towards a holistic paradigm of art education: Mind, body, spirit. *Visual Arts Research, 32*(1), 8–15.
London, P., & The Study Group for Holistic Art Education. (2004). *Towards a holistic paradigm in art education* [PDF file]. Monograph #1 Center for Art Education. Retrieved from https://assets.mica.edu/files/resources/holisticmonograph.pdf
Lord, R. (2013). Into the deep. In E. Burtynsky, W. Davis, & R. Lord (Eds.), *Burtynsky water* (pp. 186–189). Gottingen: Steidl and New Orleans, LA: New Orleans Museum of Art.
Mailer, N. (1967). Interview. In G. Plimpton (Ed.), *Writers at work: The Paris review interviews: Third series* (pp. 253–278). New York, NY: The Viking Press.

Bibliography 183

McKinney, M. (2004, Summer). Wisdom: The pauses between the notes. *Vision*, n.p. Retrieved from www.vision.org/visionmedia/article.aspx?id=289

McMahan, D. (2008). *The making of Buddhist modernism*. Oxford, UK: Oxford University Press.

McNiff, S. (2008). Art-based research. In J. G. Knowles & A. L. Cole (Eds.), *Handbook of the arts in qualitative research: Perspectives, methodologies, examples and issues* (pp. 29–40). Los Angeles, CA: Sage Publications.

Melville, H. (1922). *Moby Dick: Or, the whale*. London, UK: Constable and Company Ltd.

Merton, T. (1947). Poetry and the contemplative life. *Figures for an apocalypse* (95–111). New York, NY: New Directions.

Merton, T. (1966). *Raids on the unspeakable*. New York, NY: New Directions.

Merton, T. (1968). Zen in Japanese art. *Zen and the birds of appetite* (89–92). New York, NY: New Directions.

Merton, T. (1969). *The geography of Lograire*. New York, NY: New Directions.

Merton, T. (1972). *New seeds of contemplation*. New York, NY: New Directions.

Merton, T. (1974). *A Thomas Merton reader* (T. Mcdonnell, Ed.). Garden City, NY: Image Books.

Merton, T. (1977). *The collected poems of Thomas Merton*. New York, NY: New Directions.

Merton, T. (1979). *Love and living* (N. Burton Stone & P. Hart, Eds.). San Diego, CA: A Harvest Book-Harcourt, Inc.

Merton, T. (1981). Answers on art and freedom. In P. Hart (ed.), *The literary essays of Thomas Merton* (pp. 375–380). New York, NY: New Directions.

Merton, T. (1983). *No man is an island*. San Diego, CA: A Harvest Book-Harcourt Brace & Company.

Merton, T. (1993). *The courage for truth: The letters of Thomas Merton to writers* (C. Bochen, Ed.). New York, NY: Farrar Straus & Giroux.

Merton, T. (1998a). *The other side of the mountain: The end of the journey* (P. Hart, Ed.). New York, NY: HarperOne.

Merton, T. (1998b). *The seven storey mountain*. Orlando, FL: A Harvest Book-Harcourt, Inc.

Merton, T. (2004). *The inner experience: Notes on contemplation* (W. Shannon, Ed.). New York, NY: HarperCollins Publishers, Inc.

Merton, T. (2014). *Conjectures of a guilty bystander*. New York, NY: Image.

Miller, J. (2006). *Educating for wisdom and compassion*. Thousand Oaks, CA: Corwin Press.

Miller, J. (2008). *The holistic curriculum*. Toronto: University of Toronto Press.

Miller, J. (2010). *Whole child education*. Toronto: University of Toronto Press.

Miller, J. (2011). *Transcendental learning: The educational legacy of Alcott, Emerson, Fuller, Peabody and Thoreau*. Charlotte, NC: Information Age Publishing Inc.

Miller, J. (2014). *The contemplative practitioner: Meditation in education and the workplace*. Toronto: University of Toronto Press.

Miller, J. (2016). The embodied researcher: Meditation's role in spirituality research. In J. Lin, L. Oxford, & T. Culham (Eds.), *Towards a spiritual research paradigm* (pp. 127–139). Charlotte, NC: Information Age Publishing, Inc.

Miller, J. (2019). Holistic education: A brief introduction. In J. Miller, K. Nigh, M. Binder, B. Novak, & S. Crowell (Eds.), *International handbook of holistic education* (pp. 5–16). New York, NY: Routledge.

Montessori, M. (1970). *The child in the family* (N. Rockmore Cirillo, Trans.). Chicago, IL: Henry Regnery Company.

Bibliography

Moore, T. (2019). Care of the soul. In J. Miller, K. Nigh, M. Binder, B. Novak, & S. Crowell (Eds.), *International handbook of holistic education* (pp. 51–56). New York, NY: Routledge.

Morgan, P. (2012). Following contemplative education students' transformation through their "ground-of-being" experience. *Journal of Transformative Education, 10*(1), 42–60. doi:10.1177/1541344612455846

Nicholas of Cusa. (1996). *Of wisdom and knowledge* (J. Hopkins, Trans.). Minneapolis, MN: A.J. Banning Press.

Okri, B. (1997). *A way of being free*. London, UK: Phoenix House.

Oron Semper, J., & Blasco, M. (2018). Revealing the hidden curriculum in higher education. *Studies in Philosophy of Education*. doi:10.1007/s11217-018-9608-5

Oxford, R. (2016). Creation spirituality as a spiritual research paradigm drawing on many faiths. In J. Lin, L. Oxford, & T. Culham (Eds.), *Towards a spiritual research paradigm* (pp. 199–232). Charlotte, NC: Information Age Publishing, Inc.

Paley, W. (2009). *Natural theology: Or, evidences of the existence and attributes of the Deity, collected from the appearances of nature*. Cambridge, UK: Cambridge University Press.

Palmer, P. (1993). *To know as we are known*. New York, NY: HarperCollins.

Palmer, P. (2004). *A hidden wholeness: The journey toward an undivided life*. San Francisco, CA: Jossey-Bass.

Palmer, P., & Zajonc, A., with Scribner, M. (2010). *The heart of higher education: A call to renewal*. San Francisco, CA: Jossey-Bass.

Pinar, W. (2015). Forward. In S. Walsh, B. Bickel, & C. Leggo (Eds.), *Arts-based and contemplative practices in research and teaching: Honoring presence* (pp. xv–xx). New York, NY: Routledge.

Pinar, W., Reynolds, W., Slattery, P., & Taubman, P. (Eds.). (1995). *Understanding curriculum: An introduction to the study of historical and contemporary curriculum discourses*. New York, NY: Peter Lang.

Poincaré, H. (1914). *Science and method* (F. Maitland, Trans.). London, UK: Thomas Nelson & Sons.

Polkinghorne, D. (2007). Validity issues in narrative research. *Qualitative Inquiry, 13*(4), 471–486. doi:10.1177/1077800406297670

Randall, V. R. (1978). The mandala as structure in Thomas Merton's "The geography of Lograire". *Notre Dame English Journal, 11*(1), 1–13.

Reeve, R., Messina, R., & Scardamalia, M. (2008). Wisdom in elementary school. In M. Ferrari & G. Potworowski (Eds.), *Teaching for wisdom* (pp. 79–92). Ann Arbor, MI: Springer.

Rosch, E. (2008). Beginner's mind: Paths to the wisdom that is not learned. In M. Ferrari & G. Potworowski (Eds.), *Teaching for wisdom* (pp. 135–162). Ann Arbor, MI: Springer.

Schiller, S. A. (2014). *Sustaining the writing spirit*. Lanham, MD: Rowman & Littlefield Education.

Schützen, S. (2017). *Caravaggio: The complete works*. Köln: Taschen.

Scott, C. (2014). Buberian dialogue as an intersubjective contemplative praxis. In O. Gunnlaugson, E. Sarath, C. Scott, & H. Bai (Eds.), *Contemplative learning and inquiry across disciplines* (pp. 325–340). Albany, NY: State University of New York Press.

Simmons, S. (2006). Living the questions: Existential intelligence in the context of holistic art education. *Visual Arts Research, 32*(1), 41–52.

Stange, A., & Kunzman, U. (2008). Fostering wisdom as expertise. In M. Ferrari & G. Potworowski (Eds.), *Teaching for wisdom* (pp. 23–36). Ann Arbor, MI: Springer.

Staudinger, U. (2013). The need to distinguish personal from general wisdom: A short history and empirical evidence. In M. Ferrari & N. Weststrate (Eds.), *The scientific study of personal wisdom* (pp. 3–20). Dordrecht: Springer.

Staudinger, U. (2019). The distinction between personal and general wisdom: How far have we come? In R. Sternberg & J. Glück (Eds.), *The Cambridge handbook of wisdom* (pp. 182–201). Cambridge, UK: Cambridge University Press.

Sternberg, R., & Glück, J. (Eds.). (2019). *The Cambridge handbook of wisdom*. Cambridge, UK: Cambridge University Press.

Sternberg, R., Jarvin, L., & Reznitskaya, A. (2008). Teaching for wisdom through history: Infusing wise thinking skills in the school curriculum. In M. Ferrari & G. Potworowski (Eds.), *Teaching for wisdom* (pp. 37–58). Ann Arbor, MI: Springer.

Sternberg, R., & Jordan, J. (Eds.). (2005). *A handbook of wisdom: Psychological perspectives*. Cambridge, UK: Cambridge University Press.

Student Observations. (2011, November 15). *Arts based research and ethnography seminar*. Dr. Karyn Cooper, CTL 1018H Introduction to Qualitative Inquiry in Curriculum, Toronto Canada: Teaching and Learning, University of Toronto.

Teaching and Learning for a Sustainable Future. (n.d.). Retrieved from www.unesco.org/education/tlsf/

Thoreau, H. (1854). *Walden; or, Life in the woods,* Boston, MA: Ticknor and Fields.

Thoreau, H. (1892). *A week on the concord and Merrimack Rivers*. Boston, MA: Houghton, Mifflin and Company.

Walsh, R. (2011). The varieties of wisdom: Contemplative, cross-cultural and integral contributions. *Research in Human Development, 8*(2), 109–127.

Walsh, R. (2015). What is wisdom? Cross-cultural and cross-disciplinary syntheses. *Review of General Psychology, 19*(3), 278–293.

Walsh, S., & Bai, H. (2015). Writing witness consciousness. In S. Walsh, B. Bickel, & C. Leggo (Eds.), *Arts-based and contemplative practices in research and teaching: Honoring presence* (pp. 24–44). New York, NY: Routledge.

Walsh, S., Bickel, B., & Leggo, C. (2015). Introduction. In S. Walsh, B. Bickel, & C. Leggo (Eds.), *Arts-based and contemplative practices in research and teaching: Honoring presence* (pp. 1–19). New York, NY: Routledge.

Webb, D. (2018, July). John Coltrane: Both directions at once: The lost album. *Sungenre*. Retrieved from https://sungenre.com/review/john-coltrane-both-directions-at-once-the-lost-album/

Webster, J. (2019). Self-report wisdom measures. In R. Sternberg & J. Glück (Eds.), *The Cambridge handbook of wisdom* (pp. 297–320). Cambridge, UK: Cambridge University Press.

Weststrate, N. (2019). The mirror of wisdom: Self-reflection as a developmental precursor and core competency of wise people. In R. Sternberg & J. Glück (Eds.), *The Cambridge handbook of wisdom* (pp. 500–518). Cambridge, UK: Cambridge University Press.

Weststrate, N., Bluck, S., & Glück, J. (2019). Wisdom of the crowd: Exploring people's conceptions of wisdom. In R. Sternberg & J. Glück (Eds.), *The Cambridge handbook of wisdom* (pp. 97–121). Cambridge, UK: Cambridge University Press.

Wittkower, R. (1986). *Art and architecture in Italy 1660–1750*. Harmondsworth, UK: Penquin Books Ltd. (Original work published 1958).

Woideck, C. (1998). *The John Coltrane companion: Five decades of commentary*. New York, NY: Schirmer Books.

Yagelski, R. (2009). A thousand writers writing: Seeking change through the radical practice of writing as a way of being. *English Education, 42*(1), 6–28.

Yagelski, R. (2011). *Writing as a way of being: Writing instruction, nonduality, and the crisis of sustainability*. New York, NY: Hampton Press.

Zajonc, A. (2006). Love and knowledge: Recovering the heart of learning through contemplation. *Teachers College Record, 108*(9), 1742–1759.

Zajonc, A. (2009). *Meditation as contemplative inquiry*. Great Barrington, MA: Lindisfarne Books.

Zajonc, A. (2010). Attending to interconnection, living the lesson. In P. Palmer, A. Zajonc, & M. Scribner (Eds.), *The heart of higher education: A call to renewal* (pp. 77–99). San Francisco, CA: Jossey-Bass.

Zajonc, A. (2013). Contemplative pedagogy: A quiet revolution in higher education. *Special Issue: Contemplative Studies in Higher Education*, (134), 83–94. doi:10.1002/tl.20057

Zajonc, A. (2014). Contemplative pedagogy in higher education: Toward a more reflective academy. In O. Gunnlaugson, E. Sarath, C. Scott, & H. Bai (Eds.), *Contemplative learning and inquiry across disciplines* (pp. 15–29). Albany, NY: State University of New York Press.

Żurawska-Żyła, R., Chmielnicka-Kuter, E., & Oleś, P. (2012). Spatial organization of the dialogical self in creative writers. In H. Hermans & T. Gieser (Eds.), *Handbook of dialogical self theory* (pp. 253–263). Cambridge, UK: Cambridge University Press.

Index

Note: Page numbers in italics indicate figures on the corresponding pages.

Abramovic, M. 158
active contemplation 43
act of dialogical being 36
Adam and Eve 61
Adams, A. 65
Adoration of the Magi 72
aesthetical, the 41–43; impossible paradox and 93; intertwined with wisdom 63–65, 92–93; paradoxical relation of the spiritual and 46–51, 92–93; as summonses to awareness 77–80; transformation, contemplation and 43–44; witnessing of self through writing and encounters with 123–125
alienation in society 29
Alsubaie, M. 21
American Transcendentalism 63, 64, 65, 92, 103
Angelico, Fra 30–32, *31*, 33, 56, 104, 153, 155, 174
Answers on Art and Freedom 134
Anthropocene Project, The 65
Ardelt, M. 158
art: learning with 146; paradise imagery in 61; radical self and 59–62; relation of spirituality and 52, 54–55; relation of wisdom to 84–87, 109–111, 173; seeking the divine by visualizing connection 65–72; the soul as 51–53; as spiritual inquiry 105; spiritual presence of 67
Artist is Present, The 158
arts-based contemplative inquiry 1–2, 135, 149; paradigm of 150–151; towards artist as atman in 151–156; *see also* contemplative inquiry
Arya, R. 67

Astavakra Gita 63–64
Atlas Slave 117
Atman 152
authentic self 93, 121–122, 173–174

Babiuk, G. 164–165
Bai, H. 2, 19, 20, 83, 123, 152, 173; on character of inquiry 26; critique of dualistic thinking 20; on nuance and complexity 26–27; on self-cultivation 146; on unity of the ethical and aesthetical 172; on writing witness consciousness 4, 7, 92, 124, 125, 132, 139, 153, 155–156
Baichwal, J. 65
Bakhtin, M. 36, 89, 92, 126
Balance Theory of Wisdom 10, 107, 168
Baldwin, J. 105
Baltes, P. 49, 108, 109, 111
Barone, T. 149
Barthes, R. 66, 84
Basquiat, J.-M. 103, 105
Beattie, M. 2–3, 6
Beginning Inquiry, My Grade 3 Workbook 17
being in narrative in the world 3, 151
Berlin Wisdom model 10, 163–164, 165
Blake, W. 29, 61
Blasco, M. 21
Bohm, D. 8, 82, 126
Bonaiuto, A. di *100*
Borromini, F. 68
Borromini #21 67, 68
Botton, A. de 105
Breughel, J. 61
Briggle, A. 25, 28
Bright, P. 107

Brother Louis 7
Bruner, J. 2–3, 6, 9–10, 152; on character of narrative 17
Bruya, B. 158
Buber, M. 92
Buddhism 107, 112
Buonaguida, P. di 60
Burrows, L. 37, 41, 43–45; dialogical self theory and 132, 133; on inner alchemy 89, 133–134, 145; on non-dual mindfulness 48
Burtynsky, E. 10, 24, 65–68, *67*, 102, *157*, 157–158, 161, 168; *Borromini No. 21, 1999 67*, 68; contemplative images of 73, 164–166, *167*, 174; holism of images by 68–71; imaginal narrative of 162–163; *Pivot Irrigation No. 39* 67–68, *67*; *Manufacturing No. 18. Cankun Factory, Zhangzhou Fujian Province, 2005 157*; *Navajo Reservation/Suburb Phoenix, Arizona U.S.A. 2011* 73–77, *75*, 158; Zen-like feeling evoked by 80
Byrnes, K. 37, 41, 63, 132, 136

Cajete, G. 56, 57–58, 103, 174
Cambridge Handbook of Wisdom, The 158
Capra, F. 144
Cartesianism 25, 92; as a philosophy without mystery 27–32
Cartier-Bresson, H. 102, 104
cave story 109
The "Centred Self" 31
Cezanne, P. 103–104
child mind 9, 55, 117, 142
Chmielnicka-Kuter, E. 127
Chitwood, A. 99
Christ *31*, 33, 48–49, 56, 60–61, 104, 153, 155, 174
Christian contemplation 38, 43
Christian paradise 61
Clandinin, D. 116, 143
Clark, C. 145
Clock Mechanism 23
cogito ergo sum 29, 30
Cohen, A. 20, 123
Cole, T. 121
Collister, R. 15, 37, 41, 42, 43, 117, 137
Coltrane, J. 16, 103, 104–105, 120, 121
Connelly, F. 116, 143
Concerning the Spiritual in Art 103
Conjectures of a Guilty Bystander 56, 59–60, 62, 63

consciousness 136–137; dialogic nature of 89; as moment within encounters with text 125; transformative shifts in 41, 42–44, 116; weaving into 44–46; witness 92, 125–127
contemplation: active 43; Christian 38, 43; holistic 76; imaginal 73–77; infused 44, 49; as life 18, 147; natural 43, 44, 49; relation of the aesthetical to 49; "seamless garment" of 44–46; seeing whole as imaginal 73–77; as summonses to awareness 77–80; transformation, aesthetics and 43–44
contemplative ethos 118–120
contemplative inquiry 5, 9; begun by reflecting on one's story 12–14; dialogical speaking, narrative and 134–137; emergence of second questions in 88–93; as epistemological touch of flow 139–140; impossible paradox in 93–95; primordial character of first questions in embarking on 83–88; question of dialogical self and imaginal self in 88–90; question of solitude and the dialogical in 90–92; question of wisdom image in 92–93; as recycling of memory 16–18; solitude in 89; spirituality research paradigm and wisdom image in 93–95; voice of paradise child emerging from vague fragments onto 140–144; way of arts-based 151–156; wondrous and paradoxical journey of questions in beginning 82–83
contemplative turn 2, 15, 145–148
contextual coherence 161
Csikszentmihalyi, M. 140
Curnow, T. 1, 25, 47, 64, 65, 84, 104; on connection between wisdom and perception 109; on history of wisdom 108, 109–110

daimon 152
Dante Aligheri 61
Davis, W. 66
deeducation 123
Del Prete, T. 72, 142
Dencev, H. 15, 37, 41, 42, 43, 117, 137
Descartes, R. 27, 28, 30, 32–33, 137–138, 147
dialogical as witness consciousness 125–127
dialogical-being-in-the-world 115

Index

dialogical character of transformation 114–117
dialogical self 88–90, 126–127; solitude and 90–92
dialogical self theory (DST) 126–127, 132
dialogical speaking 134–137, 138
Diamond, C. 14, 19, 86, 153
dignity of the esthetic intuition 50
di Rezze, G. *118*, 155
Discourse on Method and Meditations 27, 28–30
Divine, the: return to seeking 173–176; severed from humanity 71, 170–171; sought through connection 65–72
Divine Comedy 61
Dostoevsky, F. 127, 171
Dutton, T. 21

earth connections 62–65
Eckhart, M. 120, 121
Educating for Wisdom and Compassion 7, 84, 102, 106–107
education: balkanization of 20; contemplative turn in 145–148; earth connections in 62–65; ethos of 21; hidden curriculum in 21; holistic 32, 42, 131, 147; loss of soul in 20; the paradisal and 54–57; relation of wisdom and art in 84–87; Rossini on his epicyclical transit through 21–24; self-cultivation in 146; spiritual deficit in 24; for sustainability 165
Education for Sustainable Development 165
Eisner, E. 14, 131, 151, 153
Electrostatic Machine 72
Elysian fields 61
embodied knowing 104–105
embodied present-moment-centered awareness 140
embodiment 43
Emerson, R. 102, 104
empiricism 134
epistemic agency 168
epistemology: of love 18–19, 62; of presence 137–139, 145; of separation 7, 171
Ergas, O. 9–10, 15, 48, 53, 88, 93–95; call for deeducation 123; on character of spirituality and spiritual research in education 122; contemplative turn and 146–147; on nonparadigm 150
Essential Elements 24, 67, 71

ethos of connection 41–43, 83
Ewing, W. 68–71
exploratory processing 161
Expulsion from the Garden of Eden, The 61

Fall and Expulsion from Paradise, The 61
felt knowing 98
Ferrari, M. 7, 84, 107–108, 158–159, 161–163, 165
"festival of rain" 38–39, 51, 92
Figures for an Apocalypse 36, 41, 113
first questions in inquiry 83–87
The Fluidity of Inquiry. A Narrow Street in Venice Known as a Calle 27
flow 139–140
Formation of My Being-in-the-Moment, A 154
frame of reference 15
Francis, Pope 37
Frodeman, R. 25, 28
From Information to Transformation 83

Galile, G. 82
Galison, P. 159
Garden of Earthly Delights, The 92
Garden of Eden with the Fall of Man, The 61
Garden of the Gods 61
Gardner, F. 142
generative dialogue 8, 89, 132–134
gentle empiricism 64–65
Geography of Lograire, The 71, 72, 176
Gieser, T. 116, 126
Gilgamesh 61
Gionitus, The Beginning of Astronomy 81, 82, 172
Giroux, R. 128
Glück, J. 159
God 43–44, 48–49; *see also* Divine, the
Grace's House 142
Grady, M. 105
grasping 44–45
ground of being experience 117, 144–145
Gunnlaugson, O. 15, 26, 26, 37, 41, 43, 83, 116, 132; on communicative and social aspects of transformation 133; on embodied present-moment-centered awareness 140; on generative dialogue 8, 89; on messiness of inquiry 134; on presence 117, 137–138; on transformational learning 134

Index

Hadot, P. 1–2, 3, 10, 157
Hagia Sophia 43, 57, 58, 60, 70–71, 76, 110–111, 131, 176
Hart, T. 4, 5, 6, 8, 14–15, 25, 26, 37, 52, 55, 73, 104, 152, 159, 174, 176; appeal for calm and silence 58–59; on character of contemplation 156; on children as natural contemplatives 117, 142–143; on consciousness 136; on contact over categorization 150; on contemplative inquiry offering another way of knowing 87; on contemporary culture 62; criticism of rationalist and empirical paradigms 79; on the divine severed from humanity 71, 170–171; on epistemology of presence 140, 145; on information flattening the world 83; on journey of questions 82–83; on metacognition 120; on vital character of words 139; on ways of knowing 116–117, 155; on the wise child 142; on words having vital presence 92
Heidegger, M. 106, 119
Heart of Higher Education, The 20, 24, 103–104
Heraclitus 99, 110
Heretic Blood 29–30, 112
Hermans, H. 116, 126
Heschel, A. 174–175
hidden curriculum 21
hidden wholeness 16
Higgins, M. 29, 58, 112
Hinduism 152
Hirst, D. *118*
holism 26, 32, 33, 42, 45, 67–72, 76, 131, 147, 174; contemplative images and 73
Holistic Curriculum, The 62, 165

idea diversity 168
imaginal, the 59–62, 88–90, 157–159; contemplation of ultimate concerns 73–77; re-imagining of wisdom and 168; think[ing]-aloud with 163–168; wisdom as narrative-imaginal stimulus and 161–163; wisdom emergent from the self-reflective mirror of narrative and 159–161; wisdom studies allusions to the artful and 109–111
imaginal dialogue 89
imaginal stimulus 161–168
impossible paradox 93–95, 122
Inchausti, R. 52, 67, 76, 112, 129

infused contemplation 44, 49
inner alchemy 89, 132–134, 145
Inner Experience, The 146
inner work 89
inquiry *see* contemplative inquiry
Integrative Mind, The 59
intuitive knowing 43, 104–105
I-Thou 126
I Turn Inwards in Order to Look out Onto the World 34

James, W. 126
Jarvin, L. 10
Job, story of 110
John's Journey 12
Jordan, J. 158
Journey, The 100
journey of questions 82–83
Jung, C. 16–17, 19

Kabat-Zinn, J. 53, 63
Kandinsky, W. 103
Kantiansim 147
Khachadourian, R. 102
Kelly, V. 102–103
Kim, J. 165
King, M. L. 59
Kuhn, T. 25, 93, 171
Kunzmann, U. 163–164

Labrie, R. 29, 50, 54, 60, 77, 112, 142
L'albero della Vita 60
Latour, B. 25
Leavy, P. 149
Leiter, S. 120–121
Letter to an Innocent Bystander 9, 113, 129
Levi, C. 13
life as contemplation 18, 147
life of inquiry 146
life reflection 166, 168
lifespan contextualism 166
Life's Sake. Be with Life! 103
Lin, J. 45, 48, 93, 122
lived exercise 3
living words 98, 117, 139–140; transformation as 137–139
London, P. 4, 76–77, 83, 106, 174
Looking Onto Others to See Myself 40
Lord, R. 66
love: embrace of wholeness and 58; epistemology of 18–19, 62
Love and Living 7, 24, 35, 55, 84, 111, 152

Mailer, N. 124
Malaquais, J. 124
Malick, T. 13
Manufacturing No. 18. Cankun Factory, Zhangzhou Fujian Province, 2005 157
maps 36–37, 100–101; of the contemplative turn 145–148; of wisdom 148–151
Masaccio 61
McClintock, B. 104
McKinney, M. 74
McNiff, S. 153
meaning-making process 162
Meditation as Contemplative Inquiry 59
Melville, H. 47
memory, recycling of 16–18
Merton, T. 1–2, 4, 7–9, 13, 25, 84, 120; aesthetical writings of 41–43; on Cartesianism 28; on the child mind 9, 55, 117, 142; as cultural theorist 134–135; on Descartes 28; and dialogue with Brother Louis as strategy for inquiry 127–130; on dignity of the esthetic intuition 50; on education and the paradisal 54–57; on essential nature of Zen 105–106, 113; on ethos of education 24; on ethos of wholeness 135; "festival of rain" 38–39, 51, 92; on hidden wholeness 16; historical interpretations of wisdom by 111–113; on holism 33, 174; on the impossible paradox 93–95, 122; on impossible paradox of Zen 78–79; inquiry as epistemological touch of flow 139–140; journey of 15; on man as soul in the form of art 51; outsider's map looking onto 36–37; on the paradisal 54–57, 112–113; on the paradoxical relation of the spiritual and the aesthetical 46–48; paradox of spiritual journey of 48–51; on rationalism 29–30; on relation between wisdom and art 84–87; Rossini's classroom encounter with 35; "seamless garment" of contemplation 44–46; seeds of organic methodology in writings of 130–132; SUM, I AM 30, 32–33, 153; on transformation, aesthetics and contemplation 43–44; Watchmaker and Artist story 169–170
Merton's "Vague Fragments," Building the Big Picture 96
Messina, R. 10
metacognition 120

metaphor 71–72
methodology of one 118–120; dialogical speaking, narrative and contemplative knowing in 134–137; dialogue with Brother Louis as strategy for inquiry in 127–130; heart of the map of wisdom in 148–151; inner alchemy of silent self in 132–134; map of contemplative turn in 145–148; seeds of organic 130–132; spiritual research paradigm in 121–123; transcendence of being in 144–145; unravelling layers of palimpsest of being in 120–121; way of arts-based contemplative inquiry in 151–156; witnessing of self through writing and encounters with the aesthetical 123–125
Michelangelo 61, 92, *114*
Miller, J. P. 2, 7, 9, 20, 33, 38, 52, 62, 84, 93, 102, 132, 137, 146, 152, 165; on restoration of earth connections 62; return to seeking the Divine and 173, 174; seeking wisdom from wisdom studies and 106–107; on the soul opening 60
Milton, J. 61
mindful awareness 63
mindfulness 44; non-dual 48
mirror of wisdom 159–161
Mocking of Christ 31, 104, 155, 174
Montessori, M. 117, 142
Moore, T. 98, 161
Morgan, P. 37, 98, 117, 123, 144–145
Mullen, C. 14, 19, 86, 153
myth of objectivity 48

narrative 2–4, 146; and contemplative knowing 134–137; as contemplative terrain 87; entering the "sacred land" of 14–16; epistemology of love and 18–19; philosophy and 19–21; retelling 140–142; self-reflective mirror of 159–161; shared 24–27
narrative accrual 17
narrative-imaginal stimulus, wisdom as 161–163
narrative theory 135
natural contemplation 43, 44, 49
Navajo Reservation/Suburb Phoenix, Arizona U.S.A. 2011 73–77, 75, 158
Navicella of St. Peter the Apostle 112
New Seeds of Contemplation 4, 15, 18, 28, 143–144, 173; epistemology of love and 18–19

Newton's Child 172
No Man Is an Island 75
non-dualism 16, 44, 84, 102, 135
non-dual mindfulness 48
nonlinearity of inquiry 26
nonparadigm 150
non-propositional knowing 94

Okri, B. 137, 139, 173
Oles´, P. 127
one-eyed lives 172
On Knowing: Essays for the Left Hand 171
ontological acts in encounters with texts 101–106
Oron Semper, J. 21
Other Side of the Mountain, The 63, 65, 76, 79, 110, 113, 137
outer work 89
outsider's map looking onto Merton 36–37
out-turning 25
Oxford, R. 2

palimpsest of being 120–121, 124; probing of authentic self in 121–122
Palmer, P. 6, 7, 8, 18, 25, 26, 33, 37, 53, 113, 130, 146, 171, 173, 174; appeal for calm and silence 58; on approaching texts in friendship 41; on complexity of inquiry 83; critique of dualistic thinking 20; dialogical self theory and 132–133; on dialogue 90–91; encouraging us to be in dialogue with texts 127; on ethos of wholeness 135; on going beyond looking 79–80; on holistic education 32; on how university has lost its soul 20; on intimacy of the personal with the subject 128; on metaphor of Mobius strip 135; on myth of objectivity 48; on nature of *how* in knowing 97–98; on nature of truth and method in spirituality studies 151; on non-propositional knowing 44; on one-eyed lives 172; on pain of disconnection in education 62; presence of Merton in writings of 55; in reintegration of broken selves 71; on seeing the world within unity of heart and mind 58; on spiritual deficit in post-secondary education 24
paradisal wisdom 54–57, 92, 112; of the radical self and the artist 59–62;

seeking the inner light of 57–58; silent self and solitudinous ethos of 58–59
paradise child, voice of 140–144
Paradise Lost 61
paradoxical ethos of the spiritual terrain 88
paradoxical relation between the spiritual and the aesthetical 46–48
paradox of Merton's spiritual journey 48–51
paradox of Zen 79
Pencier, N. de 65
Pentimento 118
personal wisdom 161–162
perspective transformation 145
Petro, P. 158
philosophy 19–21, 22–23, 25, 106; Cartesian 25, 27–32
photography 64, 65–70, 102–103, 162; *see also* Burtynsky, E.
Picasso, P. 171
Pinar, W. 153
Pivot Irrigation #39 67, *67*
Plotinus 171
poetry: metaphoric 71–72; wisdom in 109
Poetry and the Contemplative Life 36, 41–43, 49, 50, 52, 77, 92, 112–113
Poincaré, H. 171–172
Polkinghorne, D. 3
Potworowski, G. 7, 84, 107–108, 158–159
presence 117, 127; epistemology of 137–139, 145
primordial character of first questions in inquiry 83–87
Problem of Research Methodology: A Paradoxical Paradigm, The 121–123
"Prolegomena to a Spiritual Research Paradigm" 123
Prologue, The Author's Advice to the His Book 113, 128–129
Ptolemy 24
punctum 66

Quine, W. O. 172

radical self 56, 59–62
Raids on the Unspeakable 1, 9, 37, 65, 78, 92, 94, 113, 149; dialogical speaking in 138; methodology of one and 128–130
Rain and the Rhinoceros 37, 92
Randall, V. R. 72

rationalism 25–26, 29–30, 32–33, 48, 73, 134
recycling of memory 16–18
reductionism 71, 93, 171
Reeve, R. 10, 168
reflectivity 124
re-imagining of wisdom 168
relational ethos 41–43, 83
retelling 140–142
Reznitskaya, A. 10
Rosch, E. 45, 107
Rossini, G. *17*; classroom encounter with Merton 35; conversation with William Ewing on holism of Burtynsky's images 67–70; epicyclical transit through graduate and professional school by 21–24; reflection on Merton and self 35–36
Rothko, M. 67

"sacred land" of narrative 14–16
Sant'Ivo alla Sapienza 68
Scardamalia, M. 10
Schiller, S. 9, 14, 86–87, 131, 132, 152
Scott, C. 20, 64, 123
second questions, emergence of 88–93
Seeking Merton's "Festival of Rain" 38–39, 51
self: authentic 93, 121–122, 173–174; dialogical as witness consciousness of 125–127; Merton on the unclothed 56; path to core of 62; question of dialogical and imaginal 88–90; radical 56, 59–62; reintegration of 16, 105; Rossini's reflection on Merton and 35–36; silent 58–59, 62, 67, 70, 132–134; witnessed through writing and encounters with the aesthetical 123–125
self-cultivation 146
self-knowledge 47
self-reflective mirror of narrative 159–161
Seven Storey Mountain, The 29, 87, 111, 113, 143, 149
Shannon, W. 146
shared narrative 24–27
Sidereal Messenger, The 82
Signatures: Notes on the Author's Drawings 65, 78, 113
silent self 58–59, 62, 67, 70; inner alchemy of 132–134
Simmons, S. 83, 105
Sistine Chapel 92

Socrates 152
solitude 58–59, 89, 90–92
spiritual, the 46–48; holism and 67–70; impossible paradox and 93–95, 122; relation with art 52, 54–55; summonses to awareness and 77–80; wisdom in the landscape and 62–65
spiritual embryo journey 144–145, 147–148, 175
spirituality research paradigm 93–95, 121–123
Stange, A. 107, 163, 166
Staudinger, U. 166–168
Sternberg, R. 10, 159, 168
Student Group Reflections on Paper of a Burtynsky Photograph 167
Study of Zen, The 41
SUM, I AM 30, 32–33, 137–138, 153
Sumerian paradise 61
sustainability 165
synchronicity of events 18

Teaching and Learning for a Sustainable Future 165
Teaching for Wisdom 7, 84, 107, 158–159
texts 96, 97; allusion to the artful and imaginal in wisdom studies 109–111; friendship with 97–100, 127, 130–131; ontological acts in encounters with 101–106; read while seeking the aesthetical map 100–101; seeking wisdom from Brother Louis and 111–113; seeking wisdom from transformative learning paradigm 114–117; seeking wisdom from wisdom studies 106–108; writing within and between analytical and aesthetical 118–120
thinking aloud 163–168
third-person approach 8–9, 35–36, 120, 149–150
third way of knowing 4, 155
Thomas Merton and the Inclusive Imagination 29, 112
Thomas Merton Reader, A 9, 110, 128, 132, 138
Thoreau, H. D. 64, 92, 120, 121
Tillich, P. 4, 76–77
timeless learning 102
To Know as we are Known 36, 128
transcendence of being 144–146
transformation 41, 43–45, 48, 77, 174; dialogical character of 114–117;

194 Index

journey of shadows and paradoxes 134–137; as living words 137–139; perspective 145
Transformation 114
transformative learning paradigm 114–117, 128
transformative shifts in consciousness 41, 116
transforming spirit 45
transmission model of learning 102
Treasures From the Wreck of the Unbelievable 118
Tree of Life 13
Triumph of Christian Doctrine, The 100
Tycho Brahe 23, 173

ultimate concerns 76–77
UNESCO 165

vague fragments 140–144, 175
vignette-images 163–164
Viola, B. 67
Voice of Contemplative Solitude, A 91
voice of paradise child 140–144

walking the talk 146
Walsh, S. 4, 7, 92, 124, 125, 132, 139, 153, 155–156
Watchmaker and Artist story 169–170
Watermark 65
weave of inquiry 6–11, 45
Webb, D. 120
Weststrate, N. 158, 159, 168
What is Inquiry? 26
Wittkower, R. 13, 68
wholeness 58, 70–71
wholesight 6
Wilson, A. 145
wisdom 1–2, 3, 7; earth connections in 62–65; emergent from self-reflective mirror of narrative 159–161; Greek idea of 57; journey of questions and 82–83; in the landscape 62–65; map of 148–151; as narrative-imaginal stimulus 161–163; paradisal 54–59; re-imagining of 168; relation of poetry to 50; relation to art 84–87, 106, 173; sought from Brother Louis 111–113; sought from wisdom studies 106–108; visualizing connection for seeking divine 65–72
Wisdom 108, 109
Wisdom, Intuition and Ethics 64, 108, 110
Wisdom as Orchestration of Mind and Virtue 108
wisdom image 37, 92–93, 115; spirituality research paradigm and 93–95
Wisdom in the Ancient World 108
wisdom studies 106–108, 158–159
wise child 142
witness consciousness 92, 125; dialogical as 125–127
witnessing of self 123–125
Woods, Shore, Desert A Notebook, May 1968 113
Writing Witness Consciousness 4, 159

Yagelski, R. 35–36, 41, 101

Zajonc, A. 7, 14, 18, 25, 33, 37, 53, 146, 171, 173, 174; on centrality of doing interior work 89; on contemplative thinking 20–21; on creative silence 58–59, 62, 67, 70; dialogical self theory and 133; on ethics 173, 176; on gentle empiricism 64–65; on how university has lost its soul 20; on knowledge formed by love 58, 62; presence of Merton in writings of 56; on solitude 90–92; on spiritual deficit in post-secondary education 24; on transformative promise of aesthetical encounter 103
Zen and the Birds of Appetite 37, 41, 52, 92, 105, 113
Zen in Japanese Art 37, 41, 52–53, 55, 113
Zoroastrianism 109
Żurawska-Żyła, R. 127

Printed in the United States
By Bookmasters